RISK, UNCERTAINTY AND GOVERNMENT

Pat O'Malley

Carleton University, Ottawa

D1615190

London • Sydney • Portland, Oregon

First published in Great Britain 2004 by
The GlassHouse Press, The Glass House,
Wharton Street, London WC1X 9PX, United Kingdom
Telephone: + 44 (0)20 7278 8000   Facsimile: + 44 (0)20 7278 8080
Email: info@cavendishpublishing.com
Website: www.cavendishpublishing.com

Published in the United States by Cavendish Publishing
c/o International Specialized Book Services,
5824 NE Hassalo Street, Portland,
Oregon 97213-3644, USA

Published in Australia by The GlassHouse Press,
45 Beach Street, Coogee, NSW 2034, Australia
Telephone: + 61 (2)9664 0909   Facsimile: +61 (2)9664 5420
Email: info@cavendishpublishing.com.au
Website: www.cavendishpublishing.com.au

British Library Cataloguing in Publication Data
O'Malley, Pat
Risk, uncertainty and government
1 Political science 2 Risk assessment 3 Risk management
4 Uncertainty
I Title
320.1

Library of Congress Cataloguing in Publication Data
Data available

ISBN 1-90438-500-1
ISBN 978-1-904-38500-4

1 3 5 7 9 10 8 6 4 2

Printed and bound in Great Britain

Acknowledgments

This book started out as an edited collection of my writings on risk. In some ways it retains this character, although Chapters 1 to 3 and Chapter 9 are entirely new. Only a few of the other chapters correspond very closely with the papers I had hoped would just slot together. Some are very different indeed from their first published versions. In part, this is because I have become more interested in uncertainty, and the ways in which it is often passed off under the rubric of risk – as though it were just a minor variation on the theme. Of course, risk and uncertainty are no foreigners to each other: they overlap and share many family resemblances. But it seemed odd to think of Bentham talking of risk when he insisted that liberal subjects gain foresight. Likewise, it did not appear to me that 19th century judges elaborating upon the law of contract were merely performing a variant of social workers filling in risk schedules. A distinction lay in here that I felt was worth making. So, one thing led to another and eventually here is the book.

The staff at Cavendish Publishing – particularly Beverley Brown and Jon Lloyd – deserve a first and special vote of gratitude. To say they have been patient and understanding is an understatement. Of course, with a book such as this very many people earn sincere thanks for providing advice and comments, unfortunately more than could be named. My dear friends Mariana Valverde, Nikolas Rose and Stephen Mugford gave me many of 'my' ideas and saved me from a few of the more egregious errors in my thinking. Mariana, in particular, has read and commented on most of the chapters and encouraged me to keep going when I thought of giving the project away. I'm enormously grateful for her friendship, collegiality and support. The usual suspects in the risk and government area have strongly influenced this book, especially through considered criticisms of the articles and conference papers out of which it was eventually built. Richard Ericson, Jonathan Simon, Tom Baker, George Pavlich, Clifford Shearing, Lucia Zedner, Kit Carson and David Garland, especially, should be mentioned here. So too, all the faculty and graduate students at the Centre of Criminology at the University of Toronto where most chapters were first tested. I would also like to thank John Braithwaite and the Australian National University, whose award of a Sabbatical Fellowship allowed me write and think in a scholarly and friendly environment. Likewise, I owe a debt of gratitude to Christine Harrington and her colleagues in the Institute of Law and Society at New York University, who provided me with a term as a Distinguished Professor in Residence. My work there (not without irony as I was to teach a course on risk) was traumatically affected by the tragic events of September 11th. Nevertheless, it was a period where, perforce, I learned much about risk that would otherwise have remained obscure. I am indebted to my former colleagues in the School of Law and Legal Studies at La Trobe University, particularly to David Wishart. Likewise, I owe much to my new colleagues at Carleton University – Aaron Doyle, Alan Hunt, Dawn Moore and Bruce Curtis. My graduate student Chris Peters at Carleton made a heroic effort to help me write English, and together with Dan O'Malley turned a chaotic mass of references into a manageable bibliography. Margaret Foddy lived through all of this on a day to day basis, and as ever has my love and admiration.

While most of the chapters previously published in some form have been substantially revised, I would like to thank the following for giving permission to include material originally published elsewhere. Chapter 4 originally appeared in a different form in *Economy and Society* volume 29 (2000), under the title of 'Uncertain subjects' (www.tandf.co.uk). Chapter 5 is based on a paper that appeared as 'Imagining insurance. Risk thrift and insurance in Britain' in *Embracing Risk* edited by Tom Baker and Jonathan Simon (© 2002 by The University of Chicago. All rights reserved). Chapter 6 appeared in its original form as 'Moral uncertainties: contract law and the distinctions between speculation, gambling and insurance', in *Risk and Morality*, edited by Richard Ericson and Aaron Doyle, and published by the University of Toronto Press in 2003. Chapter 7 is loosely adapted from 'Risk, crime and prudentialism revisited' in *Risk, Crime and Justice* edited by Kevin Stenson and Robert Sullivan, and published by Willan Press in 2001. Chapter 8 is based on 'Drugs, risks and freedoms' that appeared in Gordon Hughes and Eugene McLaughlen's edited collection, *Crime Prevention and Community Safety: New Directions*, reprinted by permission of Sage Publications Ltd (© The Open University, 2002).

Contents

Chapter 1
Risk, Uncertainty and Government

Someone who depicts the world as risk will ultimately become incapable of action.

(Ulrich Beck, 1994, p 9)

Uncertainty makes us free.

(Peter L Bernstein, 1998, p 229)

In current sociology it is almost banal to make the claim that we live in a risk society. For the most part it seems no longer necessary to draw even a lay audience's attention to the fact that risk-based routines and practices of government pervade most areas of our lives. Techniques based on the calculation of health risks set out dietary and exercise regimes that thousands, even millions, now follow routinely. We periodically undergo diagnostic tests, in an effort to minimise or prevent the effects of pathologies that were hardly known to us a few years ago. Risk frameworks form the basis of regimes of security that attempt to turn each of us into crime prevention practitioners and in some cases to turn our homes and even communities into hi-tech fortresses. Motor vehicles are increasingly marketed in terms of their sophisticated risk-reducing features, ranging from the humble and taken-for-granted seat belt, through multiple air bags, sophisticated braking systems and side-impact bars, to a new array of proximity alarms that warn of impending collisions. On the darker side of life, psychiatric assessments are now usually framed in terms of the risks posed by patients to themselves and others, while in many jurisdictions former sex offenders are publicly identified so their neighbours may be aware of the risks they represent. Mass imprisonment is practised in some states as a way of reducing crime risks, a strategy aided by the application of risk-based sentencing tables that displace judicial decision-making. Major government projects set out to educate us in the need to practise risk assessment along these and other lines, and whole industries have been established to manufacture and sell commodities that secure us against risks to health, property, personal security and virtually every hazard that can be imagined.

This way of governing reflects a familiar model in which great bodies of data are turned into predictive formulae. Armies of crash test dummies are sacrificed, masses of information on burglaries and assaults are accumulated, endless research into the distribution of pathologies of every conceivable form is processed in order to reveal 'risk factors'. Such indicators often tell us the exact degree of probability there is of us experiencing the relevant harm, although sometimes they only approximate this statistical ideal. In all cases, the aim is to improve on the 'uncertain' prognoses of those judges, social workers, medical practitioners, psychiatrists, probation officers and so on who practise more traditional arts and sciences of judgment. They seek to make objective, standardised and exact predictions to replace subjective expectations based on such non-quantitative modes of calculation as rules of thumb, experience, foresight, estimation and professional judgment.

Much of the public discourse on risk in fields such as medicine, crime prevention and public health has emphasised the positive contribution of these new techniques toward minimising harms and increasing security. In social theory, however, the response to the spread of risk-centred government has been far more negative. In particular, a new 'risk society' orthodoxy in social theory led by Ulrich Beck and Anthony Giddens regards risk as – at best – a mixed blessing for government. In Beck's (1994, p 9) words, risk '… dims the horizon …' because it tells us only what we cannot do, not what we can do. It fixes us in the past, for an irony of risk is that its predictions will work only if in relevant respects the world is unchanging. Risk society theorists further argue that risk-based predictions deliver insecurity rather than security, for the more that science discovers, the more it demonstrates that life is saturated with risks.

Of course, the promise of risk – or of most other governmental innovations for that matter – is not often the subject of contemporary sociological investigation. Sociology is rarely an optimistic discipline. Indeed it is prone to discovering that the world is on the brink of a new crisis or catastrophe, and risk society theory is no exception. For this theory, whatever promise risk once held is regarded as largely null and void, for we are now said to live in a changed world. This is a world of new, incalculable, unpredictable and catastrophic 'modernisation risks' such as global warming, depletion of the ozone layer and nuclear contamination. These emergent risks are held to have been created by the very *success* of modernity: its scale of production, its pace of innovation and its compression of time and space. Harms created in Chernobyl are visited upon English farmers. A hole in the ozone layer generated largely by industry in the northern hemisphere delivers increased rates of cancer to 'isolated' areas in the southern hemisphere. The industrialised world, through global warming, is even melting the polar ice caps, threatening the long-term viability of almost every coastal town and city on the planet. None, not even the wealthy, can escape the global reach of these harmful effects. Nor can they buy protection. Risk-based early warning techniques are useless against catastrophic events of very low statistical frequency, and for types of event in which the processes that produce the harms usually go unrecognised until it's too late.

While these modernisation risks are said to be 'incalculable' or 'uncertain', it is argued that scientists and governments continue to assert they are knowable and governable. Official discourses, it is claimed, assert that even infrequently occurring harmful events can be predicted and minimised, that they fall within 'acceptable' risk levels, or are in some way 'insignificant'. For this reason, Beck and his colleagues regard risk as an ideology. It is used by powerful interests to mask the politically destabilising truth that we are threatened by unpredictable catastrophes. And because modernisation's catastrophes frequently prove scientific predictions and reassurances wrong, the risk society thesis suggests we are entering a new era in which the ideological authority of expertise is beginning to be undermined. Faced with the insuperable contradiction that the more it produces goods, the more it produces unpredictable catastrophes, the world of 'reflexive modernity' comes to question and reflect upon the value of its core processes. Belief in 'progress' and 'truth' gives way to fundamental doubt.[1]

---

1 A very similar position has been developed by Luhmann (1993, pp 82–100), who agrees that the harms generated by modernity's success are capable of outweighing the benefits. Likewise for Luhmann, the problem with contemporary risks is that we 'are faced … with rare, improbable causal combinations, from which, since they are so rare and unlikely to reoccur, we cannot learn' (1993, p 89). Luhmann's position thus does not centre statistical prediction, but causal prediction. In contrast to Beck – and perhaps taking a swipe at his politics – Luhmann (1993, p 100) also suggests that one response should be to avoid 'exaggerated fears and excitement' as this produces further risks – what he terms 'preventive misfortune'.

In this highly influential literature 'uncertainty' takes a key role as risk's alternative. Beck suggests that uncertainty is government of the 'incalculable'. For this reason we can only be governed by 'estimation': *possible* catastrophes are identifiable but their probability and magnitude remain unclear. Uncertainty thus appears both as a characteristic of events (that is, events that are not statistically predictable), and as a way in which the future can be imagined or predicted (that is, forecasting methods that are not based on statistical calculation). The two usages of 'uncertainty' are closely linked in this theory, since under conditions of uncertainty we cannot deploy risk and must resort to uncertain techniques. Considered as 'estimation of the possible', uncertainty is given a rather negative value, for it is made to appear as the poor cousin of risk calculation.[2] The problematic status granted to uncertainty is most evident, perhaps, in Beck's (1998) and Ewald's (2002) focus on governmental deployment of the 'precautionary principle'. The precautionary principle involves governmental proscription of certain practices – such as genetic modification of foods – even though no conclusive scientific evidence yet corroborates the claim that the process is harmful. In such cases, waiting until the level of risk has been determined is itself considered an unacceptable risk. We are forced to deploy uncertainty because the superior technology of risk is not available. However, uncertainty of this sort offers no compensating advantages because, like risk, it too paralyses us into inactivity.

Almost diametrically opposed to this vision of crisis is another account, recently exemplified by Peter Bernstein's (1998) hugely successful *Against the Gods: The Remarkable Story of Risk*. After a lengthy analysis of the history of risk and probability, Bernstein concurs with Beck's view that risk is a worrying technology. In Bernstein's view, probabilistic prediction of the future creates a 'prison' that consigns us to an endless repetition of past statistical patterns over which we have no control. 'Nothing we can do, no judgement that we make, no response to our animal spirits, is going to have the slightest influence on the final result' (1998, p 229).[3] In complete contrast to Beck, however, Bernstein *celebrates* uncertainty.

---

2 In consequence, Beck has been heavily criticised for privileging expertise over the forms of knowledge practiced by others. Brian Wynne (1996), for example, has argued at length that uncertain estimations made by 'lay' people using local knowledge (ie prognostication based on uncertainty) may provide very accurate and sophisticated diagnoses of hazardous situations. Wynne argues that in some ways this criticism goes to the heart of Beck's argument, for it suggests that uncertainty may be at least as effective as risk in revealing and governing modernisation's perils. The 'failure' of risk thus does not necessarily spell the descent into catastrophe. Nor does it imply that social order is being restructured as a result. Indeed, Wynne argues that resistance to expert definitions of risk is not at all new, and thus does not necessarily herald major shifts in consciousness in the present era.

3 In this, of course, Bernstein is not new but resuscitates and puts a new gloss on 19th century liberal concerns about the implications of statistics for the sanctity of 'free will'. As Porter (1995) argues, after the publication of Buckle's *History of Civilisation* in 1847, debates on this issue became at least as prominent and urgent as those generated by Darwin. Thus Porter quotes an outraged commentator from 1860, sounding very much like Bernstein, suggesting that '[a] protest may safely be entered against this modern superstition of arithmetic, which if acquiesced in, would seem to threaten mankind with a later and worse blight than any it has yet suffered, that not so much as a fixed destiny, as of a fate falling upon us, not personally, but in averages' (in Porter, 1995, pp 164–65).

Uncertainty appears not as the imprecise fall-back technology for dealing with impending catastrophe, but as the technique of entrepreneurial creativity. He quotes, with approval, the economist Frank Knight who – drawing on 19th century precursors – argued that uncertainty is crucial to business enterprise. This is because any given situation:

> ... is so entirely unique that there are no other or not a sufficient number to make it possible to tabulate enough like it to form any inference of value about any real probability in the case we are interested in. *The same obviously applies to the most of conduct and not to business decisions alone.* (Knight, quoted with emphasis added by Bernstein, 1998, p 221)[4]

Bernstein added the emphasis in this quotation to make his point clear. But his highest approval is retained for John Maynard Keynes. Keynes rejected the possibility of using statistical methods to forecast such significant future events as whether there will be war, or whether stock market prices will rise or fall. These are matters subject to 'uncertain knowledge'. 'About these matters' said Keynes, 'there is no scientific basis on which to form any calculable probability whatsoever. We simply do not know!' (quoted by Bernstein, 1998, p 229). Bernstein concludes that a 'tremendous idea lies buried in the conclusion that we simply do not know. Rather than frightening us, Keynes' words bring great news: we are not prisoners of an inevitable future. Uncertainty makes us free' (Bernstein, 1998, p 229). By itself, Bernstein's conclusion might be regarded as slightly anachronistic. After all, some risk society theorists such as Sanjay Reddy (1996) have argued strongly that Keynes represented the last hurrah for such thinking before it was trampled into undeserved extinction by the risk-oriented machinations of statistical economists. Reddy may be right about this subordination of uncertainty in the middle years of the 20th century, when the planned economy appeared as a rational governmental response to massive swings in the fortunes of the market. But things are rather different now. *Against the Gods* is only one example of an extensive and immensely influential managerial literature, appearing since the early 1980s, that extols the 'transformative power of the entrepreneurial spirit' and sees in this a blueprint for the 'reinvention of government' (Osborne and Gaebler, 1993).

Like Beck, many of these 'new managerial' writers see us as entering a novel world of uncertainty, produced by the forces of global modernity. But they don't see uncertainty as linked to catastrophe. In the rhetoric of Tom Peters (1987, p 5), another guru of the uncertainty industry:

> The times demand that flexibility and love of change replace our longstanding penchant for mass production and mass markets, based as it is upon a relatively predictable

---

4 The origins of this distinction go back somewhat further than Knight's work. During the late 19th century, the view began to be articulated that profit emerges not out of the complex interactions of causal laws, as positivistic theories argued, but out of the creativity of entrepreneurs. In this interpretation, expressed by von Thunen and others, '... the rewards of the entrepreneur ... [are] the returns for incurring those risks which no insurance company will cover because they are unpredictable, and in this sense, the entrepreneur is necessarily an "inventor and explorer in his field"' (Blaug, 1988, p 461). It is, of course, possible that insurers did not insure profit because of the moral hazard involved – that is, entrepreneurs would be less motivated to secure an insured profit.

environment now vanished ... Chaos and uncertainty will be market opportunities for the wise; capitalizing on fleeting market anomalies will be the successful business's greatest accomplishment ... the strategy is paradoxical – meeting uncertainty by emphasizing a set of basics: world class quality and service, enhanced responsiveness through greatly increased flexibility, and continuous short cycle innovation ...

For Peters, 'predictability is a thing of the past' because in the real world 'we don't know whether merging or de-merging makes more sense, and we have no idea who will be partners with whom tomorrow or next week, let alone next month' (1987, p 6). Uncertainty, then, is to be the fluid art of the possible. It involves techniques of flexibility and adaptability, requires a certain kind of 'vision' that may be thought of as intuition but is nevertheless capable of being explicated at great length in terms such as 'anticipatory government' and 'governing with foresight' (Osborne and Gaebler, 1993, p 229).

What also is intriguing here is the similarity between Frank Knight writing early in the 20th century and Tom Peters writing near its end, either side of the heyday of the interventionist state. In both analyses uncertainty – in the shape of the entrepreneurial reliance on practical experience, inspiration and foresight – is central to profitability and good economic governance. In this vision of enterprise, risk – the management of avoidable and statistically calculable harms through insurance and related techniques – is made subordinate to the rationalities and practices of uncertainty. Risk-centred arrangements are merely tools for governing the incidental and collateral harms (such as industrial accidents, consumer injuries or exposure to crime) generated by the *core* enterprising activities. When mathematical models of risk usurp the sovereign role of uncertainty, as in the planned economy, it is claimed that disaster and stagnation will doubtless strike. For Knight, Peters and Bernstein, the entrepreneur must be at the centre of the economy. The essence of the entrepreneur is envisaged as possession of the responsibility and skills for managing and creating not merely wealth but *the future* through techniques of uncertainty. Thus Peters 'pays tribute to the entrepreneur' by quoting George Gilder:

> ... entrepreneurs sustain the world. In their careers there is little of the optimizing calculation, nothing of the delicate balance of markets ... The prevailing theory of capitalism suffers from one central and disabling flaw: a profound distrust and incomprehension of capitalists. With its circular flows of purchasing power, its invisible handed markets, its intricate plays of goods and moneys, all modern economics, in fact, resembles a vast mathematical drama, on an elaborate stage of theory, without a protagonist to animate the play. (Peters, 1987, p 245)

This is heady stuff indeed. Peters is the promoter of a new market-based modernity, and sees the interventionist state as defeated by a resurgent capitalism driven forward to prosperity by enterprise. There are resonances with Beck, for Beck, too, feels that the day of the interventionist state is over. But Beck is the prophet of a new modernity that has lost confidence in itself. The interventionist state, he argues, can no longer be relevant because it (re)distributes goods whereas the contemporary task for government is the management of 'bads'. Peters, on the other hand, is the prophet of a new modernity that is enormously self-confident. It has defeated the twinned evils of the planned welfare state and the command economy. Peters thrives on chaos, Beck descends into it.

Let us for the moment suspend judgment about whether the world actually has leapt into a condition governable only through uncertainty, as Peters, Giddens and Beck suggest in their different ways, or whether, as Knight, Keynes and Bernstein argue, uncertainty is the timeless reality of all entrepreneurial activity. Instead, we could consider that all these discourses of risk and uncertainty, these academic analyses and economic polemics, these dire warnings about governing a catastrophic future, these optimistic manuals for born-again managers, represent diverse positions in a long-term governmental politics. Each position is focused on establishing the 'proper' way of governing through a reasoned estimation of an indeterminate future. They are unwittingly allied with each other in their suspicion of risk and related expert knowledges. They each recognise that alternative forms of knowledge, associated under the broad umbrella terms of 'uncertainty', 'foresight' or 'estimation', must necessarily be deployed in order to govern a contemporary 'incalculable' world. What is more, despite various polemics against risk, they are even in accord on the assumption that risk should not be abandoned but rather put in its 'proper' place.[5] Risk's assigned tasks are to govern security only in those domains where statistical prediction is held appropriate, and even then to be but one of multiple forms of knowledge brought to bear on the government of the future. In short, all these discourses concur that our future should governed through risk *and* uncertainty. This being so, it is striking how little time all of these authors spend on a series of questions about how past and present governments have deployed what they refer to as risk and uncertainty. All of these authors rail against the tyranny of expertise under regimes of risk, but none provides any analysis of the *variability* of techniques and knowledge of risk already deployed by government. None seems concerned to consider the differing implications of these diverse forms. Do household insurance policies deploy risk in the same way as preventative mastectomies? Does the installation of street lights to reduce the statistical risk of crime operate in the same way as using computer technologies to manage financial risk futures markets? Do these differing risk techniques have the same governmental implications for how we live our lives and what kind of people we are being made into? What do we lose analytically and politically by collapsing diverse technologies of risk into one undifferentiated category?

All these commentators, without any irony, emphasise the inevitability of having to deploy uncertainty in the future, but none provides any analysis of the *diversity* of ways in which 'uncertainty' is already imagined and governed. Surely there is a critical distinction to be made between 19th century exhortations to govern the vicissitudes of life though savings and thrift, and the neo-liberal exhortations for us all to become enterprising investors chancing our wealth on the stock market? How are we to investigate the diverse governmental visions and programmes in which uncertainty is embedded and given form, if it is reduced to merely the monolithic and generic 'incalculable' alternate to risk? None of these commentators considers

---

5 Indeed, for Bernstein this point makes up the gist of his closing remarks. In his view (1998, pp 336–37) 'we must avoid rejecting numbers when they show more promise of accuracy than intuition and hunch'. He argues, further, that the existence of probability has enabled many catastrophic errors of judgment to be avoided or their harmful effects mitigated.

that if we are to be governed through frameworks of 'risk' *and* 'uncertainty', then we should attend to how these ways of governing have been linked together in past and present practices of government. While insurance is regarded as the quintessentially risk-based institution, even it is strongly marked by educated guesswork, traditional routines and hunches (Ericson, Doyle *et al*, 2003); and to the extent that this is typical, what are the implications for how we understand the 'spread' of risk into new areas in the past few decades? Indeed, how much 'risk' is, rather, 'uncertainty' renamed?

Risk and uncertainty in governmental analysis

In the light of these observations and questions, possibilities of a rather different research orientation begin to open out. If risk and uncertainty are each recognised as diverse entities having diverse implications for government, we should develop ways of analysing that can help us recognise and understand such variability. We should consider how such variability has been created and maintained, in relation to what kinds of visions and problems of order. In this sense we would develop a genealogical approach to risk and uncertainty, attending to their natures as the products of contingency and invention rather than the effects of an inescapable 'logic' of modernity, capitalism or whatever. We should also develop some ways of analysing the governmental or political implications of the various forms and combinations of uncertainty and risk. These analyses would include examining the diverse ways in which risk and uncertainty might shape the kinds of subjects we are to be made into; the practices through which we will be expected to govern ourselves; and the ways we will be expected to imagine the world and prepare for the future.

Over the past decade or so, scholars using an analytic of government – or 'governmentality' – have been exploring the diversity of risk in these ways. Put briefly, their concern is primarily to understand risk as a complex category made up of many ways of governing problems, rather than as a unitary or monolithic technology. Great emphasis is placed on the many differences between, say, using risk techniques to structure insurance, and using risk techniques to diagnose or prevent cancer. In addition, these diverse configurations of risk are not understood as collectively generated by one vast process, such as modernisation. Instead, they are regarded as formed and deployed in diverse ways in the many governmental settings in which they are embedded. Consequently much interest is shown in studying the variety of ways in which risk is developed or elaborated in specific regimes, programmes and technologies of governance. Similarly, there is a focus on the diverse histories or genealogies of such processes and on their diverse implications as ways of governing. The concerns of analysts in this literature can roughly be grouped into three complementary and overlapping kinds of investigation.

First, many researchers have charted the increasing deployment of risk techniques across diverse fields of social life. The governance of pregnancy, for example, has been seen to shift from treating it as something akin to an illness afflicting women, toward treating it as a condition where both mother and foetus are regarded as 'at risk'. In this process, a variety of risk-management duties are invented and their performance assigned primarily to the mother. These relate to many hitherto unidentified risks associated with smoking tobacco, imbibing alcohol, ingesting caffeine and other forms of drug consumption. There is heightened attention given to the need for proper diet, physical exercise, regular medical tests and so on. All of these render the mother increasingly responsible both to the medical practitioner and to her foetus (Ruhl, 1999; Weir, 1996). As Rapp (1995, p 180) has indicated, while previous generations of women might have been aware of some of these risks, it is only the present generation of 'statistically graded pregnant women' who have been given specific risk figures and thus been led to identify 'generic pregnancy anxieties with their particular characteristics and behaviours'. In this environment, pregnant women might be thought of as governed increasingly 'through' risk.[6] That is, they are governed by means of risk technologies, and thus their present lives are shaped in terms of a *probable* future – a future that may never happen but that must be guarded against. Of course precautions characterise previous forms of government. But now, even though there are no signs of present pathology, specific interventions may be called for. Women's sexuality and reproductive capacity, more generally, have become a particularly active site for such developments. On the basis of genetic information gleaned from family history, and in the absence of any evidence of existing abnormality, radical mastectomy or removal of the ovaries or uterus may become a 'choice'. As with any other way of governing, risk can be gendered, and, as will become clear, all manner of other social and moral distinctions may be deeply embedded in this apparently 'technical' framework. Not least important in this respect is that wherever risk avoidance or minimisation is at issue, a moral judgment has been made concerning the unwanted status of an event in the future. While this may seem unproblematic with respect to the possibility of cancer, it is clearly not the case with respect to foetal 'abnormalities'. Both the congenitally deaf, and those with Down's Syndrome, have argued that related risk-based interventions in pregnancy devalue their status as fully human, and represent a form of prospective genocide.

Of course, not only women are made risk-knowledgable in order to be made responsible choice-makers in the current era. 'Drug addicts', for instance, have been recast in some jurisdictions as a new kind of subject – as 'responsible risk-takers' who must govern the effects of their risks on themselves and others. This new governmental image of the 'drug user' no longer represents them as 'addicts' enslaved by the drug and cursed with impaired rationality. Rather, drug users are made *free* by these new regimes. In this particular sense of freedom they are considered rational choice subjects, free to make choices and to take responsibilities, albeit having a 'relation of dependence' with a drug. Like other kinds of subject that have been governmentally created in the past 30 years, such as the 'welfare dependent' and 'job seekers', they come to be regarded as people in need of information about the risks they face. This information will enable them to govern

---

6 The phrase is borrowed from Jonathan Simon's (1997) 'Governing through crime'. This refers to the fact that many aspects of life in the United States are being governed through their connection to 'the problem' of crime, and thus in terms of techniques for governing crime. Streetscape design, for example, reflects current theories of situational crime prevention; invented 'communities' are formed around the task of protecting neighbourhoods against crime; and so on.

themselves in seemingly more autonomous and responsible ways through the technique of making 'informed choices' (O'Malley, 1999a). Similar developments have been studied by governmental analysts in many other contexts. Not only subjects, bodies and social relations may be recast by governing through risk, but even the environment and elements may be transformed. For example, drought in the Australian outback has been redefined by governments from being a 'natural disaster' to being a 'manageable risk'. In this new governmental guise, drought is constituted as something farmers should anticipate and make provision for, rather than regard as an unforeseen cataclysm requiring state intervention. Indeed, drought itself comes to be envisioned not as a climatic condition creating a dearth of water, but as an index of poor risk assessment reflected in inadequate alignment of farming practices and current climatic conditions (Higgins, 2001). As with many of the other examples, risk-centred government assigns new responsibilities to subjects. In turn, while risk may be regarded as constricting the future by closing off 'risky' options, ironically these new subjects can also be imagined to be free in new ways. In such government visions, risk and responsibility are taken to imply that the conduct of subjects is not predetermined by rigid laws of nature or society. They are said to reflect a particular vision of freedom: 'freedom of choice'.[7]

In such governmental studies, attention therefore is paid to the ways in which the increasingly prevalent adoption of risk as a framework of government creates new subjectivities and redefines relationships. There is a focus on how it invents new techniques for self-government and for the government of others, and creates and assigns responsibilities accordingly. These studies explore and dissect what are often 'details' of government that fall beneath the grand gaze of universal theories of risk society and global catastrophe, yet which restructure existence in many important ways.

In a second research direction, governmental analysts have been tracing the genealogies of various techniques of governing through risk. Their concern is not with mapping a teleological model of 'progress' toward the present. Nor is it with Beck's antithesis of this: the 'logical' production of risk-based government as part of modernity's dystopian evolution. Rather they are concerned with the unanticipated and sometimes contingent or arbitrary ways in which the course of risk-based government has come into being or changed direction. Thus Francois Ewald (1991) has stressed that the genealogical development of insurance reflects the contingent contribution of 'insurance imaginaries' – that is, inventive ways of applying the abstract technology of risk to some currently useful purpose. New forms of insurance appear as responses of risk to contingently emerging opportunities, as these are envisaged, defined and acted upon by insurance entrepreneurs. From this point of view there can be no linear history of insurance or of risk. This may be seen with respect to governmental research into the ongoing response of the insurance industry to the rise of global terrorism. As Ulrich Beck (1992, pp 16–28) predicted,

---

7 Niklas Luhmann (1993, pp 21–23) makes this point with particular clarity. In turn, he uses this to differentiate risk from danger. Where there is no choice, he suggests, we can speak only of danger, that is, the play of forces 'attributed to the environment'. For Luhmann (1993, p 22), what is critical to the definition of risk is that a decision can be made between alternatives 'clearly distinguishable in respect of the possibility of loss occurring'.

the reaction of much of the insurance industry has been to remove the effects of terrorism from the array of insurable risks, on the grounds that it is a high magnitude threat not statistically calculable with any confidence. Nevertheless, many reinsurers and other speculative agents have come to regard insurance against terrorism as a hazardous but potentially lucrative venture. Consequently, some parts of the insurance industry are now taking up the challenge to make catastrophe insurance workable, attracted by what is judged to be a 'make or break' opportunity. While actuaries may avoid them, these uncertain but high-stakes ventures are precisely the kinds of exercises in speculation that are the bread and butter of many practitioners in financial markets. As Bougen (2003, p 258) points out, such insurers 'operate in a calculative space invested by inescapable uncertainty', with a 'particularly fragile connection to statistical technologies'. In short, Beck misunderstands insurance when he imagines it to be governed entirely by risk technologies, for important sectors of insurance work through uncertain techniques. However, what is more important to observe is that new forms of securities are thus being *invented*. These bring together, in unanticipated ways, assemblages of insurance and speculation in 'catastrophe bonds'.[8] In Bougen's words:

> Reinsurers, capital market participants, catastrophe information systems, catastrophe-modelling agencies, investment-rating agencies, financial underwriters and existing financial products have all become imaginatively assembled. From a liberal government perspective, the very emergence of such risk networks capable of supporting securitization as an alternative method of catastrophe financing can itself be considered illustrative of the moving and creative possibilities of government. (2003, pp 262–63)

In such work, as I have mentioned, there is no sense of a linear history in which anything – such as liberalism, modernity or democracy – 'unfolds' along predetermined lines. There is no subject of history, such as 'class' or 'power', that necessitates the emergence or expansion of risk as a framework or technology of state and government. Nor is it assumed that risk techniques, or techniques of statistical probability, have a logic that steers them in such a way that modern institutions, such as insurance, must inevitably have been 'emerged'. Discontinuities and accidents, inventions and acts of imagination, are much more central to analysis in the governmental tradition. Greater attention is paid to how new ways of thinking and doing are assembled together from existing intellectual, social and material resources, in response to perceived problems of the time. Even such far-reaching governing apparatuses as the law of contract, while no doubt linked to the great intellectual schemata of 18th century economists and philosophers, is not simply their product. Instead, it seems that it was selectively plagiarised and fabricated from historical precursors and foreign texts. It was very likely a pragmatic creation intended to solve new problems of business and commerce, and was later developed in response to all sorts of unanticipated

---

8 Such innovations have much in common with what many of us would refer to as a gamble. While it may be surprising to associate insurance and gambling – if rather less so gambling and financial speculation – the three forms of financial risk have proven difficult to untangle in law. An analysis of the inventiveness of lawyers and financiers in differentiating the three, and of the struggles around the process, is the subject of Chapter 5.

eventualities.[9] In such governmental analysis, there is no judgment by hindsight that any given development was *the* solution required. It is neither the only nor necessarily the optimal response. The 18th century founders of modern marine insurance, for example, did not know that their schemes would 'work' – any more than we know whether catastrophe bonds will hold up. They did not know, any more than do we, whether some 'better' solution than insurance remains to be invented. Accordingly, what exists at any time is constantly being tinkered with, re-imagined, reinvented, 'improved', and thus becomes or is becoming something else. Governmental analysis, in short, assumes that governmental configurations are not necessary: they could have been otherwise, and can become otherwise.

It is important to recognise that governmental research of this kind has political implications by destabilising the taken-for-granted. In this way it points toward possible avenues of change and the always-alterable nature of the present. Such genealogical emphasis, however, does not imply that government can be understood only as developing through random or unanticipated events. Government is in considerable measure a matter of planning. New ways of imagining problems and the solutions invented to resolve them are thus likely to reflect each other. For example, governments that regard society as an organic whole which extensively shapes individuals, will tend to imagine problems as being due to the underdevelopment or breakdown of social processes. Accordingly they are likely to seek solutions of a collective sort. Socialist and welfare-liberal governance over long periods and across many social domains can be understood in such terms.

The examination of such patterns or overarching rationalities of governance is characteristic of a third style of governmental analyses. In particular, many writers in the governmental literature have been concerned to link changes in risk techniques with changes in broader political rationalities, such as the emergence of 'neo-liberalism'. Some of this work suggests that, rather than assuming that the risk society is inexorably extending its governmental reach, we are in the midst of a political shift in which governments are deploying risk in *changed* ways. Whereas the era of the welfare state was one in which risks to health, employment and so on were collectively governed through such techniques as social insurances, current political rationalities tend to regard the same risks as governed better by individuals and markets. Based on such a vision, many neo-liberal governments provide incentives and disincentives to persuade people to move out of social security and social insurance arrangements into private schemes. These inducements vary enormously. With respect to the provision of support for retirement and old age, it has been argued that individuals should become more independent and take command of their own futures by entering private superannuation schemes. Sometimes this is expressed more radically, proposing that fixed benefit retirement insurance should be substituted by schemes that pay benefits according to the performance of a share market portfolio. These are said to encourage private enterprise, to allow people to set their own level of financial risk, and to give them

---

9 Some key aspects of this development are the subject of Chapter 4, which focuses on the development of the common law of contracts, and are also developed in Chapter 5, dealing with insurance, gambling and speculative financial contracts.

greater control over their own futures. In other contexts it is urged that the costs of supporting the aging 'baby boomer' population will inflict a massive tax burden on the much less populous succeeding generation. Accordingly the former generation should be privately providing for their retirement years. In line with this, public pension benefits are often reduced, and tax breaks created to offset payment of premiums to private insurers. Private avenues of self-help are thereby made more attractive than reliance on social security. In still other ways it is argued that those who can afford to support themselves in old age are morally at fault by relying on public pension schemes that should be reserved for the deserving poor. In yet other accounts, it is claimed that as global competition increases we can no longer afford the forms of social security relied upon by a previous generation. The point here is neither to promote nor to cast doubt on any of these multifarious claims. Rather, it is to note that despite their number and diversity all these supposed problems are to be resolved by the same solution. In an era of neo-liberal politics, individuals deploying commercially provided programmes become far more central to the governance of risk than was the case under the socially liberal regimes of the welfare state's heyday. (See for example, O'Malley 1996, Greco 1993, Dean 1995a, Ruhl 1999.) This does not only imply that neo-liberalism imposes certain regimes of risk, although this is normally the case. It is also that such explanations and observations helped to form what is now recognised as the more or less coherent rationality of neo-liberalism. As I will later argue, ways of formulating liberalism and ways of formulating risk and uncertainty are processes that are closely bound together.[10]

Such work may sometimes appear to be concerned merely with philosophies of rule or the history of ideas. But the stress in governmental analysis is that these articulations of ideas and techniques are always practical. That is, what makes them *governmental* is that they are concerned with how to change the world, not merely to understand it. In the light of this, the literature makes a central distinction between mental and practical aspects of government. Adapting slightly from Miller and Rose (1990, pp 175–76), we can refer to the mental aspects as *'governing rationalities'*.[11] These are understood by Miller and Rose as 'discursive fields within which the exercise of power is conceptualised, the moral justifications for particular ways of exercising power by diverse authorities, notions of the appropriate forms, objects and limits of politics, and conceptions of the proper distribution of such tasks among secular, spiritual, military and familial sectors'. On the other hand, *'technologies of government'* appear as 'the complex of mundane programmes, calculations, techniques, apparatuses, documents and procedures through which

---

10 The exploration of such changes in political or governmental 'rationalities', and their relations to government through risk, will be developed most explicitly in Chapters 2 and 3, although they will be explored throughout the book.

11 Miller and Rose refer here to 'political rationalities'. Nevertheless, the term 'governing rationalities' is preferred precisely because many examples do not belong in the realm of politics, at least not in the everyday sense of the word. The example following in the text, drawn from the private insurance industry, is a good illustration of this. This is also closer to Foucault's original terminology of 'rationalities of government', which as Colin Gordon (1991, p 3) points out, means 'a way or system of thinking about the nature of the practice of government (who can govern, what governing is, what or who is governed), capable of making some form of that activity thinkable and practicable both to its practitioners and to those upon whom it is practiced'.

the authorities seek to embody and give effect to governmental ambitions'. Much governmental analysis is concerned especially with the *articulation* of such technologies and rationalities of government. As I have noted, while the emergence or ascendance of governmental rationalities is difficult or impossible to predict, certain kinds of technologies tend to be aligned with them. This is the case with the promotion by neo-liberal rationalities of commodified security techniques such as private insurance. At the same time, technologies of government have their own genealogies rather than being solely the creations of rationalities that promote them. Indeed, government rationalities themselves are in many ways themselves the product of assembling together and 'rationalising' existing elements into something approaching a consistent whole (O'Malley, 2000). Thus, for example, the neo-liberal emphasis on enterprise and risk-taking is scarcely something created *de novo*, as indicated by the following passage from the insurance industry in the United States:

> It is pertinent to my remarks that the word 'Assurance' ... means confidence, not certainty. Our pioneering ancestors had confidence as they faced an uncertain future and the hazards of an unknown country. Their confidence, courage and will to build made that unknown country our great nation. The gravest threat to our nation's survival would be the decadent loss of our ancestral pioneers' creative, adventurous spirit. One of the greatest contributions of life insurance is, I think, encouragement of that spirit. Bold adventurers in new undertakings are fortified by the assurance that risks they take will be shared by many others ... Life insurance has formed an indispensable foundation stone of individual risk-taking enterprise. It has provided a floor of security for millions of people upon which they have been able to place a ladder of opportunity. (Institute of Life Insurance, 1959, pp 13, 27)[12]

Neo-liberals fostering the 'enterprise culture' would no doubt have drawn upon such words in formulating their rather more encompassing visions of government. Yet there is another significant reason for selecting this example, for it reflects the ways in which even such a risk-oriented institution as insurance places uncertainty to the fore. Risk and uncertainty are regarded as necessary components of optimal governance – whether of nations, institutions or individual subjects. After so much attention to risk (sometimes a problematic feature of governmental analyses), it is now time to turn attention to distinguishing between risk and uncertainty.

Distinguishing risk from uncertainty

In much of the literature reviewed so far, risk appears as a way of governing in terms of aggregated futures, frequently in terms of objective measures and especially statistical probabilities. Uncertainty, on the other hand, appears as a way of governing in non-quantitative ways, by reference to experienced judgment, shrewd guesswork, rules of thumb, analogies and so forth. By implication, uncertainty therefore is a way of governing futures that are imagined as singular, infrequently recurring or unique. They can therefore only be 'likened' to other cases. Thus Beck's argument, for example, links uncertainty to non-recurring or rarely recurring events. Bernstein links uncertainty with the unique effects of human agency and the category of individual freedom. Knight associates uncertainty with

---

12 In turn, such discourses were even more common in the late 19th century than in the 1950s. For further illustrations, see Zelizer (1979).

the unique case or experience of the entrepreneur. Keynes sees uncertainty originating in his view that economic history is a single genealogical process rather than an aggregation of many equilibrating moments. Uncertainty thus stands out not only from risk, but also from those ways of thinking and governing that assume a determinate world. These would include, for example, some forms of positivist determinism in the sciences, and government, and forms of belief in *fortuna* in which it is assumed the fates have set a course which can only be divined.

Governmental studies and analyses overwhelmingly have been concerned with risk and its encroachment into contemporary governance, and have rarely examined 'uncertainty' in detail. In part, this aversion to analysing uncertainty as a way of governing is based on the general hostility to the grand theoretical character of the risk society theorists for whom uncertainty is a central concept. This takes its most specific form in a rejection of the idea of a rigid binary between calculable (risk) and 'incalculable' (uncertain) technologies of governance. As well, there is a general rejection of the idea that governance could be anything other than calculative. In one of the most influential claims, Mitchell Dean (1999, p 177) argues against Beck that:

> [r]isk is a way – or rather, a set of different ways – of ordering reality, of rendering it into a calculable form so that it might be made governable in particular ways, with particular techniques and for particular goals. It is a component of diverse forms of calculative rationality for governing the conduct of individuals, collectives and populations. It is thus not possible to speak of incalculable risks, or of risks that escape our modes of calculation, and even less possible to speak of a social order in which risk is largely calculable and contrast it with one in which risk has become largely incalculable.

It is hard to disagree with Dean's refusal of 'incalculable' governance, and easy to agree with his emphasis on the need to consider the diverse ways of calculating the future that are found in risk-centred government. But does this warrant the erasure of uncertainty from a framework of governmental analysis? Whatever Beck and others meant by asserting that uncertainty involves 'incalculability', they did not mean that *no* calculation was occurring. Neither Knight nor Keynes, for example, believed that capitalists simply entrusted their capital to *fortuna*. Knight, for example, argues that it is vital to recognise that under conditions of uncertainty,

> [t]he fact can hardly be over-emphasized, that a judgment of probability is actually made in such circumstances. The businessman himself not merely forms the best estimate he can of the outcome of his actions, but he is likely also to estimate the probability that his estimate is correct. The 'degree' of certainty or of confidence felt in the conclusion after it is reached cannot be ignored, for it is of the greatest practical significance. The action which follows upon an opinion depends as much upon the amount of confidence in that opinion as it does upon the favourableness of the opinion itself. (Knight, 1921, pp 226–27)

The problem, as Knight sees it, is simply that business decisions are 'far too unique' to allow for *statistical* calculation to occur. Nevertheless, he asserts that entrepreneurs practising uncertainty may make a 'more or less correct judgment about things' on the basis of what seems 'reasonable' (1921, p 227). Much the same line was followed by Keynes, who understood uncertainty to refer to situations where there is 'no method possible for determining a *numerical* measure of the probability relation between given hypotheses and evidence' (Keynes, in Cutler *et al*, 1986, p 913; emphasis added). It appears he considered it rational and normal to use available evidence to make a non-statistical calculation about the likely outcome of events. Even Tom Peters (1987), despite his view that prediction is a thing of the past, gives us a considerable array of instructions about how the new age manager should practice 'forward planning' in the new 'uncertain' global economy. It is likely that Peters has made a considerable fortune out of dispensing such advice on how to 'effectively' conduct business under 'incalculable' conditions.

Such writers might thus agree with Dean that uncertainty is rationally calculative, but still maintain the distinction between risk and uncertainty. One reason for resisting Dean's position – apart from the fact that he deploys the seemingly identical distinction between 'qualitative' and 'quantitative' risk (1999, p 177) – is that the protagonists of uncertainty use it as a term explicitly and pivotally denoting something they set against risk. As with Beck, those such as Keynes, Knight, and others clearly mean to state that uncertainty is not a type of risk, and a governmental analysis needs to recognise this. This is not meant to suggest that we accept their claims that the distinction reflects divergent properties of real events or situations. From a governmental standpoint, risks and uncertainties are neither real nor unreal. Rather, they are ways in which the real is imagined to be by specific regimes of government, in order that it may be governed. In this sense, if these writers are regarded as promoting certain ways of governing – as is most obviously the case with Keynes, and only slightly less so with the others – then their distinctions between uncertainty and risk are not simply academic but governmental.[13] In turn, a governmental analytic that ignores categories internal to government, such as uncertainty, is in peril of losing contact with its subject matter, for language is the form through which government gives expression to how it envisions reality.

This same point raises questions from another direction. Lorna Weir has argued that in governmental discourses:

> Risk no longer has the invariant characteristic of being calculated exclusively on probability statistics. This position, standard in the 1920s, treats risk as contrastive with uncertainty, the former consisting of events whose probability is known or knowable, the latter where future events have inestimable or unknowable probabilities. In the extraordinary growth of risk assessment and risk management over the 1980s the category of risk was extended to include areas formerly categorised as uncertainties …
> Risk has become polysemic, a discursive shift that needs to be discussed as a phenomenon rather than eliminated by definitional fiat. (1996, p 383)

Weir's point is subtle and important. While it could be read as denying the risk/uncertainty distinction, I do not read it that way. Rather, it suggests, first, that

---

13 Keynes' writings were most explicitly translated into governmental practice, but self-evidently Tom Peters also seeks to instruct business leaders on how to govern their enterprises. Likewise, it can be argued that the whole purpose of Beck's thesis is to create a politics that is oriented toward the 'false' claims of expertise, the 'real' risks to the environment and so on. For this reason, I would argue that my 'collapsing' of the theoretical into the governmental reflects the explicitly governmental nature of these authors' projects. The argument also reflects points raised more generally by Foucaultian scholarship concerning the knowledge/power couple. In particular, such arguments suggest that where truth claims are made about the world, these always imply or justify certain courses of action aimed at aligning the conduct of others with the 'real'.

the distinction exists both in rationalities and in technologies. Second, it implies that the relationships between the discourses of risk and uncertainty and the technologies of risk and uncertainty are variable. To illustrate this, Weir points to the historical process in which techniques of uncertainty have been subsumed by discourses of risk. No doubt this is so. Thus while crime prevention is routinely referred to in terms of risk minimisation, many of its practices are based on common sense or 'uncertain' assumptions about what reduces crime, rather than on demonstrated statistical probabilities (Haggerty, 2003). Equally, however, the converse may occur. Technologies may change without a corresponding change in the language used to describe them. In financial futures and derivatives markets, the discourse of 'risk' has remained fairly constant since the 19th century. Yet complex, statistically probabilistic modelling techniques have extensively displaced uncertain forms of estimation (Pryke and Allen, 2000; Green, 2000). Thus, Weir is quite correct to emphasise the importance of tracking the variable relations between technologies and discourses of risk and uncertainty But, as her own argument indicates, analytically this makes more important, rather than less so, the need to retain a distinction between risk and uncertainty.

Despite this point, it may still be argued that the distinction between discourses and technologies of risk and uncertainty should not be given any special status. There are, as already implied, many ways in which technologies may be differentiated from each other. So why is this particular distinction to be made salient? One reason is that many of the most influential studies within the governmental analytic have traced not so much the discursive shift from uncertainty to risk, but a widespread shift toward the use of risk technologies and away from professional case-by-case diagnostics. It is a movement to government through aggregated futures (risk) from government of singular futures (uncertainty). For example, the contrast between statistical risk and uncertain technologies plays a central role in Castel's (1991) landmark analysis of the transition from dangerousness to risk. For Castel, 'dangerousness'

> ... implies at once the affirmation of a quality immanent to the subject (he or she is dangerous), and a mere probability, a quantum of uncertainty, given that the proof of the danger can only be provided after the fact, should the threatened action actually occur. Strictly speaking there can only ever be *imputations of dangerousness*, postulating the hypothesis of a more or less probable relationship between certain present symptoms and a certain act to come. (1991, p 283; emphasis in original)

The result, he suggests, is that it is not possible to have 'a fully fledged policy of prevention' under the sign of dangerousness, because only those already diagnosed as dangerous could be subject to such a policy. Diagnosing dangerousness, in this sense, involves a disciplinary technology whereby the patient is diagnosed as having an existing condition, and is treated or restrained in order to govern the possibility of harm. The diagnosis produced by this disciplinary process remains uncertain, and a 'second opinion' can always be sought. This is, of course, a problem common to all diagnostics, even where positivist scientific theories are deployed. The individual, unique diagnosis or prediction is often regarded as uncertain because, it is argued, 'interfering variables' can never be eliminated. This problem haunted the positive human sciences especially, and science in general, until, after the turn of the 20th century, it was resolved by translating uncertainty into probability. This was achieved, as Ian Hacking shows (1990, p 45), by shifting scientific epistemologies from the deterministic to the stochastic. Uncertainty disappeared, to be replaced by risk. The problem of imprecise or inaccurate prediction was 'resolved' by rendering the underlying regularities probabilistic. Unpredicted outcomes in particular cases became merely part of a probabilistic distribution. For Castel, the emergence of risk in psychiatry resolved a parallel problem by making the 'diagnosis' appear objective, an effect achieved by representing the particular case as simply an instance of an aggregate with known statistical properties. This first appears in the psychiatric domain with the work of mid-19th century scientists, such as Morel, concerned with abnormalities among the poor. As Castel argues:

> Morel was already arguing in terms of *objective risks*: that is to say, statistical correlations between series of phenomena. At the level of practices, he also suggested that the public authorities undertake a special surveillance of those population groups which might by this stage already have been termed populations at risk, those located at the bottom of the social ladder. (1991, p 284; emphasis in original)

Because such aggregate 'objective' characteristics could be represented with statistical precision – that is as 'risks' – they became visible and manifest, rather than merely the hypothetical diagnoses of individuals based on medical opinion. Castel suggests preventative strategies aimed at whole categories of people henceforward became both justified and possible. In turn, as this process has advanced, Castel (1991, p 281) sees the use of uncertain technologies (diagnosing individuals by the case method) becoming progressively more marginal. The 'new strategies dissolve the notion of a *subject* or a concrete individual, and put in its place a combinatory of *factors*, the factors of risk'. At the same time, 'the essential component of intervention no longer takes the form of the direct face-to-face relationship between the carer and the cared, the helper and the helped, the professional and the client'. Under the emerging regime of risk, Castel argues, psychiatric specialists become marginalised and subordinated, merely filling in *pro forma* scales and routines provided by a remote managerial expertise. All this is achieved not simply by aggregation, for the dangerous had often been aggregated before, for example in the idea of the 'dangerous classes'. The unpredictable, dangerous classes could be governed only as unpredictable mobs or individuals. Only when the 19th century drew to a close did new technologies emerge – ranging from eugenics to social insurance – for governing them as 'actuarial' entities, statistically knowable and calculable risks.

In a parallel example, Feeley and Simon's highly influential work on the 'new penology' (1992; 1994) argues that in the governance of crime, statistically-based 'actuarial justice' has been promoted over uncertain methods of clinical or judicial decision-making. This is said to be occurring precisely because the predictive power of professional judgments about re-offending is officially regarded as inferior to statistical calculations of risk – based on such factors as offending record, employment and psychiatric indicators. In place of the once dominant influences of judicial expertise and the professional diagnoses of social workers and probation officers, actuarial justice is seen to subordinate all court officers to managerial demands. Concerns to reduce risks are translated into flows of numbers, inputs and outputs – statistical and systematic properties that pay no attention to the identity of subjects being processed.[14] In turn, in place of the uncertain ways of governing individuals through diagnosis and therapeutics, the convicted are incapacitated. The reduction in risk can thus be calculated precisely, but not in terms of 'reformed' prisoners (an always contestable category as prisoners may re-offend at some later point). Instead, risk reduction is rendered 'objective' by computations of aggregate numbers of prisoners and the average number of offences per year each would otherwise have committed – thus confirming the importance of systematic indicators such as inputs and throughputs.

In sum, foundational works in governmental analysis have focused on the importance of recognising the changing relationships between aggregating and individuating technologies of governing the present in terms of an indeterminate future. These and a host of other studies of specific fields of governance trace the transition from government by professional, expert and everyday knowledges concerned with the diagnosis of individual cases, towards the management of probabilistic – often statistical – categories with individual 'cases' considered as members of these. In short, this process is identifiable as the shift from uncertainty to risk.[15]

Articulating risk and uncertainty

It would be easy to draw the conclusion that by differentiating risk and uncertainty, a rigid binary has been established. This certainly is the case in the writings of Beck. However, there are various dimensions in terms of which risk and uncertainty may blur, converge or overlap. First among these is the statistical dimension of probability itself. Statistical calculation is an essential element of risk for many commentators. For Richard Ericson and his colleagues (2003, pp 34–35) risk is 'embedded in statistical laws of probability'; for Francois Ewald (2002, p 278) it is 'based on statistics and probabilities'; and for Mary Douglas (1986, p 19) risk turns 'uncertainties into probabilities'. An alternative governmental approach to risk has been explored by Jonathan Simon (1987, pp 66–67), who regards risk as 'a set of

---

14 Many other leading studies have been carried out along similar lines, although only a few need be mentioned. Weir's own research, while emphasising the multiplicity of discourses and practices of risk embedded in the genealogy of pregnancy, is focused primarily on the ascendancy of a particular variety of statistically-based risk – 'clinical risk' – over more traditional practices of medical diagnosis (Weir 1996). Ericson and Haggerty's (1997) research on police work attends to the ways in which the required use of incident report sheets forces officers to record their observations in a pre-coded form based on risk frameworks. A plethora of studies (eg, Ewald, 1991; Defert, 1991; Simon, 2001; Knights and Verdubakis, 1997) has mapped the extension of statistical calculations of risk across a wide array of insurance forms and practices. Most fundamentally, perhaps, Hacking (1995) and Daston (1988) have mapped the ways in which probability itself came to drift from uncertainty to risk – from the considered reasoning of wise men to the numerical reasoning of statistics.

15 Eg, Defert's (1991), Daston's (1988), Doran's (1994) and Ewald's (1986; 1991) studies of insurance chart the ways in which statistically-based actuarialism came to displace other forms of spreading 'risks' that were based on judgment and estimation. Many studies have examined similar processes in criminal justice (eg, O'Malley, 1992; Hannah-Moffat, 1999; Ericson, 1994; Ericson and Haggerty, 1997; Levi, 2000; Simon, 1998). Health and safety have also been extensively researched (see generally Green, 1997), and more recently a body of work is developing on genetics and risk (eg, Novas and Rose, 2000; Rose, 2001).

techniques for aggregating people, representing them as locations on a population distribution, and treating people on the basis of this distribution'. This allows him to include in his analysis non-statistical techniques of governing aggregates through distributions. Thus, among the ways of 'pooling resources to cover the risks generated by collectivities of people', he includes the movement in tort law toward strict liability. (That is, in relation to certain commodities, claimants need no longer establish the negligence of the manufacturer if they have suffered injury or other harm.) In such instances courts in the United States (for example in *Escola v Coca Cola Bottling of Fresno* 24 Cal 2d 462 (1944)) have come to regard incidents such as exploding glass bottles of carbonated soft drink in a new way:

> Bottles exploding are not treated as anomalies that break the rules of normal conduct, but as a regular by-product of the manufacturing process which is predictable in general, but not in its specific manifestations. The logic of this position is forward looking. Manufacturers can provide the generalized form of security needed to counteract the social cost of this risk, regardless of whether they could prevent this risk in the first place. (Simon, 1987, p 71)

Simon's argument raises a critical issue. In this light it does appear that the focus on statistics is only a special – albeit perhaps currently the most important – technique based on a governmental mentality that is predictive and governs in terms of aggregate futures. It also suggests that there is no hard and fast line to draw between risk and uncertainty in this way. As will be seen shortly, Nikolas Rose (1998a, pp 186–87) notes with respect to psychiatric assessments of risk, 'even if clinical diagnosis has become probabilistic and factoral … it is seldom numerical'. Resistant to subordinating their diagnostic skills to risk schedules, psychiatrists blur the distinction between risk and uncertainty. In Chapter 4, it will be seen that in contract law and tort law, common law judges hold fast to a model of 'reasonable foreseeability'. In so doing they frequently stray into linguistic discourses on probability but rarely, if ever, refer to statistics. In this way we might regard risk and uncertainty as end points on a continuum, with statistical probability at one extreme, although it might be better to think of statistical probability as being one form, rather than a polar (and thus defining) type, of risk.

Simon's analysis also suggests a second dimension in terms of which risk and uncertainty may converge, overlap or diverge. We may take it for granted that uncertainty focuses on avoiding or minimising harms, as in the taking of precautions on the basis of 'common sense'. But equally, as in the case of speculative investment, uncertainty may be creative, generating profit and wealth. This is the sense in which Frank Knight uses the term. Risk, on the other hand, is routinely referred to as if it is a technology only for governing harms (for example, Ewald, 1991; Beck, 1992). However, for Simon the focus of risk is on *security*. Security, in liberal government, has both a positive sense of facilitating the creative and productive liberty of the population, and a negative sense of preserving the population's safety from violence and depredation. In this specific respect, Simon's approach is aligned with that of Ericson, Doyle and Barry (2003, p 34) who argue that 'probability statistics provide knowledge of risk not only for the "taming of chance", but also for the taking of chance'. Some of the interventions of welfare states, effected under the banner of social security, can also be regarded in this light. The mass provision of dietary supplements, for instance, was founded not only in an attempt to reduce health risks to the population, but also to build the strength and constitution of its members.[16] Such measures characterised some of the earliest 'welfare' programmes in Europe, in the wake of statistical evidence of the declining physical constitution of working people (and particularly of men eligible for conscription). Considered in this way as technologies of security, the binary of risk as defensive and uncertainty as creative, as imagined by Bernstein and others, is displaced by more variable and overlapping relationships. However, there is a third dimension that is perhaps still more important in this respect. This concerns confidence.

It will be recalled that Frank Knight remarked upon the importance of the degree of certainty or 'confidence' felt by an entrepreneur about a decision. Uncertainty – as Keynes also stressed – does not necessarily imply mere guesswork, but is based on the formation of empirically-based principles or rules that provide a guide to the future. Tried and trusted routines that have 'worked' for years, theories associated with professional knowledge, rules of thumb that have proven good predictors in the past – these are associated with high degrees of confidence. As confidence increases, then ultimately indeterminacy is eclipsed, and the course of action will proceed as if the outcome is known. Conversely, unusual situations tend to generate low confidence because the applicability of familiar rules or patterns cannot be assumed. With respect to risk also, confidence is vital, usually being related to questions about sample size and appropriateness. The principles involved closely parallel those with respect to confidence in uncertainty. An illustration of the importance of this point is provided by Ulrich Beck's assumptions about

---

16 This is, perhaps, closely linked with Foucault's conception of 'the regulation of populations'. Regulation is associated with 'comprehensive measures, statistical assessments and interventions aimed at the entire social body or at groups taken as a whole' – and thus corresponds closely to 'bio-power' (Foucault, 1984, p 145). Thus he argues that government now:

> has as its purpose not the act of government in itself, but the welfare of the population, the improvement of its condition, the increase of its wealth, longevity, health, etc. and the means that the government uses to attain these ends are themselves all in some sense immanent to the populations; it is the population itself on which the government will act either directly through large-scale campaigns, or indirectly through techniques that will make possible, without the full awareness of the people, the stimulation of birth rates, the directing of the flow of population into certain regions or activities etc. (Foucault, 1991, p 100)

However, as such approaches are by no means limited to predictive and indeterminist interventions (eg, ethnic cleansing) it is mostly likely that risk is best regarded as a technology integral to – but not exhausting – regulation.

A similar point may be made with respect to the relationship between discipline and risk. Some commentators (eg, Simon, 1988) have suggested that risk displaces discipline, and it may be deduced that discipline and uncertainty are thus intimately related. In practice this is doubtful. Most government through risk is highly disciplinary. This may be seen in the responsibilities of the 'risky' pregnant mother (Weir, 1996), in the 'duty to be well' implied by new techniques of risk-based health (Greco, 1993), or in the crime prevention responsibilities of the potential victim (O'Malley, 1992). However, it is also the case that the disciplinary process of creating individuals – the separating practices, examination, normalisation and so on – are displaced where risk is introduced (O'Malley, 1992). Such aspects of disciplinarity may be seen as characteristically uncertain, rather than risk-related. But they do not characterise all uncertainty. The enterprising activities of the business operator, for example, escape this framework.

modernisation risks. For Beck, the focus on statistical prediction appears critical, for his argument is that one of the primary characteristics of modernisation risks is that they are of such low frequency that they cannot be statistically predicted with any confidence.[17] In practice, however, the statistical nature (or otherwise) of the predictions Beck is concerned about is not the relevant matter. It is quite rare to find events such as global warming or holes in the ozone layer associated with predictions based on statistical probability. Rather, they are known and discussed primarily as singular processes understood in terms of general scientific theory. In this respect Beck's problem is that he lacks confidence in the science on which the predictions are based. Despite his fetish about statistical prediction, whether predictions are made in terms of statistics, or not, evidently is more or less irrelevant. In conditions of low confidence, the distinction between risk and uncertainty becomes sufficiently unclear that even such critics become confused.

For such reasons, making the distinction between risk and uncertainty cannot be regarded as setting up a rigid binary. It may be better to regard them as related along multiple axes, with the effect that no single continuum (such as one running from statistical probability to vague hunches) will adequately represent the relationships between them. This makes all the more pressing the need to consider closely the diverse configurations that are adopted by risk and uncertainty, and the relationships between these.

Configurations of risk and uncertainty

In governmental analysis, blanket categorisations of 'government through risk', while often a useful shorthand, often give way to an interest in the diverse 'configurations of risk'. Initial advances of this sort have been made by Mitchell Dean (1999) and Lorna Weir (1996), at least with respect to classifying diverse forms of risk-based government. Both scholars suggest that analysis is hampered by the adoption of a unified category of risk. While uncertainty seems not to have entered their equation, at least explicitly, their work leads to the identification of a number of forms taken by risk technologies. The three principal forms identified are insurance, clinical, and epidemiological.

'Insurance risk' is perhaps the most familiar type, readily identified as a form of risk-spreading. Its concern is not necessarily with reducing risks – indeed under many circumstances this might be quite counterproductive to the profitability and viability of insurance. Rather, it is concerned with mitigating the impact of harms by distributing them across time and populations. They are spread over time through the mechanism of monthly or yearly premiums; and across populations through the mechanism of risk pools – categories of equivalent riskiness. Statistical probability

---

17 Beck's focus on statistics also leads him to characterise the risk society as one in which insurance becomes impossible. It is one in which, symptomatically, we are confronted by insurers refusing to insure what scientists claim to be risk-predictable events (1999, p 142). This is assumed to reveal the bogus nature of scientific estimations of risk. Beck is perhaps guilty of some naivety here, since insurers quite often refuse insurance on events that might be quite predictable but that are in their estimation unlikely to provide profitable business. Insurance redlining is precisely one such institutionalised practice, often more or less explicitly racist in nature (Heimer, 1982).

allows insurance actuaries to calculate efficient risk-spreading distributions: other things being equal, the greater the risk, the higher the premium. Insurance risk redistribution is premised, as Ewald (1991) has indicated, on the conversion of risks into capital. Typically, insurance has become a process in which a given harm is equated with a specified amount of money; financial compensation is distributed for a specific loss under specified circumstances. This set of practices is founded on an abstract technology of risk, which, translated into a wide diversity of specific forms of insurance, works through statistical distributions that indicate the frequency and magnitude of harms (Ewald, 1991).[18]

'Clinical risk' (Weir, 1996) is typified by the use of risk-based techniques in medical diagnosis and can be differentiated from insurance risk on many dimensions. In the case of pregnancy, for example, risk factors in the woman's heredity, diet and physical condition are monitored in order to locate the presence of risk factors. While it shares with insurance the technique of deploying probabilities to locate potential harms, clinical risk does not seek to spread or transfer risks; instead, it aims to reduce or minimise them. It works by identifying probabilistic indicators of future conditions. In response to the presence of these indicators, it seeks to reduce the probability, mitigate the magnitude or prevent the occurrence of the predicted harm. Thus, pregnant women may be advised to change their diet, take certain drugs, stop smoking, even abort the foetus depending on the risk factor detected and the practitioner's estimation of its impact. Evidently this type of risk technique has been adapted to many other contexts and forms the basis of interventions in developmental psychology, education, crime prevention and so forth.

Clinical risk has much in common with what Dean (1999) terms 'epidemiological risk', which includes public health interventions such as mass immunisation and drug regulation. Like clinical risk, epidemiological risk is concerned with risk identification in order to achieve risk and/or harm reduction. However, epidemiological risk differs in that, like insurance, it exhibits little interest in the individual except as a member of the risk category. Moreover, while clinical risk deploys risk techniques in order to work on specific individuals, epidemiological risk aims to reduce harms to general populations. To these three types may be added what Feeley and Simon (1994) refer to as *actuarial risk*. While sharing with insurance and clinical risk the technique of assigning individuals to risk pools, its concerns are not with reducing risks to individuals, but with reducing risks for populations. For example, in actuarial justice, high-risk potential offenders are subjected to curfews or quarantines to reduce the overall distribution of risk for all potential victims. Psychiatric interventions, discussed by Rose (1998a), partake of the same form, whereby psychiatrists may prolong or intensify the incapacitation of patients deemed to represent unacceptable risks to others.

---

18 As suggested already, and further argued in Chapters 5 and 6, this is a debatable characterisation of insurance as a contemporary and historical institution. It is probably more accurate to say that it is a very common technology of insurance, especially in the 19th and 20th centuries.

No doubt further types could be identified, and it is clearly the case that specific strategies for governing through risk may combine several or conceivably all of these. Rose's (1998a) work, for example, indicates that psychiatric patients may be kept under treatment both in relation to risks to themselves (clinical risk) and risks to others (actuarial risk). Yet for all the evident insights that it is capable of generating, this approach either ignores uncertainty or collapses it into risk, assuming risk-centredness. If risk and uncertainty are to be regarded as distinguishable ways of imagining and governing the future, then rather than analysis only in terms of configurations of risk we should also think in terms of *configurations of uncertainty*. Again, no definitive list can be attempted, but several broad configurations are readily discernable: prudential, precautionary, and diagnostic.

Prudential uncertainty is exemplified by such specific practices as thrift and saving, in which financial resources are set aside in order to provide for the effects of future harms. It is a highly moralised technology, founded in the assumption that certain adverse events are foreseeable, and should be guarded against. Like insurance risk, with which it shares much in common, this converts harms into capital. Also like insurance it spreads the harms over time in the form of regular contributions to savings. Unlike insurance, it is not based upon the probabilistic calculation of hazards, but on foresight – that is, on a prediction based on common sense knowledge of empirical frequencies. It works with possibilities rather than precise probabilities, but it can readily be seen that insurance and prudence blur together. As will be discussed in Chapter 6, in the 19th century savings and insurance were regarded as more or less interchangeable forms of prudence. Savings bank accounts and insurance policies often overlap in form, as is most evident where insurance benefits are strictly related to past contributions.

Precautionary uncertainty coincides with prudence in that it is based on the perception of possibilities rather than probabilistic prediction. It differs from prudence in that, as Ewald (2002) and Haggerty (2003) suggest, it is not concerned with harms calculated as capital. As with clinical risk and epidemiological risk, the primary aim of precaution is the avoidance or minimisation of harms. Often this is because what is to be protected is not regarded as financially compensable. Precaution can be deployed at a mass level, as with respect to prohibitions on genetically modified foods. Equally, it is deployed at an individual level where a common stock of knowledge identifies major hazards. Stanko (1990), for example, has argued that in an environment where sexual predation is common 'precaution is normal' among women. In contrast to most forms of risk, precaution and prudence do not rely on expertise of the abstract-universal kind. Often they apply under conditions in which such expertise is brought into doubt or is unavailable, and in which local and informal knowledge and techniques are deployed to achieve security.

Diagnostic uncertainty contrasts with both previous forms in that its predictions are structured by reference to expertise, usually abstract-universal expertise. As suggested above, at one extreme diagnostic uncertainty merges into certainty or determinism. However, much expert determination of futures takes an uncertain form. For example, the clinical prognosis given by the medical practitioner or psychiatrist; the advice of the lawyer on the likely outcome of a case; the investment advice of the financial expert; and so on. All these predictive exercises govern individual futures about which not all 'relevant' details are known or knowable. These are assumed to be inherently uncertain predictions. In contrast to both prudence and precaution, however, diagnostic uncertainty is not necessarily focused on the government of harms. As with certain forms of risk, diagnostic uncertainty can be put to work productively or creatively – the example of the financial adviser being one of the more salient. Diagnostic uncertainty overlaps extensively with discipline, in the sense that diagnosis involves the processes of examination, individuation, normalisation and so on that Foucault outlines as characteristic of that form of 'power'. It is this form of uncertainty that is usually at issue in studies, such as those of Castel (1991) and Rose (1998a), that chart the displacement of uncertainty by risk.[19]

No doubt other forms of technology of uncertainty could be identified. Diagnostic uncertainty implies the presence of expert judgment. But 'informal' judgments about the future may also be productive. Tom Peters' vision of *enterprising uncertainty*, for example, stridently rejects formal expertise as irrelevant and ineffective. Instead it focuses on the perceptive and adaptive capacities of the entrepreneur, and links these directly to the power to create wealth. But what is already emerging is that this way of thinking about risk and uncertainty in terms of types may be rather limited. We have already seen that various forms of insurance are difficult to classify in terms of 'insurance risk', for elements of uncertainty may be combined with the latter, as in catastrophe insurance (Bougen, 2003). Much the same seems to be true for superannuation (O'Malley, 2002) and many other forms of insurance (Ericson *et al*, 2003). Such examples indicate the limits of this kind of typological exercise, for 'hybrids' often appear more frequently than the 'pure' types. For this reason, it may be better to regard these types as sometimes useful summaries, but which focus more on risk and uncertainty as being configured together in many and complex ways – as configurations or assemblages. In Mitchell Dean's terms:

> An assemblage is made up of bits and pieces and operates in its coupling with other assemblages. It is a way of thinking about entities as multiplicities rather than unities, as complex ensembles of discontinuous elements and forces bound by heteromorphic relations. It thus makes possible a way of thinking about 'social apparatuses' ... as composed from diverse elements and relations that are irreducible to a fundamental essence, and that are composed of multiple and varying dimensions. The notion of an assemblage implies lines of continuous variation that can never be homogenised into a linear process of change or transformation. (Dean, 1996, pp 55–56)

Analyses that envision governmental technologies in terms of variable configurations, assemblages or ensembles of elements, rather than as fixed types, fit well with analyses of how governmental technologies and techniques reflect a particular vision of the problem to be solved. They allow us to make clear the distinction between risk and uncertainty without forcing analysis to make invidious omnibus decisions in classifying complex assemblages of 'risk' and 'uncertain' elements as either risk or uncertainty. They allow that the technologies will frequently be present as fragments or elements of a particular configuration. In turn,

---

19 This is further discussed at footnote 16 above.

such a framework might cast a new light on the question of the ascendancy of risk in the current era, encouraging a more partial and nuanced analysis of how risk is expanding its domain.

Using the example of 'clinical risk', this suggestion can be taken further. Configurations of clinical risk have been widely developed in many fields of government. If we accept Weir's depiction, their key characteristic is the deployment of risk to govern a specific individual. That is, the individual is treated not simply as a representative of the risk category but as a unique case to which certain risk factors apply. Now in some examples, as Deleuze (1995, pp 169–82) has suggested, 'individuality' is perhaps a misleading term, as the case becomes a particular combination of risk factors, a recombination of 'dividuals'. Here, risk is clearly the dominant organising principle. In other cases, as discussed by Weir, the risk-based information is combined with elements of professional judgment, the building up of a case record, and so on. Both variants could be thought of as 'clinical risk'. However, as Castel's (1991) analysis of psychiatry suggests, the difference between them is significant. In one the professional expert becomes merely the functionary of risk-centred governance located elsewhere. In the other, professional experience and disciplinary knowledge retain a key role, a fact also registered in the status of the individual patient as an identity. What begins to come clear in this light is that not only is clinical risk a configuration that is variable in significant ways, but also it may not simply be a configuration of *risk*. Rather it appears as a variable array of assemblages of risk and uncertain elements. In some instances, such as Castel's, risk is the dominant element. In others, such as Weir's, uncertainty appears to be the main organising technology. The implications of this seem to be quite far reaching.

Castel's analysis of psychiatry, to stay with this example, maps out a process in which the professional practitioners are increasingly marginalised, their disciplinary knowledges ever more subordinated to risk routines. Rose's (1998a, pp 186–87) work, seemingly in agreement, points to a shift towards psychiatrists assessing the risks posed by patients at the expense of the priority of therapeutic intervention. But unlike Castel, Rose found that the process did not complete the transition from dangerousness to (statistical) risk. 'Psychiatric risk', Rose suggests, is rarely a comparison of patients' risk scores to statistical tables in order to generate probabilistic predictions:

> Rather it entails calculating the consequences of a concatenation of indicators or factors co-occurring in certain regular patterns. Even if clinical diagnosis has become probabilistic and factoral, however, it is seldom numerical ... mental health professionals tend to resist the use of numerical risk assessment schedules and classifications. They stress that assessment of risk is a clinical matter, and has to take place within a clinical assessment of mental disorder ... (Rose, 1998a, pp 196–97)

Psychiatrists, it would seem, have avoided displacing or reducing their diagnostic assessments to mere numerical scores. Instead, perhaps because of the autonomy or status of their profession, they appear to have negotiated a compromise through which to govern mental illness. Castel's trajectory has been disrupted by the development of a new configuration of technologies. If Castel unwittingly slips into a mapping of an inevitable future, Rose's observations on the unanticipated emergence of a new diagram of power retain a genealogical sensibility. No outcome is inevitable, and things may become otherwise than they are. Clinical risk thus appears not as a stable type of risk, but as an unstable assemblage in which diagnostic uncertainty and predictive risk may be aligned in significantly different ways. These alignments may change according to such considerations as the resistance of practitioners, discoveries of the 'unreliable' nature of planned techniques, and so on.

As this also indicates, the existence of a plan, or of the design of a governmental technology, is quite distinct from whether or not it is translated into practice. It would be a major error of interpretation (for example, Frankel, 1997) to read governmental analyses as assuming that everyone now accepts 'enterprise culture' as the way they should govern themselves, or that everyone is 'risk conscious'. As with Rose's resistant psychiatrists, probation officers required to deploy risk schedules in making decisions regarding offenders routinely use their professional judgment instead (Kemshall, 1998). Government is always an *attempt* to create subjects of a certain kind, or achieve results of a certain form. Failure, judged internally or by external critics, is routine. To some degree, such 'failures' to translate the blueprints of rule into practice are part of the genealogies of new technologies and rationalities. For example, the resistance of many 'welfare' professionals and intellectuals to the abandonment of 'social' factors may have been instrumental in modifying British neo-liberalism in the direction of a social democratic 'Third Way'. Among other advantages, this emphasis on risk and uncertainty as being in unstable and multiple relationships with each other may also serve to restrict the tendency to overemphasise the unidirectional spread of risk.

Risk, uncertainty and the risk society

In many writings, there is a sense of an almost inexorably increasing reach of risk. This sense is readily formed from the sheer accumulation of studies identifying risk's recent appearance in new programmes and areas of government. It is most explicit, of course, in the risk society theorists' vision of an unending cycle in which new discoveries of risks give rise to increased insecurity, in turn giving rise to further risk discovery (Ericson and Haggerty, 1997; Beck, 1992). The result is a kind of fatalism about risk. This is not meant to deny that in some respects risk is becoming a more widespread and encompassing technology of governance. Rather, it is to suggest that the picture is much more complex and uneven than the theories of the 'risk society' suggest. For example, while there has been an increase in some forms of risk-centred governance, many 'social' forms of risk-centred governance, such as social insurance, have been reduced in their scale and reach by neo-liberal governments. Consequently, the undoubted increase in the more individualised and commodified technologies and programmes may be offset by this change. Risk is not simply displacing other ways of governing, and it is therefore difficult to assess whether more of the lives of more people are being governed through risk. Additionally we have no way of knowing whether current tendencies will continue. Such problems suggest that the way forward for the governmental analysis of risk is to abandon the blanket characterisation of 'risk', and to eschew the imagery of an inevitable transition into the 'risk society'. We need to forgo grand schemas of inevitable social change. Accordingly we need to develop a more nuanced analysis of the ways in which, almost everywhere that risk appears, it is assembled into complex configurations with other technologies, particularly – if not only – with uncertainty.[20] If we abandon fatalistic theories that claim to know the future, questions of *how* we are being governed through *what kind* of frameworks and technologies of government become more important. What configurations or ensembles of risk and uncertainty are being deployed, and to what end? What are their implications for how we should govern ourselves and be made responsible for others? What knowledge do these developments privilege; what truths do they assume, and which do they gag or subordinate? What kinds of subjects, communities and societies do they seek to turn us into?

These are by no means new questions, even though lately they have been somewhat silenced by a pervasive sense that risk *per se* is a new and monolithic form of government that is taking over our lives. Rather, the politics of risk and uncertainty – the raising of all these questions in relation to innovations in government – has a long genealogy. They were present in 18th and 19th century concerns about how individuals should conduct themselves in a free market society. They appeared in contemporaneous debates over how contracts of financial risk and speculation should be governed. Such politics also focused on the moral rights and wrongs of gambling and speculative futures markets. Such politics were also to the fore in the late 19th and early 20th centuries when the establishment of social insurance and social security conflicted with some foundational assumptions of classical liberal government. Subsequently, the transformation and even dismantling of these social insurance apparatuses under contemporary neo-liberalism, has become another major theme of the politics of risk and uncertainty. If today it seems daring or cruel, liberating or repressive, wise or misguided to subject people to the uncertainties of market forces, or to the technocratic domination of risk's expertise, it is to be remembered that these have also been political issues for more than two centuries.

While risk and uncertainty, and the politics they generate, are diverse in origin and form, they also are connected to variations in the forms and genealogy of political liberalism. Liberalism's constant concerns have been with the dynamics of 'freedom', in the sense of uncoerced activities of rationally calculating individuals confronting and making an indeterminate yet knowable future. Its subjects are in their basic diagram risk-assessors, performing the felicity calculus in an attempt to plot the probable and possible consequences of their actions. Its fundamental – if often troubled – reliance on the production of material wealth is based on market competition and 'risk-taking' enterprise. The rise of freedom in the context of

---

20 Much the same point is illustrated with respect to crime prevention. Kevin Haggerty (2003, pp 202–04) has pointed out correctly that much crime prevention is precautionary in nature. That is, despite the pervasive presence of a discourse of risk, exact probabilities do not exist to cover many crime situations, and many measures taken by governments and individuals are based on uncertainty. He notes that precaution is distinct from risk because, quoting Francois Ewald, it 'invites one to anticipate what one does not yet know, to take into account doubtful hypotheses and simple suspicions' (Haggerty, 2003, p 203). The category of precaution has also fallen prey to sociologists' love of identifying great sea-changes in society, for Ewald (2002) now suggests we are entering the era of precaution.

governmentally promoted market uncertainty, and the rise of probability and risk as ways of calculating indeterminacy, are historically, geographically and discursively linked with the emergence and ascendancy of liberalism. We might then profitably turn to the question of how uncertainty and risk have made us variably and *liberally free*.

Chapter 2
From Independence to Social Security

An essential and original feature of liberalism as a principle of governmental reason is that it pegs the rationality of government, of the exercise of political power, to the freedom and interested rationality of the governed themselves ... it finds the principle for limiting and rationalising the exercise of political power in the operation of the freedom and rationality of those who are to be governed. (Burchell, 1991, pp 138–40)

That risk and uncertainty have become central issues of late may have much to do with core concerns of liberalism. This view contrasts with the position adopted by theories of the risk society that envisage a government focus on risk and uncertainty as generated out of modernisation. Modernisation clearly is not irrelevant to the issue, at least in the sense of scientific and technological development. However, it would not appear that risk and uncertainty were ever strategies particularly favoured by modernist socialist and communist regimes. Their characteristic concerns have been far more with the certainties to be delivered by command economies, scientific government, five-year plans and the like. Liberalism's multifarious institutionalisations of 'individual liberty', 'freedom of choice', 'freedom of contract', the 'free market' and so on create a much greater affinity with imagining and governing a future that is more open and indeterminate than might be consistent with modernism. In particular, against the modernist desire for control, standardisation and scientific certainty, all forms of liberalism render uncertainty an essential component of good government. Through the nexus with the 'freedom' of rationally calculating subjects pursuing their own interests, uncertainty is at the core of what characterises liberalism.

Nevertheless, there are major variations in the course of historical liberalism concerning how central and large a role uncertainty is to play *vis à vis* scientific and risk-based interventions. These tensions are one expression of the dilemma of 'governing too much' that some have taken to be definitive of liberal government itself (Foucault, 1979; Gordon, 1991). Insofar as liberty can be identified as implying uncertainty, especially in the agentive figure of the liberal subject, the question of governing 'too much' can be posed as a question about how far government should restrict or regulate the play of uncertainty. As Peter Bernstein's writing on uncertainty and freedom illustrates, there is an underlying current in the liberal imagination that finds even probability a constraint of freedom. This issue is perhaps brought most sharply into focus by the struggles centred on government that are characterised by terms such as 'the mixed economy' and 'social security'. The social liberal protagonists of such strategies regarded the uncertainties generated by the supposedly untrammelled market relations of classical liberalism as problems to be governed scientifically and in the name of the social. In this sense, 'the social' refers to the collective entity, usually defined by national boundaries, that was understood to be greater than the sum of its individual members. It was seen both as a source of individual obligations and rights, and as an organic whole with sociological properties. By the end of the 19th century this was associated with a 'social' form of liberalism. Its advocates sought to reduce and contain the harms generated by cycles of boom and slump by understanding them as 'social problems' and problems of 'the economy'. Accordingly, the most characteristic interventions were made at the aggregate level by manipulating distributions such as of rates of unemployment or levels of poverty, and by inventing new forms of risk-centred technology such as social insurance. They sought to deploy the knowledge of the social sciences, especially economics, to create a more efficient and more socially 'just' society. Some uncertainty, especially in the form of market freedom, was to be retained as essential to the creation of profit and wealth, as Beveridge and Keynes had insisted; but science and risk were to tame uncertainty, to magnify its powers and minimise its harms. In making this move, social liberals set up an acute tension between their modernist and their liberal ambitions, between their faith in risk and science and liberalism's foundational faith in liberty and uncertainty.

The tensions created by these social liberal attempts to transform uncertainty are particularly visible in conflicts that opened up with classical liberals at the turn of the 20th century, and with emerging neo-liberalism toward the end of that century. By comparison, classical liberalism and neo-liberalism centre uncertainty in government to a much greater extent. The agenda of classical liberals had been to create a society in which the future was no longer to be set by governmental decrees and a moral economy. The market and 'voluntary' contractual relationships were to provide core techniques for creating and governing freedom in social and economic life. Subjects were to be exposed to uncertainties. Accordingly, freedom was shaped by attitudes and practices – especially foresight and prudence – that were deemed essential to survive independently in this environment. As a result, classical liberals' prognoses were that social liberalism would diminish those forces that stimulated enterprise and self-reliance, and that its necessary compulsions would constrain freedom. Almost a century later, neo-liberals offered a fundamentally similar diagnosis of social liberalism. Their cure for these ills was a return to greater uncertainty, but not a return to classical liberalism. Rather, 'markets' and 'enterprise' were to reconfigure governments, communities, corporations and individuals in the image of risk-taking and competition. Self-fulfilment would displace 'Victorian' self-denial, and sophisticated risk management would displace or at least modify conservative prudence.

Of course, this is a very narrow take on the genealogy of liberalism. The intention, however, is not to reduce liberalism merely to a series of configurations of risk and uncertainty. Rather, it is to explore the genealogies of risk and uncertainty in a specific light. In particular, the aim is to understand how risk and uncertainty have been deployed by diverse forms of liberalism, and how in their turn they have given a specific shape to some of the more salient characteristics of liberal government. These patterns are rarely simple, and one side of the equation cannot be 'read-off' from the other. Often the uses to which technologies are put, or the aspects of them that are valorised, could only be guessed at in advance. Social insurance, for example, often appears as a 'characteristic' technique of social liberalism, and it is easy to recognise the impact of this specific risk technology on 20th century liberal government. However, the actuarial or 'risk-based' elements of insurance were no more critical in this process than the contractual elements. Specifically liberal sensibilities were attracted to the valorisation of social insurance benefits as a legal right linked to contributions – an exchange between equals that did not vitiate independence. Indeed, the resulting configurations of social insurance themselves often proved unstable. Emerging liberal concerns such as with 'social justice' and 'efficiency' sometimes translated social insurance into forms of social security – such as universal access to benefits – bearing little resemblance to insurance. Neither risk and uncertainty, nor liberalism, are reducible to the other, but much can be learned from examining their nexus.

Classical liberalism and the 'yoke of foresight'

According to Jeremy Bentham, security was the primary object of law precisely because it 'necessarily embraces the future' (1962, p 302). Security appeared to him as the condition of existence upon which rests rational calculation of the future and all that follows from this foundational attribute of liberal subjects:

> In order to form a clear idea of the whole extent which ought to be given to the principle of security, it is necessary to consider, that man is not like the brutes, limited to the present time either in enjoyment or suffering, but that he is susceptible of pleasure and pain by anticipation, and that it is not enough to guard him against an actual loss, but also to guarantee to him, as much as possible, his possessions against future losses. The idea of his security must be prolonged to him throughout the whole vista that his imagination can measure. This disposition to look forward, which has so marked an influence on the condition of man, may be called expectation – expectation of the future. It is by means of this that we are able to form a general plan of conduct. (Bentham, 1962, p 308)

Bentham's vision was rather less optimistic than Adam Smith's serene landscape where rational choice actors operated to the mutual benefit of all. As Bentham suggests, and the first half of the 19th century illustrates, a central concern of liberals was that the future had to be made more politically certain in order to create the peaceable and free society that could deliver economic security. Only under the protection of law's security will 'want and enjoyment' between them provide for 'subsistence and abundance' (1962, p 303). But already Bentham has put his finger on a liberal paradox – perhaps its central paradox. The liberty of the individual is thought to be curtailed in order to guarantee the conditions whereby liberty will create security. Bentham's primary problem regarding security appears to be focused on the coercion needed to protect property from depredation. Having envisioned rational choice as human nature, it followed that those who 'have not' would – on the principle of least effort – take from those who 'have'. The problem was all the more acute because so much of the populace was regarded as undisciplined and uncivilised. The 'barbarious hordes' of Bentham's discourse gave way to the 'dangerous classes' of the Victorians but the sense persisted over the first half of the century, and well beyond, that the threatening masses were in need of *civilising*. They had to be coerced in order to become free. Thus, as Mariana Valverde (1996) has shown, even late into the 19th century, popular and governmental imageries of working class areas bore close resemblance to imageries of the uncivilised colonies, as did some of the techniques (notably missionary work) used to bring light into these 'dark places'.

Depredation did not only take the form of criminal appropriation of property. An equally, perhaps more pressing, problem was how to minimise the drain on wealth created by relief for the poor. The principal solution to this was to train these segments of the population in the ways of independence or 'self-reliance' – a theme that became almost the defining characteristic of classical liberal problematics. In turn, a key technique in this process of liberation and civilisation, as Foucault has observed, was discipline. Discipline, in the sense explored by Foucault in *Discipline and Punish* (1977), works on the soul as the seat of habit, and the factory, the workhouse and the prison were key institutions where habits of labour and diligence were to be instilled – coercively if necessary; but the account delivered in *Discipline and Punish* overemphasises the importance of inculcating unthinking obedience and toil. Bentham's Panopticon, for example, certainly can be read, as Foucault suggests, in terms of the delivery of a multitude of tiny moments of correction that eventually creates docile bodies. This is a rather slanted account, as in *Discipline and Punish* the emphasis was on exploring techniques of domination. Only later did Foucault's attention turn to 'techniques of the self', through which self-government is exercised. Yet the instilling of these latter techniques was critical to the formation of the liberal subjectivity that disciplinary institutions, even the Panopticon, were to produce. In Bentham's view a vital task was to impart a particular kind of rationality, the 'disposition to look forward'. Discipline was not only (and perhaps not even) intended to create habits of blind obedience. Even more importantly it was to '*accustom men to submit to the yoke of foresight*, at first painful to be borne, but afterwards agreeable and mild: it alone could encourage them in labour – superfluous at present, and [the benefits of] which they are not to enjoy till the future' (Bentham, 1962, p 307; emphasis added). These liberal subjects were not to be mindless automatons, but rational calculators of a certain sort. Foresight involved an attitude to the future which, *inter alia*, took account of the possible calamities that were regarded as a corollary of being free. It was closely linked with the application of prudent techniques for governing this uncertain future. Foresight – by aligning labour with frugality and thrift – secured the means to relief 'from accident, from the revolutions of commerce, from natural calamities and especially from disease' (Bentham, 1962, p 316). Whatever imageries of entrepreneurship may have been current, Bentham's main concern for liberal subjects, and the concern of liberal regimes throughout the 19th century, was that they were to be 'risk averse'. Insecurity in the face of uncertainty was the spur to action that secured the independence of the subject. Thus, for Bentham, a principal justification for illiberal despotism over the masses – the coercion implicit in disciplinary institutions such as the prison and the Poor Law – was the necessity of 'encouraging the spirit of economy and foresight among the inferior classes of society' (1962, p 316).

This initial focus on Bentham is not intended to establish him as the architect of liberal governance, nor as the inventor of that autonomous subject who is possessed of foresight – which has roots going back at least to the English Civil War.[1] Rather, it is that Bentham illustrates the extent to which foresight, as a technique of freedom, is deeply embedded in liberal government. Freedom was primarily thought of in terms of confronting a world characterised in its most vital respects by uncertainty –

1 In addition, foresight and its governance emerged in discourses of common law of the liberal era without any apparent reference to the works of Bentham or any of the theorists of liberalism. This will be discussed in more detail in Chapter 4. It is also the case that Bentham's vision of governing the poor was particularly severe when contrasted with prevailing views on the continent and in some colonies (Zohlner, 1982; Kewley, 1973). In Australia, for example, perhaps reflecting labour shortages from an early time, the view generally seems to have been that unemployment and poverty were likely to be temporary phenomena that required tiding-over support rather than the rigorous regimen Bentham regarded as necessary.

and most particularly by the uncertain perils and windfalls created by the free market. In the vision of 19th century governments the perils were far more salient than the windfalls. Consequently the liberal subjects' first civic responsibility was prudence, manifest in diligence, self-denial and thrift. For the most part pleasure was suspect, always teetering on the edge of hedonism and irresponsibility (O'Malley and Valverde, forthcoming). The bulk of the citizenry – who in the divergent visions of both Bentham and Marx possessed only their labour – were to be risk minimisers. More accurately they were to be practitioners of a defensive form of uncertainty. Even insurance appeared within a framework of thrift and self-denial.[2] In the form of 'industrial life assurance', developed in England and exported elsewhere, an army of collectors would exert moral pressure on families, and especially women, to pay their weekly contributions. The poor, it was assumed, could not resist the temptations that interfered with thrift and saving, and required this semi-coercive regime to enforce prudence. This kind of freedom bestowed upon the subjects of 19th century liberalism is, as Isaiah Berlin (1969) famously noted, a negative freedom, a freedom 'from'. It is a markedly different sense of freedom to that intended by Peter Bernstein when, at the close of the 20th century, he asserted that uncertainty makes us free. While for Bernstein uncertainty gives to liberal subjects unbounded freedom, a freedom 'to', for Bentham and the classical liberals, the principal problem was to make the masses guard against the uncertain and destructive forces of the future. For most subjects of classical liberalism freedom *subjected* them to uncertainty.

In marked contrast to their neo-liberal descendants, classical liberals never imagined all, or even a substantial proportion, of their subjects to be entrepreneurs. Indeed, against Bentham's vision that the market could deliver wealth to all, in the 1830s it was being argued by Chadwick that the poverty of some was essential to the wealth of others and necessary for the good of all (Poovey, 1995, pp 10–11). The entrepreneur was thus imagined as a special category of citizen. Of course, there is an assumption that everyone *could* become an entrepreneur, but mass entrepreneurship could hardly have been further from anyone's minds. Between the two uncertain worlds of Bentham and Bernstein, a gulf exists. In 19th century liberalism, entrepreneurs were those who had amassed sufficient capital to bear the loss of failure without becoming a burden on others – without subjecting their families to hardship, or the state to maintenance.[3] Even after the end of the 19th century, critics such as Max Weber (1978, p 374) were arguing that such a condition of accumulated wealth should be a *requirement* for entry into the ranks of market speculators. Entrepreneurs were the happy few who could afford to engage in practices of creative uncertainty. Notwithstanding more pressing concerns with poverty and pauperism, the state did much to foster this practice of freedom. Innovations such as limited liability encouraged risk-taking by protecting the financial security of capitalist adventurers. Stock exchanges were allowed considerable powers of self-government. The heroic status of the entrepreneur as the creator of social good through risk to his own capital served to protect this class from regulation aimed at protecting consumers from adulterated food and

---

2   This topic is the focus of Chapter 5.
3   This was a view still adhered to well into the 20th century and promoted even by Max Weber (1978), as will be discussed shortly.

drugs.[4] Naturally, such risk-takers were required to behave responsibly. They were expected to be prudent in the sense of investing within their means, for the spectre of dependency loomed even over these subjects. In addition, there were periodic moral crises likening more speculative forms of investment to 'gambling' – especially in the United States (Cowing, 1965). But the argument that capitalist risk-taking provided fundamental benefits to society was a trump card that could usually be played to forestall intervention.[5] Entrepreneurs were thus a privileged and exceptional class, given special licence and protection in order to engage in the creative uncertainty that effectively was inaccessible to most.

Configuring foresight

Accordingly, set against the often grim – coercive, morally restrictive and self-denying – side of classical liberalism, is the equally central and salient figure of 'freedom of contract'. Here – in many representations at least – it is as though we enter another world. We move from the benighted and hazardous internal colonies of the poor into the peaceable world of civilisation and the gentleman's club. Individuals, assumed to be free and rational males, make voluntary agreements in good faith about their respective best interests. Especially in the discourses of contract law the techniques of government appear to concern the elaboration and refinement of the nature of reasonable expectations, rather than the instilling of foresight into a resistant multitude. Harking back to Bentham, these are the ways in which free and equal subjects *should* govern each other, with law administering only an occasional and gentle hand – usually compensatory – when called upon by an aggrieved party. As the 19th century progressed, punitive elements of contract law and the law of torts inherited from the 1700s were erased, and compensation for unintentional harm became the overriding issue (Kercher and Noone, 1990).[6]

---

4 Ingeborg Paulus' (1975) study of the fate of pure food and drug legislation in the late 19th century provides fascinating insights into the sense of moral outrage that was generated by efforts to criminalise manufacturers' adulteration of food and drugs – even where this resulted in the poisoning of many consumers. As she shows, effective governance of this problem came into being only when the criminal status of such regulation was dropped in favour of administrative regulation.

5 It should be stressed that insurance did not always escape these moral crises, and that there was considerable unevenness across jurisdictional boundaries. Again, while in Britain there were few qualms about either speculation or insurance, especially after the early 19th century, in the US both areas of finance were prone to moralised assaults. Viviana Zelizer's (1979) study of the fate of life insurance in America is still the best account available.

6 In practice, it was well into the second half of the 19th century before most contracts other than those between entrepreneurs were formally subjected to this imagery. When workers broke contracts, this was often enforced in the criminal and quasi-criminal contexts of the master and servant legislation that governed contractual arrangements with respect to employment. Under this law, not abolished until 1875, some cases of breach of the employment contract could be punished by imprisonment. Where workers associated together to defend collective interests, the coercive machinery of anti-combination laws ensured they would engage in 'free' relations of wage bargaining in a labour market imagined as composed only of individuals. Contract was, of course, also gendered. Until close to the end of the 19th century, married women had no common law capacity to enter into contracts, nor to own property in their own right, nor could they be declared bankrupt except where trading independently of their husband. Many stock exchanges excluded women. Even at the end of the century concerns were raised about the impact of their suspect rationality on the economy, and – more paternalistically – about their vulnerability in the cut-throat environment of speculative investment (O'Malley, 2003). In its formal design, let alone its realisation in practice, contract was not an equal but a socially circumscribed, classed and gendered technology of uncertainty.

The imagery of equal individuals making rational-choice voluntary bargains formed the cellular relationship of liberal individualism.[7] It underpinned *laissez faire* economics, in which the state supposedly 'intrudes' only to ensure the rules of the market are adhered to. Of course, this is not a literal description of things. From the early 19th century, states intruded in the economy in all manner of ways: to ban truck as payment to workers; to set required standards of space, ventilation and light in factories; to establish minimum age limits for workers; and so on. Therefore, to the extent that *laissez faire* and 'freedom of contract' are at all useful images for analytical purposes, it is as an indication of a governmental vision that accorded a central place to uncertainty in the form of 'free' or 'voluntary' relations and their outcomes. In contract's self-image the operations of the laws of supply and demand – reflecting a multitude of individual decisions – displaced the command processes associated with the remnants of mercantilism and the moral economy. Thereby contract supposedly rendered the future free, open and uncertain.

However mythological its assumptions, contract law took on a key role in shaping and distributing the role and effects of uncertainty in this emerging liberal regime. From the late 18th century, to enter into a contract increasingly became an agreement about futurities. Contracts were to 'assign risks' by specifying what would happen under specified conditions whose future occurrence was uncertain at the time of the agreement. Thus, business contracts often specified agreed prices to be paid at some future date, whatever unpredictable fluctuations might occur in market prices. Employers took on employees at a mutually agreed wage, and both parties supposedly factored into account the potential cost of exposure to the foreseeable 'risks' of workplace injury.[8] In this sense, contract law was a characteristic invention of the classical liberal era: a way of rendering the future more calculable, while at the same time creating a space in which uncertainty could deliver profit. At the core of the contractual relationship is *foresight*. It remains the responsibility of the contracting parties to make their own estimations of the future, to bear the consequences of error or the fruits of accuracy – for the law now would enforce the outcomes of these uncertain calculations. Contract law took its place in the apparatuses of security, providing a legal basis for Bentham's 'expectations of the future' upon which plans of conduct could be developed. More than this, during the 19th century, in contract law especially, the 'yoke of foresight' and the practices of prudence were to be elaborated and mobilised in new, legally sanctioned disciplines of the self that took account of the security of others. However, the formation of expectations and estimations, developed and articulated under the terminology of 'reasonable foresight' in contract law, were not imagined as *new* skills for dealing with uncertain situations. As Bentham argues (1962, p 308), the

---

7 In Burchell's terms, 'At the end of the eighteenth century, the terms liberty and security had become almost synonymous. At the heart of the processes whose self-regulation government must secure is the individual, the essential atomic element of its mechanics, whose freedom to pursue his or her private interests is absolutely necessary to these processes' (1991, p 139).

8 In practice this probably happened infrequently. The 'voluntary assumption of risk' by employees was often contested as a description of what actually happened, and this was to become a major trigger for the development of workers' compensation schemes, as will be discussed shortly.

disposition to look forward was regarded as a human characteristic available to all. It was essential for rational action. Contract law was to be a key institution for generalising and refining this practice. What was new was a legal requirement that this disposition be deployed by all legal subjects, at all times, across a wide array of activities. Foresight became a legally enforceable duty owed not only to the self (as in the discourses of prudence and independence) but to others. In contract law this expectation was developed primarily in relation to the requirement that subjects take into account the foreseeable impact of a breach of contract on contractual partners. The converse of this was that no one should be accountable for outcomes that were not 'reasonably' foreseeable. Much contract law in the 19th century, and beyond, thus came to focus on the elaboration of exactly what 'reasonable foresight' entailed. What kinds of eventuality should be foreseen? How unlikely should a possible event appear in order that it can be ignored? What should parties tell each other so that each can make 'reasonable' forecasts of the future? What should count as the level of prudence and foresight that can be expected of reasonable people? As Chapter 4 will outline in more detail, in this way contract law became a site where *newly required* techniques for governing uncertainty would be elaborated and enforced.

The generalisation of contractual models across social relations also meant that such standards of foresight were to be applied with respect to 'accidents'. In tort law, *negligence* emerged as a key requirement for attributing responsibility and liability in relation to accidental harm. In Baron Alderson's words, negligence is 'the omission to do something that a reasonable man, guided by those considerations which ordinarily regulate the prudent conduct of affairs, would do, or doing something which a prudent and reasonable man would not do' (*Blyth v Birmingham Waterworks* (1856) 11 Exchequer Division 784). Foresight had entered the governance of 'accidental' harm: people should be held responsible for those events they could foresee, but are responsible only for those events. With respect to accidental harms, the influence of contractual ideas in the 19th century meant that foreseeability in tort came to be restricted in its range when compared with the standards of the more harm-focused law of the previous century (Kercher and Noone, 1990). Formerly, responsibility lay with whoever caused a harm. Now, under the doctrines of 'privity of contract' and 'negligence' it was restricted primarily to those in contractual relations, and in situations where an ordinary person should have foreseen the possibility of the harmful event. Thus, if the driver of a coach and horses were injured in an accident resulting from faulty manufacture of the vehicle there would be no legal remedy available to the victim, because there was no contract existing between the driver and the manufacturer. The manufacturer, it was reasoned, had not been negligent toward the driver, with whom no relationship was thought to exist. If a bottle of beer contained impurities that caused illness, the consumer would, likewise, have no right to remedy as their contract was with the retailer, who might have no way of knowing about the problem and thus could also not be regarded as negligent. How could such restrictive applications of responsibility appear 'reasonable'?

For Horwitz (1977), this 19th century development in Britain and America was an indication of the extent to which the courts were biased in favour of capitalists. Capitalists, as owners of factories and means of transport, as the producers and distributors of commodities, created most injuries in industrial societies. Under the emerging regime of negligence and privity of contract, capitalists would be liable to compensate for only a small fraction of these harms. Effectively, Horwitz suggests, this operated as a massive subsidy to capital at the expense of ordinary people. There can be little doubt that Horwitz is right as to the effect of these changes in law, for they certainly narrowed legal liability. But another way of regarding this development is that it was consistent with a general liberal technology for governing the future. In the case concerning injuries to the coach driver, the presiding judge, Lord Abinger, was able to argue that denial of remedy was essential. In his view, if '... the plaintiff can sue, every passenger or even any person passing along the road, who was injured by the upsetting of the coach might bring a similar action. Unless we confine the operation of such contracts as this to the parties that enter into them, the most absurd and outrageous consequences to which I see no limit, would ensue' (*Winterbottom v Wright* (1842) 152 ER 402). Even though this might now be regarded as an outrageous view, it made sufficient sense at the time to set a precedent that was to last for nearly a century. It appeared reasonable because it embodied a specific vision of freedom and responsibility in an uncertain world. That is, we should be responsible only for those eventualities we can 'reasonably' foresee, and for which we voluntarily assume responsibility. Harm to an unknown driver, at some time and place in the possibly distant future, appeared unforeseeable: a remote event, an 'accident' rather than the consequence of a negligent act.

This same mentality that valorised disciplined foresight informed the so-called 'fellow servant' or 'common employment' rule. In 1837 Lord Abinger ruled that a worker injured as a result of the negligence of fellow employees should have no right of recovery from the employer.[9] How could the employer foresee or be held responsible for injuries resulting from the negligence of a worker's fellow employees? As freely acting agents, the employees were expected to be responsible individuals in their own right. In addition, they were best placed to act preventatively. To relieve employees of the duty to apply reasonable foresight and take appropriate precautions would, it appeared to the court, be likely to create more rather than fewer accidents. To assign responsibility to the employer thus seemed an unreasonable, unrealistic and inefficient way of governing accidents in the workplace. By extension, similar rules were created whereby a worker injured as the result of an accident that she or he should have foreseen thereby became responsible for the injury. It was his or her own failure to exercise foresight and prudence that resulted in the accident, and while other factors may have been relevant, the person on the spot was regarded as having the best opportunity to avoid trouble. This doctrine of 'contributory negligence' followed the pattern of creating 'self-reliant' and 'independent' subjects, whose responsibilities in these respects were a 'natural' corollary of their freedom. Finally, the law had much to say about accidents that followed from the nature of the work, such as chemical injury in the tanning industry, or burns in a metal foundry. These harms, it was

---

9 Lord Abinger in *Priestley v Fowler* (1837) 150 ER 1030 had ruled that '[if] the master be liable to his servant in this action, the principle of the liability will be found to carry us to an alarming extent'.

argued, must have been regarded as more than a remote possibility by the employee at the time of forming the contract of employment. The worker was thereby assumed to have made a 'voluntary assumption of risk' (*volenti non fit injuria*, or *'volenti'*), and offset this against a higher negotiated wage. To seek compensation from the employer after injury thus appeared as double dipping. Having been paid a premium for taking a risk, the employee could have no right to compensation. This thinking made many assumptions that later came to be regarded as unreasonable.[10] But in terms of a contractual environment assuming rational choice actors, it appeared to be no more than the responsibility that should gladly be accepted by a free person. In this kind of issue the courts felt they had no business 'paternalistically interfering', for the contracting parties had, at the time of the contract, 'reasonably' allocated risks to their mutual satisfaction.

Making security 'social'

By the late 19th century, many of these assumptions and techniques were to be challenged. New developments treated compensation for accidents, sickness, unemployment and death, as better governable through insurance, as properties of statistical distribution rather than effects of individual negligence. Yet it would be a mistake to locate the origins of such shifts entirely within the late 19th century, or in terms of the sudden breakdown of *laissez faire* liberalism and contractualism. While the ascendancy of 'social' ways of governing, and particularly social insurances, can be dated to 20 years either side of the *fin de siècle*, its genealogical origins lie in the heart of the classical liberal era. Statistical data began to take a major place in government by the second quarter of the 19th century. In Prussia, these data emerged out of the work of bourgeois philanthropists and reformers as early as the 1830s. In Britain much of this development focused on the health of the population and linked this with the concerns that underlay the New Poor Law, making the social body visible in new ways (Poovey, 1995, p 12). Apparatuses such as workhouses, prisons, hospitals and charitable agencies began to generate information that was statistically to link indigence with disease, malnourishment and poor education, rather than with idleness. At the same time, statistical societies began their investigations in schools, churches and workhouses – following the Malthusian directive to 'prepare some of the most important rules of political economy for practical application' (quoted by Abrams, 1968, p 14). Ironically, far from supporting Malthusian assumptions, such research began to indicate that it was not enough

---

10 Nevertheless, these later standards cannot be imagined as progressing to a more 'realistic' standard. In the era of neo-liberalism, it is now not uncommon to find 19th century views proffered as an efficient response to legislation that had virtually abolished *volenti* a century before. Viscusi (1983, pp 3–4) – tying his claim in with familiar criticisms of social liberalism, suggested that the:

> ... central difficulty with the traditional approach to risk regulation is the assumption that a no-risk society is desirable. The policy approach I advocate here attempts to promote efficient, nonzero risk levels by augmenting market forces. If workers understand the risks they face on hazardous jobs, they will demand additional compensation to take such jobs ... Providing job risk information to workers to enable them to select jobs that are appropriate for their own risk preferences is a promising strategy for augmenting market forces and promoting outcomes that are responsive to the diversity of attitudes toward risk.

to work upon the will to labour and save. Disease, ignorance, cyclical fluctuations in employment and underemployment, the conditions of labour and productivity in certain industries, and a host of other privative conditions meant that even many of the *labouring* poor could not achieve a relative degree of security (Poovey, 1995, pp 98–114).

Such statistical development came to be associated with a vision of society as having an *organic* existence that required understanding and governing in terms of its own laws and customs. This was not in any simple sense a 'statistical' discovery, for statistics do not speak for themselves. With reference to Germany, Eghigian (2000, pp 43–44) argues that elementary statistics had long been compiled by the absolutist states, although even at the end of the 18th century governments:

> remained individualistic, psychological, and prescriptive in their approaches. The statistics and probability theories applied to social life in nineteenth-century Europe were of a profoundly different character. Advanced by individuals and groups from government, industry and science, the new statistics was part of a self-consciously social science of social motion ... It was offered as an eminently empirical, quantitative method for discerning the laws of a changing society. Yet equally important were its political implications. Statisticians of the early nineteenth century saw their science as an attempt to bring a measure of expertise to social questions, to replace the contradictory preconceptions of the interested parties by the certainty of careful empirical observation. They believed that the confusion of politics could be replaced by an orderly reign of facts.

The specificity of the discovery of the social, and its implications for liberal government, had to do with the nexus – forged around the middle of the 19th century – between statistics and the social and related sciences. Perhaps not surprisingly, it was not 'risks' that were 'discovered' through statistics, so much as social causation. The linking of positivist social science and statistics made it possible to regard society as a causal agent in its own right, scientifically discoverable by experts. The conditions of the poor appeared to have social, as well as individual, correlates and origins (Dean, 1991). As a modernist confidence in scientific knowledge and progress gathered strength, so too did a sense that such knowledge could be applied to society in expert and technical ways.[11]

Perhaps, also, it is no coincidence that the first of these developments was from a direction heavily influenced by the natural sciences. Tom Osborne has argued that late 18th century governance of public health had been characterised by interventions that focused on 'the inculcation of good habits, proper practice and discipline' (1996, p 109). By the middle of the 19th century a more organic vision was taking hold alongside this, particularly with respect to the health of the population, and especially regarding the provision of sewerage disposal and water supplies. Osborne argues that this development represented an attempt to

---

11 'Scientific' disciplines, such as sociology and economics, were extending their reach and governmental credibility, the latter especially, from the middle of the 19th century. Particularly through influential thinkers such as Quetelet in France and Rawson in Britain, they had begun to argue that the social was an entity visible only in terms of statistics. As such, it was argued to have properties and regularities that need not – or even could not – be reduced to the actions of individuals.

resolve tensions within classical liberalism (1996, p 110). Such tensions concerned issues of compulsion and of invasion of the private domain that were implicit in many proposed interventionist practices – such as the invasion of the homes of the sick by domestic sanitisers. For Osborne, drains and sewers contrasted with these technologies because they are:

> embodiments of an essentially political distinction between public and private spheres ... pipes are literally neutral and anonymous; they supply the home as a private space, and although by their presence they clearly have a certain moralising impact upon conduct, this is achieved essentially through non-disciplinary means and not by imposing rules of conduct on the occupants but only by leaving the home and the family to itself. (1996, pp 114–15)

This may have played some role in Britain but as a general account it is not altogether convincing. For one thing, as those arguing against fluoridation of water supplies were later to claim, there is an objection of compulsion that can be raised even about such interventions. In addition, this project to improve water supplies and sewerage occurred just as the armies of charitable volunteers and social workers were forming and penetrating the domestic sphere against seemingly little effective resistance. More to the point, there is little sense that such concerns troubled public authorities introducing similar reforms in other liberal countries such as Australia, France and Germany – where it was more generally accepted that the state should intervene in private lives where public good was concerned.[12] In Prussia, for example, employers in various industries had been required to insure their workers against accidents since the 1830s (Zollner, 1982, p 32). For all that Osborne's account may reflect the nuances of installing sewers in England, there were other things afoot than the ingenious sidestepping of liberal sensibilities. With characteristic acuteness, Patrick Atiyah (1979, p 628) pinpoints the fact that:

> it began to be discovered that it was often easier to solve social problems by changing the laws and physical environment in which people lived and worked, than it was to change the people themselves. It had been discovered that people lived cleaner and healthier lives when the public health, water and sanitation facilities were forced upon them, than when they were merely exhorted to live more salubriously or to rent better accommodation. It was discovered that it was easier to cut down drunkenness by limiting licensing hours than by moral persuasion. Poverty itself was more easily controlled when many of its causes – sickness, unemployment, old age – were directly tackled by the state.

---

12 In Australia, the history of the country as a convict settlement, and as a settlement of exploitation in which native peoples (to say nothing of disaffected Irish) had to be subdued, had meant that the state had, from the first, played an overtly 'interventionist' role. This is exhibited in innumerable ways, but perhaps most transparently in the fact that police of the 'civilian' Peelite model were only a much later introduction on the scene. Instead, as also in Canada, the model for policing had been the more militaristic model provided by the Royal Ulster Constabulary. *Laissez faire* applied, to a much greater extent than in Britain, to the field of the economy alone. In Germany, as Eghigian (2000, p 61) indicates, much the same was true with respect to health issues including nutrition and the control of contagious diseases. In a striking contrast to Britain, where continental police had been anathema, he notes that like 'policing before it, hygiene made "population" its chief unit of analysis and object of intervention'. Liberal regimes appear to have arrived at the point of the social by rather different genealogical routes.

Even in England, the virtues of state compulsion – which in any case had a respectable lineage in Bentham and the New Poor Law – were becoming evident. The justification for such intervention, scarcely challenged in the 19th century, was that the compulsions of sanitation were for the good of all. This was a utilitarian 'fact' demonstrable through the objectivity of statistical demonstration and rendered intelligible through scientific knowledge. In turn, the scale and costs of the enterprises meant that, for the most part, only the state could undertake them. Hence, these were rightly a state project. By the middle of the 19th century, this imagery of the social body as an organic whole made visible through statistics, governable in terms of positivistic science, and for which the state took responsibility, was already appearing from *within* the (utilitarian) rationality of classical liberalism. The example also suggests that the discovery of the social was not simply a self-generating quirk of liberalism. Equally it reflected the ascendancy of science and a faith in scientific expertise, in which probability and risk were imbricated. The 'invention' of the social thus binds together liberalism and modernism in an uneasy melange in which issues of freedom and compulsion are never far from the surface.

The response of liberal governments to these newly 'discovered' problems was complex. While Atiyah's observations are undoubtedly correct, many problems were not amenable to such regulatory solutions. Social insurance, likewise, while mooted, was not an obvious solution nor one that applied to many situations. Nor was the response simply to abandon attempts to discipline people into better ways, as Atiyah might be interpreted as saying. Indeed, one of the principal responses involved a recognition that, paradoxically, achieving good governance would require a more far-reaching disciplining of individuals. The poor laws, the prisons and the asylums had been designed to intervene once subjects had demonstrated a failure to govern themselves. The new civil initiatives focusing on hygiene, diet, domestic management, exercise and leisure habits were intended to raise the bar rather than attend only to those who fell beneath it. It was no longer enough to toil and be frugal. Cleanliness, proper and 'efficient' nutrition, 'rational' use of leisure time, and educational improvement were all to become targets of government that sought to improve freedom scientifically (O'Malley and Valverde, 2004). By the closing years of the 19th century new 'applied' social sciences, such as social work, were being synthesised out of amateur expertise and professional knowledge. In turn, they were generating new information that deepened the disciplinary reach of the project of security (Donzelot, 1979).[13] On the face of things, however, none of these developments implied anything other than the extension and intensification of prudential techniques for governing uncertainty. Statistical distributions were certainly an important tool of government. But while Castel may have been correct to identify the potential of

13 As Rose (1993) notes, what is referred to as the 'welfare state' might be better regarded as a network of agencies which are for the most part in the 'private' sector. While a generation of earlier social scientists (eg, Abel, 1982) regarded the development of such networks as evidence of the spread of the state and its control, Rose adopts the more Foucaultian view that government has been becoming more and more decentred and, thus, occurs increasingly 'beyond the state' in more senses than one.

such changes to displace a focus on individuals with a focus on risk, as in psychiatry, this was rarely translated into practice. Rather, statistics came to be deployed primarily as techniques whereby individuals could be identified as in need of correction, and through which the greater or lesser effectiveness of techniques of correction could be made demonstrable. While prevention came more to the fore, if anything, these developments confirmed the individual as a site for expert intervention. In the name of science and the social, social workers and their allies worked on more and more individuals, addressing their personal problems in terms of their *social* context, as effects or corollaries of *social* pathologies and *social* problems as well as individual inadequacies. Scientifically guided intervention began to displace the deterrent and moralising discipline of the poor laws. In new ways the world shaped by uncertainty was being subjected to the work of knowledges and techniques of science. The emergence of social government, in short, did not automatically centre risk, for it is just as much associated with other forms of expert-dominated, scientific government. These forms of scientific knowledge, the judgments and interventions made by professionals of the social sciences, remained a major technology of the welfare state throughout its course. As the mass of governmental analyses of risk have indicated, the irony is that while risk in the form of probability was critical to the invention of the social, it did not begin to displace such expertise until after the decline of social liberalism.

Perhaps this state of affairs can be explained in terms of a robust faith in sciences, and especially in the social sciences and their professions – a faith that wore thin only by the late 20th century (Garland, 2000). Perhaps it is because, despite this faith in science, the liberal focus on the individual also was too robust yet to be overridden. Certainly this would be consistent with David Garland's (1985) analysis of the emergence of the 'welfare sanction' in late 19th century criminal justice. In this process the conflicting demands of liberal moralists and the expertise of scientists – who attributed crime to social and psychological causes – was resolved in a compromise. This retained individual criminal responsibility and linked it with individually tailored 'scientific' correctionalism. The result was considerably removed from the kinds of risk-based techniques, such as actuarial justice, that were to present a challenge in the late 20th century. If these speculations are accurate, it is almost surprising that alongside such developments, the risk-centred technology of social insurance moved to the forefront as a governing technology at about the same time.

'Social' insurance

At the end of the nineteenth century, insurance is thus not only one of the ways the provident person can guard against certain risks. The technology of risk, in its different epistemological, economic, moral, juridical and political dimensions becomes the principle of a new political and social economy. Insurance becomes *social*, not just in the sense that new kinds of risk become insurable, but because European societies come to analyse themselves and their problems in terms of the generalised technology of risk. Insurance, at the end of the nineteenth century, signifies at once an ensemble of institutions and the diagram with which industrial societies conceive their principle of organization, functioning and regulation. Societies envisage themselves as a vast system of insurance, and, by overtly adopting insurance's forms they suppose that they are thus conforming to their own nature. (Ewald, 1991, p 210; emphasis in original)

Ewald's observation is critical, for it is the formation of social insurance apparatuses and technologies that is taken by many others, as well as Ewald, to be almost definitive of social liberalism (Defert, 1991; O'Malley, 1996; Beck, 1992; Rose, 1996a, 1996b). Within the period 1885–1915, much of Western Europe, Canada and Australasia put into place some variant of social insurance to govern such areas as health, old age, unemployment and industrial accidents. Over the succeeding 60 years these were extended, articulated and elaborated in many ways, eventually being taken up – if in somewhat limited ways – in the United States.

For Ewald, it is the combination of insurance and the social that is critical to understanding this uptake. As far as the insurance element is concerned, Ewald sees its contribution to the attractiveness of social insurance as lying in the fact that 'the technique of probabilistic calculation ... ensures the certainty of the operations, disciplining the future and ensuring that their combinations are more than a mere lottery' (Ewald, 1991, p 210). This is hard to disagree with, but it is not at all the only relevant property of insurance that was vital to the acceptance or invention of social insurance. Another, as I will suggest shortly, was its contractual nature. Ewald, however, focuses more on the 'social' aspect of social insurance rather than on this 'individualistic' side of things. Social insurance, he suggests, emerged by wedding insurance technology to the discovery of the social, for *social* insurance 'gives concrete form' to this 'social' solidarity. More than this, he argues that social insurance had to be aligned with the state for two main reasons. First was the realisation that the financial guarantee of insurance can be provided optimally and with most certainty by the state. Second was the fact that the state has the longevity to ensure this insurance will function over a 'span not just (of) one generation or lifetime but several, and thus positing the survival of society for an indefinite future' (Ewald, 1991, p 209).

It is possible to pick fault with various aspects of this account, perhaps most obviously with his observation that only the state has the longevity to operate such a scheme. Very many social insurance schemes were only initiated and co-ordinated by states, the insurance technology itself being operated by private sector insurance companies or mutual societies.[14] However, the principal problem with his account is that Ewald privileges the attractions to liberals of the socialisation of risk, over all other components of the assemblage of social insurance. I would suggest instead that there are other characteristics associated with the individuating nature of insurance (that is, rather than its social or its risk-centred characteristics) which rendered it attractive to very many liberals of the time. To begin with, because insurance requires contributions from the beneficiary, and these payments are made regularly over time, it appeared as a form of thrift. More than this, insurance has a *contractual* form which provides a legal right of benefit to the insured party in the event of specified events occurring. This benefit is not in the gift of the benefactor, for the insured party has contributed something in consideration: it is *earned security*. In turn, a relation of mutual obligation is

---

14 This was the case with the Bismarck's foundational scheme, the English national insurances established in 1911, the Australian workers' compensation scheme, and so on. It is still the case that many such schemes operate in this fashion.

established, a legally enforceable right rather than a relationship of dependence on a benefactor. In most of these respects there was a marked and governmentally salient contrast with the operation of poor laws and charitable relief.[15] The recipients of benefits from such agencies made no contribution to their security, nor were they required to exercise self-reliance, foresight and discipline. They could not establish any legal right to support, but rather established relations of dependency. It is thus no coincidence that the social insurances introduced after the early 1880s were contributory in nature: the members of the scheme paid regular premiums from their wages. This was true, significantly, for Bismarck's pioneering 'Sickness Insurance Law' of 1884–85. While compulsory (the source of most objections to social insurance), this insurance scheme required two-thirds of the contributions be paid by the worker and one-third by the employer. The Disability Insurance Pension of 1889 was to be funded more or less equally by the employee, employer and state. As all three parties were understood to be beneficiaries, all three were required to contribute (Zollner, 1982, pp 23–57).[16] The National Insurance Act of 1911 in England – partially modelled on Bismarck's scheme – introduced compulsory contributory insurance relating to health and unemployment. Many other diagrams of contributory social insurance developed along similar lines over the next half-century. In this way such schemes not only helped to define what is 'social' about social liberalism, as Ewald suggests; at the same time they carried into the core institutions of social liberalism an underlying concern with individual independence and prudence, which more than anything else had characterised classical liberalism.[17] As Ogus (1982, p 183) put it, social insurance – like the welfare sanction – represented a compromise:

> It maintained, in a somewhat modified form, the exchange or reciprocal basis to social welfare: it was based on past performance in employment, and from financial contributions from the individual himself; benefit could thus be justified as having been 'earned'. In legal terms it gave rise to something akin to a contractual right. In moral, cultural terms, it incorporated the traditional puritan, capitalist virtues of thrift and foresight.

Nevertheless, things were not totally unambiguous and stable. As Ewald implies, the model of social insurance does not necessarily require contributions to be made directly by the insured in the form of a premium. The technology of social insurance includes other variants. Using actuarial technology, states can calculate the financial burden imposed by benefit schemes and collect taxes accordingly.

---

15 See Chapter 6 for a discussion of this in 19th century Britain.

16 Half a century later, Beveridge also felt strongly about this formula, in particular on the reasons why employers should contribute, for they were at least partly responsible in effect for the problem, were morally responsible for their workers' welfare, benefited from having healthy workers, and should pay for a scheme which they had helped design (George, 1968, pp 46–47).

17 It is for this reason that unemployment assistance was routinely contrasted unfavourably with unemployment insurance. Thus in France in the 1920s, when assistance was provided for those whose contributions had expired, it was urged that it was 'essential, in the interests of the workers themselves, as well as that of industry and the public purse, that this assistance should never become a right which might encourage idleness, or a refusal to accept economic conditions to which all men must adapt; for this reason it is absolutely necessary not to call it insurance' (Colson, 1926, quoted by Saint-Jours, 1982, p 120).

The 'premiums', in this process, are paid through income tax. However, such indirect-contribution schemes can represent a particularly acute affront to the principles of individual self-help and independence if it is the case that the beneficiary has not contributed in the form of taxation and productivity. Thus the non-contributory pension scheme introduced under Britain's Old Age Pension Act of 1908 – initially planned by Beveridge as a contributory scheme – still required that the applicant have a good working history and thus did not fall into the category of the undeserving poor. Those receiving the pension would have to prove that they had not received poor relief since 1907, had not been convicted during the previous decade (including convictions for drunkenness), and be able to demonstrate that they had neither been habitually unemployed nor failed to support their dependent relatives. The same was true in the pioneering schemes developed a few years earlier in Australia, where the New South Wales (NSW) Old Age Pensions Act of 1900 had excluded persons who had not led a 'sober and reputable life' or were not of good moral character. As the preamble to the NSW Act suggested, the assumption was that:

> It is equitable that deserving persons who during the prime of their life have helped to bear the public burdens of the Colony by the payment of taxes, and by the opening up of its resources by their labour and skill, should receive from the Colony pensions in their old age. (Quoted in Conley, 1986, p 286)

Is this justification an expression of the emergent social, in which the individual is regarded as a contributor to the organic unity? Or does it reflect the classical liberal view that a person earned whatever rewards were duly theirs according to their exertions? I would suggest that both are the case. While this can be regarded, as Ewald suggests, as just a different diagram of social insurance, it reveals rather clearly the extent to which social insurance was a configuration created at the intersection between social and classical liberal views. Thus, rather than regarding social insurance as a technology that characterises or expresses 'the social', and that 'naturally' emerged as the default technology of government in the era of social security, we could focus on the *contingent* nature of its emergence in this role. It is a compromise in which the risk-based elements of insurance clearly are important, as are its 'social' and collective implications; but they are not all-important: individual responsibility, prudence and independence are also vital. This is also a characteristic of social liberalism more generally, for much of its historical course. William Beveridge, for example, writing in the 1940s, was adamant that his blueprint for the post-war welfare state carried through the central principle of social insurance, '... benefit in return for contributions rather than free allowances from the state'.[18] He was personally opposed to the means-tested forms of unemployment assistance, introduced in the 1920s and 1930s as a benefit for those whose unemployment insurance coverage had been exhausted. In his eyes this penalised those who had 'come to regard as the duty and pleasure of thrift, of putting pennies away for a rainy day' (Beveridge, 1942, pp 182–85). Most importantly, Beveridge was clear that 'the State, in organising security

---

18 Among other changes, Beveridge reformed the system of workers' compensation to become part of the national insurance scheme. Basically, this followed the formula established by Bismarck, of the employee, employer and state making contributions.

should not stifle incentive, opportunity, responsibility; in establishing a national minimum, it should leave room and encouragement for voluntary action by each individual to provide more than a minimum for himself and his family'.[19]

Social liberalism was, in this sense, multivocal, incorporating 'individual' and 'social' (risk) discourses. Accordingly there is considerable scope for variation and mutation. This is illustrated in the contrasts between the 'individualist' social liberalism that emerged in the USA in the wake of the New Deal, and the increasingly statist and 'socialist' forms adopted by countries such as France and Britain (for example, Rose, 1999a). Equally, we can register a contrast between the social liberalism of the early 1900s and that which came to fruition after the Second World War (and which Beveridge ushered into being in Britain and strongly influenced in France).[20] Both pre-war and wartime variants emphasise the individual's responsibility to govern life's uncertainties through self-help. Before the war, however, most social insurance had been contributory, and concerned with securing independence by risk-centred technologies of compulsory thrift. While Beveridge's language retains much of this spirit, and although he was personally committed to contributory social insurance, the idea of a 'national minimum' began to take the governance of risk and uncertainty in a rather different direction after the war.[21] Many states, primarily through techniques of taxation, began to provide either means-tested welfare benefits, or universal access to basic facilities. The latter occurred, for example, with the creation of the British National Health Service in 1946. In this process, new kinds of solidarity emerge. In social insurance, as Defert (1991) has suggested, there is a kind of passive solidarity established between contributors, but this is little different from that existing among contributors to a private insurance scheme. The emergence of welfare assistance, however, redistributes risk on the basis of membership in 'the social'. In this arrangement, the state becomes central not because it is permanent and can administer contributory insurance perpetually and on a grand scale. Rather, it becomes central because of the identification of the social with the nation. The result was that being a subject of the state, rather than earning a contractual right, gave a citizen *entitlement* to support. Beveridge's apparatuses of the 'national minimum' had been mutated. Only the most abstract and superficial resemblance to insurance remained, in the form of an attenuated model of risk-spreading. As neo-liberals were to argue, the liberal emphasis on individualism, and especially on individual responsibility and prudence, was being submerged under a more *modernist* agenda in which the state governed primarily through bureaucratic or administrative regulation. A new understanding of 'rationality' and 'efficiency' was thereby ushered in under the name of the social. Unevenly, in the period from about 1945 to 1980, many countries in the 'West' developed welfare apparatuses based to a greater or lesser

---

19 It is not difficult to see in this the ghost of 'less eligibility'.

20 Saint-Jours (1982, pp 120–22) points out that Beveridge's influence began even during the war years, when his report was regarded favourably by the political arm of the French Resistance.

21 Thus, for example, he insisted that 'whatever money is required for provision of insurance benefits ... should come from a fund to which the recipients have contributed and to which they may be required to make larger contributions if the Fund proves inadequate' (1942, p 12).

degree on this model. This should not lead to the evolutionary conclusion that this state of affairs represented the 'high water mark' of social liberalism. In other words, it is not that social insurance represented a compromise between 19th century classical liberalism and some 'fully social' form, which finally emerged after the Second World War. The high water mark represented by such versions of post-war social security, rather, were the high water mark of modernist – scientific even more than risk-based – government in liberal societies. Social liberalism cannot be identified with modernism, but with the unstable compromise of modernism and liberalism.[22]

For this reason, some depictions of the transition from social liberalism to neo-liberalism as a movement from socialised to privatised risk apparatuses (O'Malley, 1992) are somewhat misleading. Their valid claim is that the socialised risk arrangements of social insurance have been transformed in many ways, and that much risk management has been transferred to individuals and private sector agencies and commodities. It is also the case that, as this implies, uncertainty – especially market competition – has been emphasised far more in neo-liberalism. This will be discussed at length in the following chapter. However, many of the welfare apparatuses that have been subject to the most determined assault are not, strictly speaking, based on technologies of risk. Rather, they were founded in the provision of certainty, in which the state guaranteed social security. It is in this sense that the description of welfare as 'the no risk society' (Aharoni, 1981) has some degree of appropriateness, for the post-war welfare project was aimed at removing risk *and* uncertainty, at least below the level set as the national minimum. The social distributions of wealth, health and education, in particular, were to be altered so that the forces of market competition would no longer threaten individual security. It was a grand refiguring of Bentham's vision of security as embracing the future, for the future was to be guaranteed from 'want', while offering the possibility of 'abundance' as a reward for voluntary action and initiative.

Regulation and the fall of freedom of contract

It was argued earlier that the responses of liberal governments to the discovery of the social have been complex. They involve at least three divergent kinds of project. The first two – social insurance and 'clinical' social expertise – reflect in rather different ways a compromise struck between modernism and liberal individualism. With respect to social insurance this retention of liberalism was manifest primarily per medium of its contractual nature. With respect to 'clinical' interventions, this was primarily through the retention of the individual as the focus of reform and improvement. Much the same form of compromise, I will argue, applies also to the third of these characteristic social liberal responses: regulation.

The 'fall of freedom of contract' is a striking imagery through which critics have represented the emergence of social liberalism. But it is a term that obscures

---

22 See also further discussion in the following chapter.

more than it reveals. As it stands, the term is normally associated with the encroachment on contractual freedom by governmental regulation, in particular the replacement or modification of market uncertainty and voluntarism by bureaucratic and expert decision-making. Obvious difficulties with this vision have been adverted to already, with respect to 'interferences' dating back to the early years of classical liberalism – such as regulation of factory working conditions. But many of the changes lamented by commentators, such as Atiyah (1979), relate not only to the emergence of new impositions by government. In addition, they concern the 'shrinking' of the domain of contract and uncertainty in the face of the expansion of organisations and their command mechanisms. The emergence of giant corporations and cartels, nationalised industries, and large-scale trades unions all removed areas of life from the sweep of market forces and replaced them with bureaucratic or related forms of command-based governance. In some cases, clearly, these changes were aimed at the reduction of market-based uncertainty. But the connection of these to the problematics and rationalities of social liberalism were quite diverse and often took contradictory forms. Consequently, simply associating social liberalism with the erosion of competitive market relations, as Atiyah's interpretation implies, is misleading. It is true that much corporate expansion and monopolisation was intended to reduce market uncertainty. However, throughout the 20th century, governments with a social liberal agenda attempted to revitalise markets and to reassert the centrality of governance through uncertainty. From anti-trust laws in the United States at the turn of the 20th century through to trade practices legislation in Australia during the 1970s, states attempted to *promote* a certain level of market competition in the corporate sector, on the explicit understanding that competition was vital to an array of social benefits ranging from price minimisation to increasing productivity and efficiency.[23]

By contrast, other regulatory interventions, such as the establishment of minimum wages, were also clearly planned responses by liberal governments to *contain* the play of market uncertainties. Indeed, in some countries such as Australia this strategy functionally displaced certain kinds of social insurance. Given chronic labour shortages in Australia, guaranteeing minimum wages for the (male) breadwinner was regarded as a more relevant way of creating a 'national minimum' than providing these same male breadwinners with unemployment insurance (Carney and Hanks, 1994, pp 32–39). In other variations, market uncertainties were to be *stabilised*. Keynesian economics envisioned government interventions as mitigating the vicissitudes of the market by such strategies as state expenditure on infrastructure. The aim here was to provide employment in recessions, to 'kickstart' the 'free' economy and – most significantly – to spread the social cost of uncertainty across time by 'moving' demand for labour from the future into the present. This would be achieved, for

---

23 The Trade Practice Act (Cth) 1974 of Australia, for example, contained sections that disallowed any 'contract, arrangement or understanding [that] has the purpose or would have or be likely to have the effect of substantially lessening competition' (s 42(2)), and that prevented a corporation 'substantially in a position to control a market' to take advantage of this in order to exclude competition (s 46(1)).

example, by investing in infrastructure creation during recessions (see generally Cutler, Williams and Williams, 1986). Such interventions did not abandon the disciplinary governance of unemployed subjects, although this became rather secondary to working on the 'economy'. In particular they involved working on aggregate levels of demand as a means of reducing 'unemployment', which itself came to be understood primarily as a characteristic of the economy rather than of individuals (Walters, 2000). Later still, in a further variation of regulatory activity, the rules of market competition were changed, most especially with respect to consumer protection law. Consumers were provided with a battery of legal resources that provided them with 'protections'. These included: 'cooling off periods' in contracts of sale; broader definitions of unconscionable conduct by companies; stricter control of misleading advertising on the part of manufacturers and retailers; and granting tribunals the right to go 'inside' contracts and assess whether consumers were placed at a competitive disadvantage by an imbalance of power (see generally Kercher and Noone, 1990). Exposure to uncertainty was thereby redistributed in the name of a socially just and efficiently competitive market. Industry and the retail sector were assigned an increased burden because of the assumption that they were better placed to assume and absorb the related costs, and because the relative imbalance of power reduced competition and its beneficial effects (Collins, 1997).

All these ways of regulating in the name of the social were intended to *redistribute, channel and modify* uncertainty rather than to remove it. Such 'interventions', while labouring under the common epithet of undermining freedom of contract, sought instead to allocate contractual individualism and market forces to certain domains. Their broadly modernist aim was to retain but improve upon the market, to sustain or enhance competition where desired, to change the balance of competitive advantage, or to channel competition into certain domains – all in order to magnify the production of social utility. As Hugh Collins (1997) argues, the market was not to be obliterated, but to be rendered 'social' and 'efficient'.

Consumption and 'indirect' social insurance

Another difficulty with the 'freedom of contract' imagery is that by focusing on contract *per se*, it obscures the fact that during the 20th century the rise of social liberalism and the social market was closely associated with the rise of an economy increasingly focused on consumption. In particular, this latter change witnesses the appearance of an image of the liberal subject as consumer as well as producer. In turn, this shift creates a much expanded governmental focus on the risks that 'freedom of contract' poses to a society and its subjects. Classical liberalism was overwhelmingly concerned with the productive activity of the bulk of it subjects. Its interest was in their capacity to labour and earn, to be disciplined and to accept factory life and its demands, to be frugal and save to protect themselves against adversity. The capacity to consume was largely ignored, and – especially in imageries of pleasure and 'hedonism' – even regarded as potentially dangerous, an interference with the focus on independence. Social liberalism was much more concerned with consumption, a change of focus explicit in liberal discourses of the period. Keynes' focal concern, for example, was with a demand-led image of the economy, for he related fluctuations in employment primarily to chronic deficiencies in aggregate consumption. He opposed the classical economists' production-focused assumptions that unemployment resulted from (organised) workers' ability to demand wages higher than the market justified. Instead, Keynes' attention was focused on the need to govern – indeed promote – consumption and the forces that stimulated it. For Beveridge, the question of social insurance likewise was shifted in the direction of consumption. Denying that wealth redistribution and changes in the productive order were central, Beveridge urged that:

> Correct distribution does not mean what it has been taken to mean in the past – distribution between the different agents of production, between land, capital, management and labour. Better distribution of purchasing power is required among wage earners themselves, as between times of earning and not earning and between times of heavy family responsibilities and of light or no family responsibilities. (1942, p 167)

Consumption, in other words, was to become both a central problem to be governed, and a means whereby social liberal governments could achieve their effects. Among other things, the rise of consumption made possible new configurations of social insurance, first evidenced in the domain of workers' compensation. In its pioneering German form, the cost of such compensation was to be shared by state, employer and employee in a contributory social insurance scheme. In the legislation set up in Australia during the ensuing years – for example the Workers' Compensation Act (Vic) 1914 – a new diagram of social insurance was invented. Until this time, in Australia, accidents in the workplace were still governed by the disciplinary techniques wrapped up in doctrines of negligence and contributory negligence, voluntary assumption of risk, and common employment. The new legislation largely displaced these with a scheme legally requiring employers to take out insurance to cover such risks with one of a number of private insurance companies.[24] The assumption here, unlike that in the pioneering German examples, was not that the beneficiaries (worker, employer, state) should pay for the insurance. As a contemporary commentator noted, this was merely the starting point:

---

24 Contrast this with the original Workmen's Compensation Act 1897 in England, where the considerations of uncertainty and tort law were abandoned in favour of a compensation payment by the employer. In practice, while this may be regarded as a form of loss shifting, it is better understood as one of loss sharing. This follows from the fact that the employee was entitled to only half of his weekly earnings, and even then only to a fairly minimal ceiling – then of £1. This established a formula of mutual sharing of the costs – and thus a sense of 'contributions' paid by the worker that was to reappear in contributory social insurance. Of course, it also partook of the Poor Law principles of deterrence and less eligibility. While there is no insurance element in this, the employer could choose to build the anticipated costs into the costs of production. It should be noted that the poor law legacy became considerably more salient when the scheme was based on the assumption that the worker was effectively penalised. In tort law, at about the same time, the rule had become that 'where any injury is to be compensated by damages, in settling the sum of money to be given for ... damages you should as nearly as possible get at that sum of money which will put the party who has been injured, or who has suffered, in the same position as he would have been in had he not sustained the wrong' (*Livingstone v Raywards Coal Co* (1880) 5 App Cas 39, *per* Lord Blackburn).

> … the object is to make the trade, business or industry in which accidents happen bear the burden of responsibility of providing for those injured or for the dependents of those killed in the course of working operations; [but it is also] that the employer will necessarily add the cost of such compensation or the insurance to provide for it to the expense of the trade, business or industry and pass it on to his customers and thereby to the community generally. (Quick, 1915, p 23)

By passing the risk of injury to compulsory insurance, and by passing the cost of this insurance indirectly but wholly onto the consumer, a form of indirect social insurance was established which subsequently has become widespread.

Elsewhere, this model was to be elaborated in some of the foundational developments in the emerging field of 'consumer law'. In the United States case of *MacPherson v Buick Motor Co* 217 NYCA 382 (1916), motor vehicles were defined as part of a class of 'imminently dangerous' products. While this discourse of dangerousness had not yet harnessed a statistical component, it nevertheless implied that manufacturers would need to take their expanded liability into account, with a strong implication that they would have to insure against it. Likewise, in England, Lord Atkin's landmark ruling in *Donoghue v Stevenson* displaced the narrow duty of care imposed on manufacturers by privity of contract (in *Winterbottom v Wright* (1842) 152 ER 402). In its place was established a far more expansive duty that strengthened – rather than weakened – the requirement for disciplined foresight. This required that subjects:

> … must take reasonable care to avoid acts or omissions which you can reasonably foresee would be likely to injure your neighbour. Who then in law is my neighbour? The answer seems to be – persons who are so closely and directly affected by my act that I ought reasonably have them in contemplation as being so affected when I am directing my mind to the acts or omissions that are called into question. ([1932] AC 580)

Here, the explicit assumption was that the rise of a consumer society (the case involved contaminated soft drink) was no longer compatible with a narrow contractual form of liability for harm. Manufacturers, among others, could no longer be protected by the chain of contractual relations that separated them from their ultimate consumers. In the wake of such rulings, manufacturers' liability was sufficiently increased so that again, in practice, virtually all would take out insurance (and later would be legally required to do so) and pass these costs on to customers. In 1944 *Escola v Coca Cola Bottling* had introduced strict liability – which has been taken up in many jurisdictions across the USA – by centring the consumer. The judge in that case argued that 'consumers no longer approach products warily but accept them on faith, relying on the reputation of the manufacturer or trade mark … The manufacturer's obligation to the consumer must keep pace with the changing relationship between them' (quoted in Simon, 1987, p 71). As was the case in *Donoghue v Stevenson*, negligence was by no means always abandoned. Individual (or corporate) responsibility retained its place in most of the law of torts, but increasingly it has been combined with – or substituted by – a risk-based technique for distributing the cost of harms 'socially'. Here, as elsewhere in the technologies of social liberalism, an assemblage has been formed that reflects a compromise between liberal individualism (and the uncertain techniques of foresight) on the one hand, and on the other a more modernist emphasis on formulae of distributive efficiency and justice.

As elsewhere, this social liberal compromise proved unstable, with the direction of change being away from the emphasis on individual foresight and responsibility. As this insurance characterisation of tort law came more and more to be taken for granted, arguments gathered strength to displace tort law altogether. If, through the commodity market, most accidental harms were being insured and the cost being distributed across the whole society, then – in the name of efficiency – why not introduce a direct insurance system to displace tort law? These arguments, increasing in prominence through to the 1970s, as they moved from the academic margins to policy-making commissions and inquiries, centred on four main points. First, tort law, considered as a social risk-distributing apparatus, has transaction costs roughly equal to benefits: that is, it absorbs as much money in determining rights to redress as it distributes in compensation. From a 'social' viewpoint this is costly and inefficient as the costs can be viewed as costs to society 'as a whole'. Secondly, because of the complexities of tort law, for example determining negligence in its various forms, outcomes are always uncertain. In consequence, many injuries remain uncompensated while others are perhaps more lavishly compensated than necessary. Thirdly, some stressed that the process is slow and compensation is often deferred for many years. Both problems, it is argued, create social costs down the line. Medical expenses have to be paid in the interim, substitute sources of income may have to be found, many claimants – and especially the poor – may be forced to settle to their detriment, and so on. Finally, payment in tort law is on a once-and-for-all basis. This creates inefficiencies and possibly uncompensated costs that emerge only later. Conversely, because they are calculated on a lifetime basis such awards cannot take account of possible recovery or diminution of incapacitation. Insurance, it was argued, could improve on all these problems.[25] On the basis of this social imager of torts and compensation, in New Zealand during the early 1970s most of tort law was displaced by a social insurance scheme. This provided compensation for the majority of accidental injuries, including those associated with criminal victimisation, as well as accidents in the workplace, and domestic and recreational settings. The model proved tremendously influential, and gave rise to much talk of the 'death of tort' (see, for example, Sugarman, 1989). The Australian, Canadian, United States and British governments, among others, set up inquiries to investigate the promise of such a scheme (Keeler, 1994).

By the end of the 1970s, therefore, yet another area in which liberal individualism and the technologies of foresight had long been ascendant, now appeared to be undergoing transformation. New applications of what Ewald refers to as the 'insurance imaginary' (1991, p 198) were being deployed to invent a new form of insurance that would push risk to the foreground, taming the future. The limited impact of the New Zealand example should caution us against any naive form of evolutionary thought – for this was, after all, only a minor modification of the original social insurance developed in Germany in the 1880s.

---

25 These arguments are reviewed and rehearsed, challenged and rejected in a huge and still growing literature, as will also be seen in the next chapter. Succinct reviews are provided by Cane 1993 and Atiyah 1998, although Atiyah has an axe to grind and is a strong advocate of first-party insurance rather than social insurance.

Nevertheless, it capped a general sequence of change that had witnessed few reversals in nearly a century. Uncertainty – if not always in practice then almost always in intent – was to be subordinated: to technologies that were the domain of experts; to knowledges that sought predictability and control; to science and to risk.

From independence to social security

Article 22: Everyone, as a member of society, has the right to social security and is entitled to the realisation, through national effort and international cooperation and in accordance with the organisation and resources of each state, of the economic, social and cultural rights indispensable for his dignity and the free development of his personality.

Article 25: Everyone has the right to a standard of living adequate for the health and well being of himself and of his family, including food, clothing, housing and medical care and necessary social services and the right to security in the event of unemployment, sickness, disability, widowhood, old age or other lack of livelihood in circumstances beyond his control. (Universal Declaration of Human Rights 1948)

In social security, as defined for the post-war era by the Universal Declaration of Human Rights 1948, subjects are regarded as 'members of society' with *rights* to social security that follow from this fact. The contrast with Bentham's vision of security could hardly be greater. Bentham's major concerns were with guaranteeing protection of the accumulated property of individuals, and inculcating in individuals the capacity of foresight that would generate such property. Security centred individuals and their responsibilities, which in their turn centred production, self-denial and prudence. Want, or the prospect of want, was an essential spur to action. For the authors of the Universal Declaration, however, security was intrinsically social in nature. Their concern was that the state should abolish want, and guarantee adequate material and social conditions for members of society (Beveridge's 'national minimum'). While uncertainty was the primary feature of Bentham's freedom, neither risk nor uncertainty appears central to the Universal Declaration, for the state is to guarantee security with respect to all major aspects of life.

What is intriguing about the landscape this chapter has charted between these two points is that it is difficult to find any decisive moment of rupture between them. For example, the emergence of compulsory social insurances around the turn of the 20th century was certainly a pivotal moment, and generated considerable political opposition. But it makes almost as much sense to regard it as occurring within the parameters of classical liberalism as it does to see it as heralding the arrival of a new order. Classical liberals, from the late 18th century onwards, regarded insurance as an admirable technique for instilling virtues of thrift and foresight. Compulsion had long been justified in the name of social good. As a specific form of 'compulsory thrift', social insurance was certainly a new assemblage, but its elements were familiar enough. It did, however, require planners, equipped with what Ewald (1991, p 198) terms an 'insurantial imaginary', to put the elements together into a solution that resolved the dilemma of providing security for the poor without compromising their independence. The emergence of social insurance thus appears as historically contingent, but not as a major break with the past.

As this suggests, things could have been otherwise, and certainly alternatives to managing social risks through national insurance existed. At one extreme is the 'complete' socialisation of risk and uncertainty. *The Communist Manifesto*, after all, was published in the first half of the 19th century, and as many have argued, the 'spectre' of communism possibly contributed to the 'defensive' formation of social liberalism in the 1880s (for example, Zollner, 1982, pp 12–15). This is a familiar story, and invariably told with reference to the same time-worn quotations from a handful of late 19th century politicians. Rather than concern itself with such questions, this chapter has been more concerned with what can be thought of as the 'creative' nature of social liberalism. Weaving together available ideas, technologies and evidence, its proponents opened up new ambiguities and lines of development that were closed or constricted in the context of a confrontation between classical liberalism and socialism. The contributory character of social insurance, for instance, rendered it palatable to many liberals. Once installed, however, it was soon destabilised by arguments that a 'contribution' was made by all wage-earning members of a society in the form of taxation, and then further transformed by bringing to the fore the 'social' contribution made by unpaid housewives and mothers. By such incremental translations of the principles of social insurance, the abstraction of the social could come to be associated with practices that treated membership of society itself as creating an entitlement to assistance, a right to social security. During the third quarter of the 20th century, many liberals came to believe that liberalism itself had become compromised in the process, and that socialism had arrived. Of course, not all social liberal regimes travelled very far in this direction. Social insurance created new possibilities and opportunities, but in many instances and for many reasons these often were not taken up. Social liberalism thus cannot be represented by social insurance, no matter how pivotal its place, any more than it can be by the Universal Declaration. Each is a modality for governing risks and uncertainties in a social fashion.

The importance of this particular strand in the genealogy of social liberalism should be offset by the recognition that social insurance was only ever *one* of the ways in which social liberalism governed risk and uncertainty. If social liberalism had a special nexus with the social, this in turn created a special nexus with a certain kind of expertise. In particular, expertise in the social and economic sciences became a critical part of 20th century liberalism. Individuals were no longer the best judges of their interests: the felicity calculus became suspect. New sciences of human behaviour transformed the failure to act with foresight, diligence and thrift into pathologies of short-term hedonism, deficient socialisation and fecklessness that required expert diagnosis and intervention. Much of this occurred at the level of the individual and the family, in the form of psychological and social work. But expertise in the social was at work on broader levels also, diagnosing and prescribing remedies for all manner of social pathologies that could be traced back to deficiencies in the distribution of resources by the free market. In response to such observations of social expertise, and the discourses of 'social justice' that they engendered and reflected, changes were also introduced at what became known as the 'structural level'. Industry subsidisation, economic planning, trade protection, anti-trust legislation, compulsory wage arbitration, the minimum wage, consumer law and a host of other techniques associated with the idea of the 'fall of freedom of contract' were all *invented* by social expertise during the 20th century. Selectively encouraging, channelling or closing down market freedom and contractual bargaining, changing the balance of competitive advantages among classes of subjects, and so on, such inventions were designed to shape and direct the distribution of uncertainty and risk in order to maximise social benefit. A (shrinking) place was always left open for the play of the free market, and for individuals to practise thrift and precaution. But the course of social liberalism is perhaps best understood in terms of the displacement of uncertainty by technologies of risk, and by an array of scientific and expert designed apparatuses and practices intended to eliminate the potential harms delivered by an *uncertain* future, and to displace the technologies that governed in uncertain ways. It was precisely this trend that neo-liberalism – under the 'uncertain' banner of the enterprising society – set out to halt and turn back.

We compete in a global economy that is spinning with change.

(Prime Minister Tony Blair, speech to the Trades Union Congress, 1997)

The figure of the entrepreneur occupies a diagnostic place in the genealogies of liberalism. Associated with the Protestant ethic in the 19th century, the entrepreneur was a mythic figure. A self-made man full of energy, character and resourcefulness, he practised frugality and thrift, investing everything into the success of the business. During the 20th century, this classically liberal figure rather slipped into the shadows, displaced at centre stage by government scientists and statisticians directing a planned economy. Risk and science displaced uncertainty and foresight. However, by the late 1900s the entrepreneur was resurrected, recast as the emblematic hero of neo-liberalism. Yet in place of a handful of men of character, neo-liberals imagined an ideal world in which every man, woman and child became enterprising, speculatively adventurous, constantly in search of self-fulfilment though invention and achievement. Thus, the uncertain world of competition is once again the ideal and the figure of the entrepreneur is once again its hero; but now the entrepreneur has to be all of us. In this chapter, therefore, a genealogy of uncertainty and risk is explored through examining the changing governmental fortunes of the entrepreneurial subject. In this neo-liberal narrative not only is uncertainty valorised; risk also undergoes a noteworthy transformation, from a technique for providing social security, to a responsibility to be assumed by self-governing individuals aided by an empowering and enabling state.

Reinventing entrepreneurs

For most of the 19th century, only a tiny minority of the population were in any sense investors or entrepreneurs, and most subjects were counselled to be risk averse. At beginning of the following century, however, even Max Weber (1978, p 374) was driven to comment on the appearance of 'the great host of small speculators, equipped with little more than a good pair of lungs, a notebook and a pencil'. In Germany, as in the United States, one of the frequently mentioned benefits of futures trading and associated forms of stock market speculation was understood to be the maximisation of entrepreneurial opportunity and activity, and through this, the 'quickening' of the spirit of enterprise (US Congress, 1892a, pp 158–61). Several observations that surfaced during the *fin de siècle* period conditioned these asserted benefits by raising moral and technical concerns. The defenders of speculation had argued that the hordes of small speculators who were now beginning to enter the market provided an unforeseen benefit. Their sheer numbers, coupled with their individually small holdings, were thought to spread speculative losses with minimal social and economic impact. However, it began to be observed that these people (particularly professionals and women) were often the victims of sharp practitioners who made their careers on the market and were experts at stock speculation. One response was a series of efforts to minimise fraud. Another, more technical, concern was that if speculation performed such an essential function for commerce, then was it right for this to be put in the hands of so many – clearly inept or ignorant – amateurs rather than those of means and experience whose activities were based on reliable intelligence?

As Cowing (1965) and Brenner and Brenner (1990) have suggested, three criteria for 'speculative competence' emerged during the early 20th century, largely influenced by these considerations and inspired by the creation of bureaucratic regulations developed in Germany (where a register had been created of those permitted to engage in futures transactions). First, as the function of speculators is to effect risk-spreading and market stability, they were to be of sufficient financial means to trade without putting family or business at risk – since this would otherwise affect their judgment and their stability. Secondly, speculators had to have adequate knowledge of the commercial markets, so that their expertise could beneficially hold sway over the performance of the economy. The third was that speculators had to possess 'character' – a bundle of attributes that insulated them from the emotional impact of successes and failures and thus operated to effect rationality and stability. Such criteria became the object of various legislative experiments and stock market rules in Europe and America during the early years of the 20th century.

These initiatives did not seek to regulate the market by transforming uncertainty into risk, as was occurring with respect to the socialising of security, although they reflected a similar mentality of rule. Seeking to eliminate what was regarded as the haphazard and irrational operation of commodity markets, the aim was to identify and deploy 'experts in uncertainty', thereby rendering the performance of the economy more efficient. At the time, even Weber (1978, pp 375–76) supported the project. If, in much of the 19th century, speculative risk-taking was the preserve of a restricted class of the wealthy, now it was being reinvented as a profession – in the sense of a technical specialisation that brought together certain knowledgable, social and moral qualities in the interests of economy and society. Speculative enterprise was to become a self-governing but state-regulated preserve. Government departments and stock exchanges would admit to the ranks of the entrepreneurs only those demonstrably fit and qualified to take charge of a role so critical to the social good.

At the time such attempts to rationalise investment faced considerable opposition, which eventually led to their frustration and demise. They were said to interfere with the right of individuals to invest their funds in profitable enterprises, creating a closed and privileged community which alone could enjoy the fruits of speculation. As a new generation of critics have remarked, it was said that such regulation must fail in practice because market uncertainty could not be subordinated to expertise and bureaucracy:

> Administrators had no way of telling better than the rest of the public whether a price change would be followed by a further movement in the same direction, let alone by how much, or for how long, and whether a fluctuation was of shorter or longer duration. Not only did the administrators have no advantage over the speculators in making predictions, they were worse at it. They had less incentive to make an effort. Hidden in the anonymous labyrinth of a government bureaucracy, they had neither reputation nor money at stake. In contrast, the opportunity cost to the speculator of making a bad prediction was higher: either to lose wealth or miss the opportunity of accumulating it. (Brenner and Brenner, 1990, p 111)

Perhaps not surprisingly, the *fin de siècle* initiative to restrict access to enterprise had little impact and was of short duration. But it is starkly illustrative of a profound clash that still resonates within modern liberalism between diverse kinds of calculation. On the one side, destined to become ascendant in the apparatus of the 'welfare-interventionist state', is the calculative rationality that attempts to create certainty through a combination of science, statistics and bureaucracy. By taming uncertainty, government would tame the future, achieve stability and efficiency and thereby maximise freedom for all. From the standpoint of its protagonists, this rationality was and still is an immensely optimistic project. Set against it, however, is a governmental rationality that regarded it – and still regards it – as immensely conservative, counterproductive and anti-democratic. For its present day neo-liberal opponents, uncertainty is a creative force. Through the charismatic figure of the entrepreneur, the *risk-taker*, neo-liberals supplant 'rigid' calculative knowledges with an agentive subject that valorises flexibility, imagination, inspiration, acuity and inventiveness.

The trajectory of social liberalism was to take it very far from the charismatic image of the entrepreneur. Instead, in most discourses of government, the figure of the entrepreneur almost disappeared. In its place, the 'economy' took centre stage, imagined as a system of forces – as Tom Peters (1987, p 245) saw it, a 'vast mathematical drama lacking a protagonist'. It was to be governed through such systematic properties as levels of demand and rates of unemployment, rather than the activity of individual agents. As seen in the previous chapter, the architects of social liberalism had not intended that enterprise and uncertainty should be stifled. It was, rather, that the socially harmful side effects would be moderated by technologies of risk minimisation and redistribution, while the creative potential would be magnified by scientific planning and statistical modelling. By the 1970s, however, a new generation of neo-liberal and managerial critics were arguing that the 'welfare-interventionist state' had become a defensive and negative formation, privileging risk reduction and risk-spreading over the creative forces of enterprising uncertainty. It was in the light of this perspective that neo-liberals came to valorise enterprise and the free market. These entities appeared as symbolic and practicable *techniques* for turning what they regarded as stagnating economies and passive populations into dynamic forces. By thus subjecting both economy and society to competitive and less predictable influences, the hope was that this new regime would enliven a society whose 'stagnation' was seen as the direct consequence of the 'no risk' welfare state. The uncompetitive nature of economies would be resolved by removing stifling regulation, privatising nationalised industries and eliminating protectionist subsidies and trade barriers. State bureaucracies that had become cumbersome and counterproductive would be made more responsive and flexible though the application of business principles and techniques. The mass of subjects who had become 'welfare dependent' would be exposed to market forces and be required to become self-reliant. The whole population would be stimulated to become more 'enterprising'. The supposed fiscal crisis of the state, generated by the burgeoning cost of providing social security, would be resolved by a corresponding restriction of access to benefits to a reincarnated 'deserving poor'. Technocratic domination by paternalistic experts of 'the social' sort would be tamed by making professional monopolies answerable to their 'customers'. Where this was not possible, expertise would be made more responsible to government and public through regimes of financial accounting and consumer audit. A new force for freedom was about to be unleashed.

While some social liberals also recognised and sought to resolve many similar perceived problems of the welfare state, most of their proposals for reform centred on an intensification of the social. Social democratic and socialist planners, in particular, were profoundly suspicious of the market – to the point where economic uncertainty appeared as the principal obstruction to progress.[1] For neo-liberals, however, the solution was almost at the polar extreme. Uncertainty – in the form of market forces, competitive practices and related entrepreneurial techniques – was to become the dominant technology of government. As this implies, the market was no longer imagined as a space, as it had been under previous liberal rationalities. Instead it was understood as an 'enterprising' mentality articulated with an array of techniques that could be applied anywhere. While these are derived from an ideal-type vision of the competitive marketplace, enterprise in this sense includes, but is not exhausted by, economic activity. Instead, one could say that the economically founded imagery of enterprise and the entrepreneur has been applied as the ideal model for all or most subjects and organisations. It is in this broader sense of enterprise that uncertainty, as a way of imagining the world and as a technique for governing it, has become more central to neo-liberalism than it was even to classical liberalism in the 19th century. As Tony Blair recently expressed it, 'in government, in business, in our universities we must do much more to foster a new entrepreneurial spirit, equipping ourselves for the long term, prepared to seize opportunities, committed to constant innovation and improved performance' (quoted in du Gay, 2000, p 78).[2] This point was put even more clearly by his advisor, Anthony Giddens:

> Successful entrepreneurs ... are innovators, because they spot possibilities that others miss, or take risks that others decline, or both. A society that doesn't encourage entrepreneurial culture won't generate the economic energy that comes from the most creative ideas. Social and civic entrepreneurs are just as important as those working

---

1 See, eg, Gough, 1979. Some of these, especially the Marxist oriented accounts, argued that the fiscal crisis of the state would result in the collapse of capitalism and force the socialisation of production (O'Connor, 1973). On the other hand it is clear that many other 'Left' critiques were emerging at the same time that emphasised greater individual liberty, although few regarded the market as the route to this end. It is with considerable irony (and historical hindsight) that we can now read James O'Connor's (1973, pp 255–56) concluding words to his enormously influential book *The Fiscal Crisis of the State*:

> Precisely because we live at a time when all strata of the working class relate to each other more and more politically (and at a time when [the] ultimate contradiction is the use of political or social means to achieve individual ends), what is needed is a socialist perspective that seeks to redefine needs in collective terms. The fact is that even if the working class socialized the entire share of income going to profits, the fiscal crisis would reappear in a new form – unless both social investment and social consumption and individual consumption and individualist modes of life are redefined. Stokely Carmichael's saying 'individualism is a luxury we can no longer afford', is becoming true in a political as well as economic sense.

2 This should not be taken to suggest that the emergence of the cult of the entrepreneur – or 'enterprise culture' – is a more recent development in neo-liberalism. As Keat (1991) has mapped out in detail, this is identified with the early years of British neo-liberal ascendancy, and of course in the United States it draws upon, or even reproduces, a very strong tradition of lionising entrepreneurs. As will be argued shortly, what distinguishes the neo-liberal valorisation of enterprise is the belief that virtually all organisations – state, private or voluntary – should be characterised by the spirit of enterprise.

directly in the market context, since the same drive and creativity are needed in the public sector, and in civil society, as in the economic sphere. (Giddens, 2000, p 75)

In this sense, entrepreneurs are those who practice the art of uncertainty through risk-taking – that is, as those who identify, create and take advantage of possibilities and opportunities. Possibility prevails over probability. In Giddens' words, 'most of the key sources of growth … are also sources of uncertainty, and anyone who wants to contribute to them must engage with it … as the uncertainties grow so too do the opportunities for innovation and profit' (2000, pp 67–68). In this way, liberalism itself is to be 'enterprised'.

Underlying much of this push toward enterprising governance has been a series of interlocking discourses about globalisation as an unavoidable, already present future that renders existing institutions and arrangements obsolete. It is argued that the autonomy and boundaries of national economies have been fractured, the result being that all economic relations have become subject to an international competition that does not permit tradition, protectionism or other special pleading. In this 'post-traditional' world, it is also argued that the pace of change has quickened immeasurably. Improvements in communications instantaneously bring to bear multiple innovations from every corner of the world. A discursive 'tyranny of transformation' has been ushered in, with the result that 'things which at first appeared to be terrifying inversions of older certainties [have come] to be a normal part of everyday practice' (Clarke and Newman, 1997, p 39).

Whether or not these 'global' changes, to which I refer, are real or unavoidable, or even whether they can summed up in the concept of 'globalisation', are questions that are probably neither here nor there. Considerable transformation already has been effected in its name. Indeed, not only particular state regimes, but 'global' organisations such as the International Monetary Fund (IMF) and the World Bank have exerted pressure to ensure that appropriate reforms are introduced to deal with it, along the lines of the so-called Washington Consensus that emerged during the 1980s. Centring the now taken-for-granted assumptions that markets are the optimal form of economic organisation, and the idea that the best course for states is to foster an internationally competitive economy, the Consensus brought together a series of elements that represented a formula for good government in the globalised economy. This neo-liberal recipe utilises as its ingredients:

> Trade liberalisation, financial liberalisation, privatisation, 'deregulation', foreign capital liberalisation (elimination of barriers to FDI [foreign direct investment]), secure property rights, unified and competitive exchange rates, diminished public spending (fiscal discipline), public expenditure switching (to health, schooling and infrastructure), tax reform (broadening the tax base, cutting marginal tax rates, less progressive tax), and a 'social safety net' (selective state transfers to the needy). A twelfth element, expressed in World Bank and IMF (and OECD) reports is labour market flexibility, by which is meant decentralised labour relations coupled with cutbacks in protective and collective regulations. (Stanning, quoted by Fine, 2001, p 134)

As this makes clear, the kinds of change envisaged and implemented from the 1980s onward scarcely mention 'the social'. A gulf has opened up between the present, with its restricted view of a 'social safety net', and the expansive discourses reflected by the Universal Declaration of Human Rights and its focus on rights of social, cultural and economic security and dignity. In place of the organic bonds of society, both states and subjects are reconstituted by changing economic 'necessities'. In turn, the forms of relationship between states, businesses and citizens are said to be dictated by a global economic imperative, rather than following assumptions about collective solidarity. By the late 1980s, in much of the OECD world, discourses of the social had been subsumed, or overwhelmed, by those of the economic.[3]

As this also makes evident, 'the economic' as imagined in neo-liberal programmes is not simply a reproduction or generalisation of any existing economy. It is an ideal type of competition, the realisation or achievement of which is the aim of the governmental project. Clearly, pre-existing economic relations in the 'interventionist state' were regarded, and continue to be regarded, as a major part of the problem rather than the solution. But there is much more going on than just removing the impediments created in the era of the social. It is not just a matter of allowing natural market forces to produce their effects. Indeed, once expressed in this fashion it becomes clear that 'markets' and the creation of an 'entrepreneurial' society are not identical aspects of the neo-liberal imagination. Certainly early neo-liberalism was greatly influenced by neo-classical economics, especially of the Chicago School style, and this has retained considerable influence. It is an approach, typified in the work of Gary Becker, that 'is concerned to treat as much as possible as a market, as if life was a virtual world with individual choices being made in the context in which everything else is or is equivalent to a price or income. As a result the market is analytically privileged and unquestioned. It is always there to be used as a prism for understanding any social phenomenon' (Fine, 2001, p 42). But during the 1990s these kinds of economistic frameworks for rethinking economy and society were joined by new discourses that are rather distinct. Consider, for example, Osborne and Gaebler's now classic formula for creating 'innovative, entrepreneurial organisations':

> Most entrepreneurial governments promote *competition* between service providers. They *empower* citizens by pushing control out of the bureaucracy, into the community. They measure the performance of their agencies, focusing not on inputs but on *outcomes*. They are driven by their goals – their *missions* – not by their rules and regulations. They define their clients as *customers* and offer them choices – between schools, between training programs, between housing options. They *prevent* problems before they emerge, rather than simply offering services afterward. They put their energies into *earning money*, not simply spending it. They *decentralize* authority, embracing participatory management. They prefer *market* mechanisms to bureaucratic mechanisms. And they focus not simply on providing public services, but on *catalysing* all sectors – public, private and voluntary – into action to solve their community's problems. (1993, pp 20–21; emphasis in original)

---

3 It should go without saying that there are exceptions to this. Canada is one of the more interesting examples, for neo-liberal economic and market reforms have been effected with comparatively little disruption to discourses of the social and to the apparatuses of social welfare (although for another view, see Crossman and Fudge, 2002). It is not at all unlikely that this is related to the proximity of the United States in which the 'social' perhaps obtained least grip, while Canada developed a fairly extensive welfare apparatus. Canadian political discourse often centres the positive evaluation of contrasts between Canadian ways and those of the USA.

Such thinking owes comparatively little to contemporary neo-classical economics. Many of the terms and all of the governmental assumptions and practices to which they refer have became standard in neo-liberal discourses only since the 1980s. 'Empowerment', 'outcomes', 'dependency', 'missions', 'decentralisation', 'performance', 'participation', 'communities', 'prevention', and so on are categories that do not exist in economic theory and did not exist – or meant something substantially different – in government 30 years ago. Many of these terms are imported from the 'new managerial' literature which arose during the ascendance of neo-liberal politics, and 'changed the face of managers away from their previous image as dull organisational time-servers to those of entrepreneurial and inspirational change agents' (Clarke and Newman, 1997, p 37).[4] Even so, it is not simply the case that these discourses were all cut out of the same cloth. Their origins are complex and often contradictory – as in the categories of 'empowerment', 'participation' and 'community', whose genealogies are marked by their contested embrace by both the political Left and Right (Fraser and Gordon, 1994). The result, as Osborne and Gaebler's list indicates, takes the rather cobbled-together look of a set of principles that have emerged more from pragmatic empiricism and political opportunism than the appearance of a tightly organised 'market' rationality deduced from economic theory. Perhaps this is fitting for a framework of governance that emphasises pragmatic adaptability in the face of constant change and reformulates the constitution of liberal government in 'enterprising' ways, both with respect to organisations and with respect to individuals.

Enterprising organisations

Max Weber's concerns about the generalisation of enterprise in the early 1900s perhaps reflect his convoluted romanticism, troubled as it was about the loss of spontaneity and enchantment characteristic of previous centuries. Yet he was himself prone to privilege rational calculability of a hard-edged kind. His theoretical account of increasing rationalisation as the main characteristic of modernity created a vision of governance that would progressively render the future predictable and thus controllable. Bureaucrats – hierarchical, routinised, impersonal – are represented as performing the optimally calculable mode of administration; capitalists are represented as the optimal rational calculators of the economy; formal rational legality appears as the most predictable form of legal thought; and science appears as the form of knowledge dedicated to predicting the outcomes of natural events. It is a strikingly modernist sociological theorisation, one consistent with the project of social liberalism, which envisions the world as ever-intensifying the value placed upon rational calculability in the future. If we attend only to the advance of risk technologies in government today, arguably it still makes sense. But it seems

---

4   This was the era of the emergence of the MBA as a major qualification, of the challenges thrown out to orthodox economics by the 'voodoo economics' of management and the development of such novel academic subjects as 'entrepreneurship'. A new and highly influential literature sprang up with this. Perhaps beginning with Peters and Waterman's (1982) *In Search of Excellence*, it was soon to be followed by a long line of best-selling iconoclastic works such as Peters' (1987) *Thriving on Chaos. Handbook for a Management Revolution*, Handy's (1989) *The Age of Unreason*, Kanter's (1990) *When Giants Learn to Dance*, and of course Osborne and Gaebler's (1993) *Reinventing Government*.

strangely at odds with current governmental discourses on the 'enterprising society'.[5] In this latter view:

> We are entering an Age of Unreason, a time when the future, in so many areas, is to be shaped by us and for us; a time when the only prediction that will hold true is that no predictions will hold true; a time therefore for bold imaginings in private life as well as public; for thinking the unlikely and doing the unreasonable. (Handy, 1989, p 1)

Reflecting such visions, bureaucracy, in particular, has become an object of considerably execration. Tom Peters (1992, p 2), with characteristic hyperbole, declaims 'I beg each and every one of you to develop a passionate and enthusiastic hatred of bureaucracy'. For Osborne and Gaebler (1993, p 15), bureaucracy can no longer operate as the model for government because the conditions of its existence are past. Rather, like British Prime Minister Tony Blair, they argue that the modern, globalised world can be characterised as an 'era of breathtaking change'. In these circumstances, they say, bureaucracy must fail us – for it was designed for the 20th century, a hierarchical, stable and mass-oriented economy and society. 'Today's environment demands institutions that are extremely flexible and adaptable', say Osborne and Gaebler (1993, p 5). These conditions '… require people to exercise discretion, take initiative and assume a much greater responsibility for their own organisation and management'. Uncertain times, in short, require uncertain methods: 'organisations must either move away from bureaucratic guarantees to entrepreneurial flexibility or stagnate' (Kanter, 1990, p 356). Even in such apparently autonomous and entrenched fields as policing, 'new managerialism' is being fostered by increasing the autonomy of police managers to act as chief executive officers and to run their forces increasingly along enterprise lines – and there are clear signs that many senior police are relishing the change (for example, Hunt, 1995; Palmer, 1995). Police managers in Canada and Australia, for example, are encouraged, even required, to act increasingly in innovative ways, to be 'change masters' and 'architects of social change' (Etter, 1995; Normandeau and Leighton, 1990).

More than this, as du Gay (1994, p 660) argues, private sector organisations and state departments now accept this necessary change in organisational style requires a different kind of managerial self. The personal detachment that is imbricated in the bureaucratic administrative persona appears as inimical to the entrepreneurial spirit. The separation of reason and emotion has come to be regarded as a deeply flawed characteristic of bureaucracy. 'In this reading, inefficiency, waste and inertia are directly related to the fact that the bureaucratic organisation does not function as an instrument of self realisation for its members.' Instead, argues du Gay, 'its very essence lies in the separation of work and life, reason and emotion, pleasure and duty which is disastrous for the productive health of the nation and the corporation' (1994, p 661). In place of this coldly calculating, rule-bound ideal type, the modern managerial critics of bureaucracy imagine a different way of governing the future that embraces – if not the irrational – then at least the passionate, intuitive, daring and imaginative. Managers not only bring emotion back in, but are mobilised by it,

---

5   It is also possible that Weber used the framework against himself – when observing that the flexibility of substantively irrational elements in common law probably rendered it more compatible with dynamic capitalist growth than did the predictable but more rigid and systematic legal codes in place on the continent.

pursuing excellence while at the same moment achieving personal fulfilment. The inflexible pursuit of certainty is overridden by the exploitation of opportunity and a positive engagement with uncertainty. 'Unreconstructed' managers and bureaucrats thereby are rendered as too risk averse. Not only is this aversion seen as an effect of bureaucratic rigidity and hierarchy, but also it is assumed to be related to the protected and complacent corporate environment characteristic of the 'no risk society'. The remedies for this state of affairs are identified as countless and complex. To begin with, the problem is seen to lie at the level of state policy. Thus, when he was the British Minister for Trade and Industry Peter Mandelson urged that there is a need 'to examine all our regulatory systems to ensure that they do not needlessly deter our entrepreneurs'. This implies a need 'fundamentally to reassess our attitude in Britain to business failure. Rather than condemning it and discouraging anyone from risking failure, we need to encourage entrepreneurs to take further risks in the future'. Risk-taking 'enables you constantly to innovate and adapt to changing economic conditions' (quoted by Wilson, 2000, pp 171, 176).

By itself, however, facilitative deregulation was never expected to create the cultural and behavioural changes required to make state and industry organisations come to terms with globalisation. New techniques were to be introduced that would *require* flexibility and inventiveness. Undoubtedly the most prominent of these has been the promotion of quasi-markets – a term that covers a multitude of specific techniques. To begin with, outsourcing and competitive tendering were promoted. Under such schemes governments introduced extensive *de facto* privatisation – or outsourcing to the 'profit-making sector' – even in such sensitive areas as criminal justice. But they were also intended as means to allow administrators to set rules for competition, whether in terms of the provision of a set task for least cost, or in terms of the delivery of additional or innovative services for the same cost. In Australia, for example, the construction and operation of private prisons was merely the tip of the privatisation iceberg. In the many prisons that remain under direct state management, competitive tendering has meant that multiple functions are performed by private sector and non-profit organisations. These include the transport of prisoners, provision of catering for institutional inmates and staff, staffing of therapeutic and other correctional procedures and the operation of electronic security. Specific standards of performance are defined by departments of correction, in terms of numbers and experience of staff, provision of educational and retraining programmes, acceptable numbers of prisoner escapes and periods of lock-down. As well as the externalising of costs from the state sector to the private sector, such manoeuvres have as a major purpose the encouragement of innovation in pursuit of cost reduction, improved services and increased efficiency through market techniques. As Considine (2001, pp 10–15) argues, the formation of 'quasi-markets' in this fashion allows for *experimental* implementations of policy by distributing governmental tasks across an array of agencies that may have distinctive capacities, resources and orientations. That is, they allow policymakers to observe, and to select from among, a variety of innovative efforts made by decentred concerns, each driven by the need to survive economically. Within organisations such as government departments, these developments have been mimicked by rendering internal sections relatively autonomous, providing them with 'ownership' of problems and processes, giving one-line budgets, encouraging them to become fiscally autonomous, setting them up in competition with parallel sections elsewhere in the organisation and so on. Thus schools are set to compete with each other for students and funds, and are evaluated in terms of the competency levels of students rather than number of bodies. Departments are also encouraged to be innovative revenue-generators. For instance, government employment services are given greater autonomy, treated as separate agencies, put into direct competition for funding with private sector agencies or accorded funding on the basis of successful job placements. Taxation departments are given one-line budgets and required to become 'revenue neutral', encouraging a cost-benefit approach to routine tax collection.

As part of the same process, the neo-liberal pioneers of revitalised uncertainty began to reconstitute 'employees into entrepreneurs' (Rose, 1999a, pp 156–58). 'Workers' and 'employees' came to be replaced by 'representatives', 'members', 'consultants' and 'assistant managers'. In the entrepreneurial organisation 'there are no "subordinates", there are only "associates"' (Drucker, 1993, p 108). In many instances this no doubt represents only a semantic shift in which autonomy and space for innovation are substantially unchanged. Nevertheless, new managerial discourses have been associated with changes such as the flattening of hierarchies, the 'autonomisation' of workers and the provision of incentives to individual employees for innovations that generate cost savings and new profit-bearing outcomes. But if the 'upside' of becoming an employee/entrepreneur is more flexibility and leeway to innovate, its downside is constant pressure to perform. In the process work has 'become a vulnerable zone, one in which continued employment must ceaselessly be earned ... Perpetual insecurity becomes the normal form of labour' (Rose, 1999a, p 158).

Underlying each of these managerial reforms is a shift in emphasis away from process and toward outcomes. The achievement of goals is prioritised over rules and regulations, and governmental processes become subject to meeting contractual and quasi-contractual performance indicators, as in the example of prison privatisation. The process here is purposely Janus-faced. On the one side, the setting of 'performance targets', 'benchmarks', 'aims and objectives' is intended to encourage innovation, especially where – as has often been the case – this has been linked with budgetary strategies that are exemplified by such labels as 'doing more with less'. On the other side, this has allowed senior management to retain control over planning in a working environment that has become more fluid and less subject to hierarchical overview on a day-to-day basis (Considine, 2001, p 13). Such 'government at a distance' is thus thought to improve performance through granting a kind of freedom to innovate, but in a form that renders the liberated agency and its individual members responsible and accountable.[6]

Closely linked with this shift is what Osborne and Gaebler (1993, p 20) refer to in their blueprint as 'redefining clients as customers and offering them choices' – and

---

6   In the words of American management guru Peter Drucker (1993, p 108), this implies a top to bottom revamping of the ideas and practices of responsibility; '[it] requires, in other words that all members act as responsible decision makers. All members have to see themselves as "executives"'.

by this technique shifting the locus of control 'out of the bureaucracy and into the community'. The creation and mobilisation of choice is regarded as a critical technique underlying the push for marketisation; a vital resource in rendering organisations enterprising. It is choice, the argument goes, that breaks down the perceived inflexibility of bureaucracies. More generally it forces all organisations to adapt to changing environments and to provide diverse services: '[s]timulating the development of non-statutory service providers will result in a range of benefits to the consumer … a wider range of choice of services; services which meet individual needs in a more flexible and innovative way' (Secretaries of State, 1989). In a strong sense, this is merely a reconfiguration of the diagram involved in outsourcing and competitive tendering. They are techniques whereby the government or corporation establishes *itself* as a customer, makes clear its demands, and then sets an array of potential service providers into competition with the aim of maximising innovation. As with outsourcing and tendering, creating clients as customers implies that multiple suppliers must be created if they do not already exist. Both configurations are intended to lead to the fragmentation of monopoly suppliers, for organisations will have no incentive to innovate if their 'customers' have no alternatives among which to choose. Such fragmentation is not always possible, or straightforward, as for example with law and medicine. In the case of law, however, a frequent response has been to identify 'core functions' which only the legal profession can perform, while allowing competition or displacement by paralegals in peripheral areas such as property conveyancing. Restrictions on market competition within the profession have likewise eroded, as advertising and 'ambulance chasing' have become commonplace in countries such as Australia and England where they were previously restricted or prohibited. The same can be witnessed in medicine, where all manner of alternative medicines and therapies have been allowed to compete in the market. Even core areas of professions may become subject to 'market' pressures. In particular, as Nikolas Rose points out, these 'enclosures of expertise are to be penetrated through a range of new techniques for exercising critical scrutiny over authority, among which accountancy and audit are the most salient' (1996a, p 54). Accordingly, there has been a veritable 'audit explosion' (Power, 1994), not only in assessing performance along such lines, but in mobilising newly invented technologies of 'quality assurance' and, increasingly, audits of consumer satisfaction. Thus, with many police forces, consumer audit outcomes may directly affect funding levels or even lead to reallocation of some functions to alternative government agencies (McLaughlin and Murji, 1995).[7]

Yet this focus on making organisations more innovative by making them more customer oriented is only half the story. At least equally important is the expectation that this process of making subjects into customers will 'build resources in themselves rather than simply to rely on others to take risks and endure uncertainties on their behalf' (du Gay, 2000, p 66). Accordingly, it is assumed that

---

7 This should not be taken to imply that other changes have not swept the police. For example, in Britain McLaughlin (1992) has pointed to official policy changes involving 'the reconceptualising of policing as a service and the redesignation of the community as customers' linked with 'the prioritisation of customer needs'. For an account of related changes in Australia, see Hunt, 1995.

customers will make their decisions with more care and responsibility. In the case of Australian educational reforms, Meredyth (1998, p 35) notes that 'governments emphasised the choices of education consumers within an expanding educational market. Students, families and employers were treated as customers and clients of education: choosing the product, taking the risk and hoping to gain comparative advantage in an inflating market for "positional" goods'. At the same time, then, this is a process through which citizens are 'empowered' and – as choice makers – simultaneously made responsible for regulating the services they receive. As will be discussed later, this is one of the major lines of thinking behind the neo-liberal promotion of the 'sovereign consumer' as one facet of the enterprising subject. The implication is that the reformation of unresponsive, unenterprising states and organisations will only occur to the extent that subjects *qua* customers, themselves, become more demanding and less passive.

Enterprising subjects

The malaise that was held to have followed from the years of social liberal governance was by no means restricted to bloated and rigid state apparatuses and uncompetitive industries. Neo-liberalism identified the effects of the 'no risk society' as having affected the psyche of the population at large. It is said that people came to regard the state as responsible for their needs, and accordingly lost the spirit of enterprise and self reliance held to have characterised the Victorian era. Nowhere was this more egregiously exemplified, so the claim went, than with respect to social security. 'Welfare dependency' was diagnosed during the early 1980s as an enduring effect of social security interventions (Fraser and Gordon, 1994). As Margaret Thatcher was to argue, many of those on welfare had become trapped in a 'dependency culture'. The cure for those who had 'lost the will or habit of work and self improvement' lay in a return to 'Victorian virtues': 'the purpose of help must not be to allow people merely to live a half-life, but to restore their self discipline and through that their self esteem' (Thatcher, 1993, p 627). To this end, access to welfare benefits was to be restricted in order to liberate them from dependency and make them become 'active' on their own behalf.[8] In the words of social security minister Frank Field, 'the majority want to get off welfare but need active help to do so ... Sanctions need to be part of the New Deal. The threat of penalisation begins to affect the culture in which people consider how they should respond and indeed, what their responsibilities are' (quoted by King, 1999, p 237). But, comparatively speaking, these are blunt instruments. It was not supposed that such subjects already had the resources of will and skill that would enable them to reinvent themselves and take up their responsibilities. In place of the 'nanny state' came the 'empowering state' or the 'enabling state'. To this end many former welfare departments began to implement changes in their relationships with their clients. In Australia, as in Britain and the United States, the notion of a set of rights

---

8   It is also, of course, the case that such measures are justified in terms of fiscal restraint and
    responsibility by the state – another key element in neo-liberal governance. Thus in Sweden,
    such fiscal arguments have been used to justify reductions in benefits and increases in
    qualifying periods for workers' compensation, unemployment insurance, sickness benefits
    and old age pensions (Ryden, 1993).

which the state owes to defined classes of citizens under a single programme, was 'being supplanted by a notion of "reciprocal bargains", tailor-made for the particular citizen, and which integrate or span multiple programs' (Carney and Hanks, 1994, p 247). Such individuated, contractual imageries were intended to make clear that there no longer existed a universal entitlement to support which could be extended indefinitely. In place of benefits emerged 'allowances', provided on condition that the recipient performs various activities. Renamed 'job seekers' or 'trainees', the unemployed subject's side of the quasi-contract is now to report regularly to agencies assigned to the task of making them 'job ready', to write *curricula vitae*, to attend training in job interview techniques, and to generate journals registering their daily efforts to gain employment. In such ways 'welfare' for the unemployed came to be re-imagined as 'skilling' and 'training', as working on the recipient's self-esteem and thereby creating subjects engaged in the project of forming themselves into subjects active on their own behalf (Dean, 1995a). Echoing its forebears from two centuries ago, this has meant creating an attitude and capacity for 'market preparedness'.[9] Of course, central to this entire vision is that full citizenship assumes participation in the employment market. Consequently, the long-term unemployed, in particular, become a source of social risk. This was particularly the case in the USA and Britain where the figure of the 'underclass' was deployed to suggest that these populations existed culturally and socially outside of society. So much had the economic subsumed the social that poverty and unemployment came to be re-coded as 'exclusion', and programmes to reclaim lost souls back into the market were bestowed with the sobriquet of 'social justice'.

Yet this is not simply an updated Poor Law, nor are the associated agencies transferring the former recipients of welfare to new age workhouses. The prevailing discourses do not regard the subject merely as becoming a wage slave, a passive commodity selling a body to labour. Rather, the new subjects are to become entrepreneurs of themselves, exploiting all opportunities to acquire new competencies and to enrich their lives through new-found knowledge and experience, whether through work itself or as part of a government's empowerment programme. Government programmes have even provided encouragement and training to the unemployed and others to establish and operate small business – to become practitioners of a kind of 'democratic capitalism'. In Thatcher's Britain, housing policy was developed with this in mind. Council housing was condemned by Thatcher as bringing together those who 'are out of work but enjoy security of tenure at subsidised rents'. The result, in this view of public housing, was that residents 'have every incentive to stay where they are: they mutually reinforce each other's passivity and undermine each other's initiative'. The solution was to sell public housing, thereby compelling – or at least strongly inducing – renters to become investors: 'however pervasive an enterprise culture is, most people are not born entrepreneurs ... buying a house is for many people the gateway to other

---

9 The same is true for 'lifelong learning'. In the global economy, jobs for life are no longer to be expected or even desired. Unemployment is even represented as a normal part of a subject's trajectory – akin to the actor's status of being 'between jobs'. Accordingly, subjects must always be ready to learn new skills and update or change their knowledge base in accordance with market demands. (See, for example, Walters, 2000.)

investments' (Thatcher, 1993, p 671). In turn, this was part of a broader vision of a society in which 'it is everywhere thought morally right for as many people as possible to acquire capital' (Thatcher in *The Economist*, 19 October 1985). Generalised enterprise, in other words, was to be taken literally rather than as a figure of speech.

In this and many other ways, the contrast to either the poor laws or social security could hardly be greater. The aim is not merely to accustom subjects to the yoke of foresight, to render them 'docile bodies', or to sustain the casualties at a 'national minimum'. As Margaret Thatcher observed, the aim is to lift people out of the 'half life' they are imagined to inhabit. Government projects aimed at creating new dynamic citizens during the 1990s extended their reach well beyond the poor or unemployed, precisely because the active subject provided a model for how *all* responsible citizens should reinvent themselves.[10] Self-esteem, as Barbara Cruickshank (1993) has pointed out, has come to be regarded as an essential attribute, possession of which is a social duty understood to increase productivity while decreasing vulnerability to educational failure, welfare dependency, crime and a host of other malaises. As with the process of valorising and enlisting the emotional life of managers, now all subjects were to focus on improving their levels of self-fulfilment and engagement in the interests of an enterprising society.

In all of this, consumption came to be centred in historically new ways. This was by no means merely to be a continuation of the limited vision of the citizen as consumer, the vision that gave rise to consumer protection measures in the 1960s and after. The new consumers were not to be passive purchasers, nor were they imagined as the weaker parties confronting powerful suppliers, in need of legislative strengthening so they could relate as equals in the market. Indeed, recent legislative changes have often sought to make the consumer the *advantaged* party. Wightman (1996, pp 93–94) points out that the Supply of Goods Act 1994 'strengthens the position of the buyer in relation to the rejection of goods which are defective by providing that the right to reject is not lost until the buyer has had a reasonable opportunity to examine the goods'. As Wightman stresses, this goes considerably beyond the co-operative 'equalising' logic of the idea of a social market as identified by Collins (1997) in relation to the first wave of consumer protection law. Rather, 'consumers are allowed to be more selfish than is consistent with the idea of co-operation' (Wightman, 1996, p 194). Reborn as 'customers' they became the focal point of a new demand-centred economy. If the state's role was to empower subjects to become entrepreneurs, equally salient was its role to encourage and facilitate customers to become aggressive and self-interested. They were to require 'providers', whether in the state or private sector, to take up a customer orientation. At the same time, consumption shifted ground from being merely the purchase of commodities, in which some commodities could be regarded as necessities and others as luxuries, to be an expression of 'lifestyle'. Commodities became part of the process of forming and expressing an identity. The

---

10 Margaret Thatcher saw the aim of her government as being 'to reinvigorate not just the economy and industry but the whole body of voluntary associations, loyalties and activities' (Thatcher, 1980, p 10).

distinction between necessities and luxuries seems almost to have disappeared from some of these governmental discourses – in part because of the centring of 'choice', but also because even conspicuous consumption came to be justified in terms of a reward for enterprise. 'Customers' were re-imaged as subjects who lived and in some ways were brought into a full life through the marketplace. As with enterprise, consumption also creates our freedom:

> Rather than being tied rigidly into publicly espoused forms of conduct imposed through legislation or coercive intervention into personal conduct, forms of life, types of 'lifestyle' are on offer, bounded by law only at the margins forms of conduct are governed by a personal labour to assemble a way of life within the sphere of consumption ... Consumption requires each individual to choose from among a variety of products in response to a repertoire of wants that may be shaped and legitimated by advertising and promotion but must be experienced and justified as personal desires. (Rose, 1989, pp 226–27)

With this imagery came a political rejection of what was characterised as 'one-size-fits-all' and 'take it or leave it' markets, imageries associated with supply-centred economies. Niche and short-term markets were to become more important, introducing a new climate of uncertainty into the marketplace and requiring manufacturers to adopt a mode of continuous innovation. Mass production – no matter how important it might remain in practice – came to be regarded by government with the same disdain heaped upon bureaucracy.

This focus on the sovereign consumer should not be separated from that on the enterprising subject. Neo-liberalism's dream is that through the figure of enterprise it achieves the resolution of all those binaries that plagued previous liberal rationalities: state versus civil society; capitalist versus worker; retailer versus consumer. In this new discourse, all subjects – from government departments to schoolchildren – are simultaneously entrepreneurs and sovereign consumers. The difference becomes one of different points in 'activity' rather than of potentially conflict-laden distinctions between class-divided subjects. A sovereign consumer in one relationship or at one time, is at another moment an entrepreneur providing services or products to a customer or a 'partner'. Enterprise and freedom thus come to be bound together in a new form that bears little relationship to the dogma of the Protestant ethic with its suspicion of consumption, its valorisation of self-denial and frugality and its promotion of unremitting diligence. Two regimes of uncertainty, separated by more than a century, are thus associated with quite distinct, even opposed, technologies of the self. In the brave new world of neo-liberalism, entrepreneur-consumers are encouraged to take risks. Deterred from being docile bodies, they are expected to reinvent themselves and given license to consume in proportion to their success. All of this is to be delivered by embracing the spirit of enterprise and the technologies of the market. It is a mentality that has rejected attitudes, social policies and business plans in which taking risks is abhorred. It regards the future as waiting to be formed by the power of will and imagination. In such ways, uncertainty is made to appear as a technology of liberation.

Risk and responsibility

Given the importance of uncertainty in neo-liberal governance, it would be too simplistic to argue that changes in government since the 1970s can be characterised adequately in terms of the 'socialised' forms of risk-centred government being transformed into a privatised 'new prudentialism' (cf O'Malley, 1992). Changes with respect to risk do in large measure follow such a pattern, but are only one side of the coin, and, as much of this chapter has argued, a comparatively secondary one. Nevertheless it is doubtless the case that across many jurisdictions pressures have been set up to encourage – or sometimes to economically coerce – the population to transfer from reliance on social insurance and related schemes of social security to membership of private sector alternatives (O'Malley, 1996). In some instances, things have moved even further in this direction, as with respect to protection against crime. Most evident in this respect is the rise of private security as a supplement to public policing. In England, for example, local government areas, as well as residential communities, are given the 'opportunity' to opt for private alternatives to policing, especially in the light of consumer audits assessing levels of satisfaction with public police provision. States may encourage 'community' involvement as a reflection of their taking up a 'proper' responsibility for local order – for example through Neighbourhood Watch. This goes along with an implication that these 'natural' responsibilities of the community were shrugged off onto police during the welfare era (O'Malley and Palmer, 1996):

> The prevention of crime and the detection and punishment of offenders, the protection of life and property and the preservation of public tranquility are the direct responsibilities of ordinary citizens. The police are given certain functions to assist the public to do its work but it simply cannot be left to the police. It is destructive both of police and public social health to attempt to pass over to the police the obligations and duties associated with the prevention of crime and the preservation of public tranquility. These are the obligations and duties of the public, aided by the police and not the police occasionally aided by some public spirited citizens. (Avery, 1981, p 3)

Citizens are exhorted to minimise their risk of burglary or assault by identifying 'criminogenic' situations and avoiding or displacing them through routines of practice or the purchase of security commodities. States, police and insurance companies may join hands to empower subjects to become skilled in securing their property and persons (O'Malley, 1992). In this process, communities may become *de facto* subjects – envisaged as voluntary associations with the same moral responsibilities for self government as individuals, or more precisely, like markets, regarded as a technique for government. Communities take up an important space, providing for the co-operative governance of crime risks where this is not a function to be carried out by individuals, or where the 'community' adds to the capacity of individuals acting alone (O'Malley and Palmer, 1996).[11]

The same kind of 'responsibilisation' of subjects with respect to risk now occurs in many other fields. Government campaigns, backed up by commercial advertising and endless media reports on scientific research, abound, all aiming to render citizens free from risks associated with eating too much of the wrong kind of fat and too little of the right kind, consuming too little calcium or iron, too much salt or alcohol. Everyone is exhorted to 'find 20 minutes a day' to walk, swim, run or jog in

---

11 For a more general discussion of communities as a technology of government, see Rose, 1999, pp 166–96.

the interests of reducing the risk of heart attack or stroke. Obesity becomes a national problem, bringing with it risks to every organ and to the future of every developed nation. Precautionary medical tests for a multitude of diseases or malfunctions become a duty of those in high risk groups. Still more services are made available on the market to those whose 'choices' and 'needs' lead them to prefer a heightened level of biological security. In turn, a new 'duty to be well' appears. Succumbing to 'avoidable' sickness and injury – that is, pathologies identifiable through risk-based predictive models – now appears as a new form of psychosomatics. 'Avoidable' medical problems increasingly appear as produced by a mentality that is not adequately attuned to the empowering information provided commercially, by professional experts and government agencies (Greco, 1993). Increasingly, blame is attached to these conditions. The overweight are made responsible for their heart conditions, and those who contract liver problems through excessive alcohol consumption may now find that they are put to the end of transplant 'queues'. In such ways, choice and responsibility permeate almost every corner of life. Even the consumption of illicit drugs may become the subject of government through 'informed choices'. 'Addicts' may be rendered 'responsible drug users', by mobilising 'empowering' information about reducing the risks associated with drug use (O'Malley, 1999a, and see Chapter 8).

With respect to risk, therefore, it is not only that 'socialised' forms of government through risk are partly displaced by those that operate in the private and voluntary sectors. A key part of the process is that *responsibility* for risk management is devolved 'downward'. The bearers of risks become the individuals, families and communities who are provided with 'choices' as to which risks they will govern, to what extent and by what means; and, of course, they must bear the consequences of any misjudgments in these respects. In this much, again, there is a significant contrast not only between the governance of risk in neo-liberalism and social liberalism, but equally with respect to classical liberalism. For all practical purposes, insurance – primarily life insurance – provided the only way of governing through risk available to most people in the 19th century. It was a form of security that was bought at the cost of many little sacrifices, and often needed to be re-enforced by insurance agents and state pressures. The erosion of social security after about 1980 did not cast subjects of the late 20th century back into this negative form of prudence. Instead, many risk techniques, routines and commodities have become an avenue for enterprising the self. Risk has so entered the fabric of life, and especially of commodified existence, that it ceases to become merely a defensive formation, a cost to existence. While it might be an exaggeration to suggest that lifestyles are increasingly constructed around risk minimisation itself, risk does enter lifestyle construction as a component or theme in the commodities of the self. Exercise and fitness, and the clothing, personalised expertise and equipment associated with them, become risk-related markers of individuality. Diets that have the lowering of health risks as one of their trumpeted benefits become New Age statements about the self. Expensive cars are advertised as much in terms of their safety and security features as of their performance and style. Reliance on private rather than public medicine, and on commercially available alternative medicine, become markers of social distinction. The sovereign consumer, and the customer orientation to which it is wedded, *personalise* risk. Risk becomes an enterprise of self-fulfilment, no longer only a responsibility for security that is a duty of the obedient subject.

Neo-liberalism as 'responsible risk-taking'

Giddens' commentaries on the Third Way are notable in that they differentiate generalised entrepreneurship from neo-liberalism. He distinguishes between the Third Way, that he advocates, and neo-liberalism, on the grounds that 'the neo-liberal idea that markets should almost everywhere stand in place of public goods is ridiculous' (2000, p 32). Among the many things he finds 'ridiculous' about this proposition is that markets produce self-interested competition and do nothing to foster community responsibility and engagement. Yet in his eyes an ethical involvement of the population must go beyond self-interest in order to secure a minimum of social cohesion and social justice. The neo-liberal emphasis on deregulated markets created 'social problems' and 'serious threats to social cohesion' which now need to be addressed by responsible government. He is critical of the welfare state because in his view social benefits 'often subdued enterprise as well as community spirit. Rights were elevated above responsibilities, resulting in a decline in mutual obligation and support' (2000, p 6).[12] What is held to distinguish the Third Way from both of these alternative forms of liberal government is thus held to be its *generalised promotion of enterprise* coupled with an emphasis on a morally-focused concern with social responsibility.

It is easy to take issue with Giddens' depiction of neo-liberalism. The Thatcher regime, which he regards as talismanic of neo-liberalism, clearly placed much stress on social cohesion and responsibility. Thus, despite her infamous remark that 'there is no such thing as society', Margaret Thatcher made it evident that by this she referred specifically to the 'social' role of the state as the port of first call by all in need of support or security:

> My meaning, clear at the time but subsequently distorted beyond recognition, was that society was not an abstraction, separate from the men and women who composed it, but a living structure of individuals, families, neighbours and voluntary associations ... The error to which I was objecting was the confusion of society with the helper of first resort. I expected great things from society in this sense because I believed that as economic wealth grew, individuals and voluntary groups should assume more responsibility for their neighbours' misfortunes. ... Society for me was not an excuse, it was a source of obligation. (Thatcher, 1993, p 626)

Social obligation was very much to the fore in successive conservative government platforms over the years, in many OECD nations. It has been manifested in a wide diversity of realms, but notably in the responsibility individuals owed to society for their families of procreation (for example, regarding wayward young men and teenage unwed mothers), and the responsibilities owed to their communities (including such virtual communities as the 'gay community'). To wit, Margaret

---

12 Thus while Giddens argues that Third Way politics represents a 'modernised' form of social democracy, he is insistent that this does not mean a reversion to social liberalism and the welfare state. In keeping with his stress on the importance of entrepreneurialism, his critique is that social democracy of that era 'became associated with a dull conformity, rather than with creativity, diversity and achievement' (2000, p 6).

Thatcher, during the 1980s, articulated her preferred world as one 'where people accept their responsibilities to others. After all you are here to use your talents and abilities, and you really only use them as part of a community' (quoted by Heelas, 1991, p 75). Likewise, as has been seen, it is not at all the case that neo-liberal regimes regarded marketisation and privatising as the only ways to make states 'enterprising'. This is not meant just to discredit Giddens' account or his politics. Rather, it is to suggest that from a governmental perspective it might be better to recognise that the difference between the Third Way and the 'neo-liberal' regimes of the 1980s has to do with how neo-liberalism has been melded with other political rationalities, rather than with regarding – as does Giddens – the various 'post social' regimes as widely divergent.

From this viewpoint, Thatcher's political rationality of the 'New Right' was very much a mix of social authoritarianism and neo-liberalism. Hence the sense of 'social obligation' that is central to her discourses was strongly marked by a moral agenda that demanded obedience or obligation to higher moral authority that was represented by the state (O'Malley, 1999b). Regimes such as those of Thatcher and Reagan, and more recently of Howard in Australia and George W Bush in America, would never have identified themselves as remotely 'social democratic' (even 'modernised' social democrats), as has been the case with those of Blair, the Keating government in Australia, and a number of European adherents to Third Way politics. The Third Way, on the other hand, is readily understood as an amalgam of neo-liberal and social democratic rationalities. Third Way politics concurs with the neo-liberal emphasis on increased risk-taking in the market, and with the generalisation of the enterprise subject. Where it differs most markedly from the New Right and neo-conservatives is in its self-styled social democratic emphasis on 'social solidarity' and 'social justice'. As Giddens makes clear, however, this is not the same as the idea of the organic social. Nor is it to be identified with the New Right vision of social authoritarianism. Rather, the social exists in the form of 'civil society', which is set against both the state and the economy, and which can loosely be associated with the idea of 'community'.[13] That is, civil society exists as a moral collectivity and a voluntary association. It is a governmental space in which 'social and civic entrepreneurs' can mobilise the self-governing desires of the 'active' populace.

For such reasons I think it useful to denote the diverse rationalities that have emerged largely in reaction against social liberalism collectively as *neo-liberal*. Clearly this runs against those who prefer the term of 'advanced liberalism' because

---

13 As noted already, Rose (1996b, 1999a) has argued that 'community' tends to replace 'the social' in advanced liberal politics. As a category of government, it differs from the social especially, if not only, in the greater specificity of its referents (as, eg, in the 'small business community', etc) and its voluntaristic and responsibilising implications. Despite distancing himself from communitarianism, and preferring the category of 'civil society', Giddens repeatedly deploys 'community' as a synonym for civil society.

of the diversity of post-social liberalism (Rose, 1999a; Dean, 1999).[14] However, the diverse 'social liberal' regimes also differed along similar lines – notably also, between specific regimes that allied conservative with social liberal, and social democrat or even socialist with social liberal. What they shared in common – to a greater or lesser degree according to the configuration with other rationalities – was a certain orientation toward the social; that is, a focus on social insurance, on the organic social as a nexus of rights and responsibilities, and on value of social and human sciences. These can all be summed up in the idea of 'social security'. Among the principal features that neo-liberal configurations share is a focus on 'responsible risk-taking'.[15] On the one hand this entails the valorisation of uncertainty in the form of enterprise and 'risk-taking', an historically unprecedented valorisation of *embracing risk* as an ideal, in terms of which, in important ways, *all* subjects should constitute their lives. Significantly, it is argued governmentally that there now should be an increased tolerance for failure where innovation is at stake. The domain of responsibility is thus reduced with respect to uncertainty, taking chances in relation to innovation that is potentially productive is to be encouraged. On the other hand 'responsible risk-taking' equally entails valorising risk. However, with respect to risk – that is, risk minimisation or avoidance of harmful risks – responsibility is expanded and personalised. Both elements, risk and uncertainty, in this specific assemblage, together constitute neo-liberalism. That there is a 'new prudentialism' is hardly to be disputed. But that this is matched by a new adventurism – a new entrepreneurialism – must equally be self-evident.

---

14 To a degree this is merely a terminological difference, and not a matter over which I want to spill much ink. However, one difficulty with the concept of 'advanced liberalism' is that it tends to imply – like the concept of 'late capitalism' does for capitalism – that liberalism is reaching its zenith and possibly its end. Both assumptions are deeply problematic, and set up the next terminological problem – relating to whatever might follow after 'advanced liberalism' but yet still remain liberal. While the concept of 'enterprise liberalism' might be a better alternative to neo-liberalism, reflecting the centrality of enterprise, yet another neologism would be hard to bear.

15 As in the previous chapter, I am not here attempting a general characterisation of this form of liberalism, many aspects or components of which do not bear directly on matters of risk and uncertainty. Broader and far more detailed characterisations exist already, especially in Nikolas Rose's (1999a) *Powers of Freedom,* and more briefly in Mitchell Dean's work (1999), and other essays of Rose (1996a, 1996b).

It is only to be expected that in a field such as the common law of contract, the rational choice subject would play a key role in formulating visions of legal subjectivity. However, what is rather surprising is that in foundational legal formulations, the treatises of Bentham and Smith are never mentioned. Indeed, Bentham complained of the fact that his central concerns were ignored (Atiyah, 1979, p 428). The same might be said with respect to Bentham's considerable emphasis on the 'yolk of foresight', with which he sought to burden – or liberate – the mass of the populace. While the courts were concerned directly with the ways in which legal subjects should calculate the uncertain future, and how they should be held responsible for the consequences of their actions where they had failed to act with 'reasonable' foresight, there is once again a deafening silence concerning the theoretical treatises of economic theory. Although this chapter examines why this might have been, more central to its concerns is examination of certain strands of contract law as sites in which uncertainty was developed as a liberal technology of government in ways other than as an application of liberal economic and political theory. In this genealogy we can trace the development of certain legal categories and techniques of government and self-government – such as 'reasonable foreseeability' and 'expectations' – which drew on lawyers' constructions of what was a common sense, situated model of 'rational calculation'. In turn, these constructions were created to govern subjects who confront futures that are held not to be calculable in any precise way. Coupled with the possibility of legal sanctions, they operated not merely as philosophical speculations, but as practical governmental tools that both solved disputes and provided a didactic model of how one is to govern life 'reasonably' under such conditions. In this way common law is one of a number of sources inventing and assembling the technologies and discourses of uncertainty that have become central to liberal governance.

As might be anticipated, 19th century legal and liberal discourses of uncertainty were not created entirely *de novo*. Concepts such as those of 'the reasonable man' and 'expectations' were central to the emergence of mathematical probability, and came to play a role in innovative ideas of jurisprudence during the 1700s. As Daston (1988, p 55) has argued, in these contexts 'reasonableness' was understood to be a 'rationality of daily life', although not the daily life typically practised by the masses. It was, rather, the exemplary rationality made manifest in the actions and deliberations of an elite of subjects epitomised by prudent and successful businessmen and learned magistrates, whose 'judgment and past experience guided practice and justified belief'. They constituted the best available criteria of proof against which the judgment of other decisions could be calibrated, and given degrees of certainty or 'probabilities'. Such techniques of 'epistemological probability' were applied to judgments under conditions of uncertainty in the domains of law, commerce and religion, as much as in science (Daston, 1988, pp 58–59). The task of mathematical probability was to determine those forms of statistical reasoning-generating predictions that most closely conformed to the truths pronounced in the wise calculations of the 'reasonable men'. In turn, the category of 'expectations' referred to the predictions of future events made in conformity with these calculative techniques:

> Once the calculus of probabilities adopted the conduct of reasonable men as its subject matter, the descriptive orientation of mixed mathematics required that probabilists accept that conduct as the final test of its results. If a mathematical theory of lunar motion failed to predict the observed orbit, the mathematicians challenged the theory. Similarly when the conventional solution to ... [a given] problem, ran counter to the judgment of reasonable men, probabilists re-examined their definition of expectation. Mathematical expectation expressed a theory about the way in which reasonable men comported themselves in the face of uncertainty, just as the mathematical formulation of the law of gravitation expressed a theory about ponderable matter. (Daston, 1988, p 56)

From this foundation, it was proposed that mathematical probability could become the means for constructing generalised formulae of 'right reasoning' or rational calculation. Thus, it was supposed that a mathematics of veracity could be generated to act as a basis upon which courts could calculate truth with maximal certainty over a wide variety of decisions. Such calculations would involve, for example, determining the optimal number of jurors that would produce a valid verdict, or the relative 'probabilities' of the veracity of the evidence given by combinations of different kinds of witness. In turn, it was hoped, the mathematics of truth could be turned to a didactic purpose, used to instruct the mass of the population from the models of correct reasoning, thereby raising their capacity for rationality and prudence.

By the early 19th century, this project had been abandoned as nonsensical,[1] but as Daston stresses, this was not through any failure of the project of statistical probabilities. Rather it was because it was concluded that probability theory 'was no longer about that kind of problem'. Instead, linked with the invention of population and the economy, a paradigmatic shift lifted judgments on the norm of truth from criteria set by the elite 'reasonable men' to regularities 'revealed' by statistics at the level of society and economy. The focus became the aggregate performance of large numbers of subjects and actions. Yet these new criteria for establishing the norm were to be unevenly applied across different fields of knowledge and government. In this way, Daston suggests, as the 19th century wore on the once-adjacent disciplines of jurisprudence and economics drifted apart. Economics began drifting in the direction of risk: favouring mathematical and statistically aggregated technologies that were to reveal the natural laws of the economy. Common law and

---

1 It must be stressed this does not imply that the project was in any uncomplicated way actually nonsensical. As Daston states, the issue was that what 'made sense' changed. Thus as Hacking (1990) has stressed, epistemological probability does not disappear from the operations and assumptions of statistical reasoning. Rather it becomes submerged, but always remains in a ghostly form as the criterion in terms of which statistical reasoning is validated. Recent work has paid considerable attention to this issue in the area of financial risk and uncertainty. For example, Maurer (2002, p 29) has argued that in the field of financial speculation, '[t]he separation of stochastic probability and epistemological probability was a traumatic event, and ... the repressed epistemology returns to haunt contemporary accounts of financial derivatives'. In his view – as in the notions of classical probabilists – the mathematical model 'is a deontology of the way things ought to be, not an ontology of the way things are'.

jurisprudence, on the other hand, began more concertedly than ever to elaborate the epistemological side of classical probability, abandoning mathematical statistics and – under the sign of the 'reasonable man' – developing new and didactic criteria to dictate the terms by which rational life should be lived.

Crucial to this divergence was the invention of economic utility by early 18th century probabilists such as Daniel Bernoulli. For Bernoulli, 'utility' implied that expectations are to be understood not as the predictions of wise men, but as 'the power of a thing to procure us felicity' (quoted by Daston, 1988, p 71).[2] His understanding of utility began from a proposed inverse proportionality between the pleasure produced by an acquisition and the amount of goods already owned, an assumption that generated a logarithmetic curve based on the inverse proportionality of the two elements. This property of utility would emerge not by examining the reasoning or the expectations of a successful businessman, but by studying the aggregated decisions of many anonymous rational choice individuals. These latter subjects increasingly would be envisioned in terms of the precisely calculating, abstract *homo economicus*, and the outcomes of their combined actions reckoned in terms of statistical probabilities. It was to be a long road from Bernoulli's invention of utility to the formation of a deterministic discipline of economics based on laws that were 'revealed' by the operation of statistical probability.[3] But by the 1830s, a statistical understanding of the laws of economy had been established and mythologised in the nexus between the actions of rational choice actors and the invisible hand of the market. On the other hand, jurisprudence had abandoned its flirtations with statistics, instead building the reasonable man as a normative figure. The result was that while the *statistical* domain severed its ties with the epistemological project of classical probabilism – establishing the norm as merely distributional – the *legal* domain severed its ties with the statistical project, focusing instead on epistemological probability's project of establishing the moral norm as a criterion of individual competence in dealing with uncertainty.

It should be stressed that this legal move had little or nothing to do with rejecting a model of the rational choice actor. As will be seen, this abstract kind of subject was the foundation of the contractual form of law, for it came to be assumed that when legal subjects voluntarily entered into binding agreements this was because they thought it – rightly or wrongly – to their advantage. While this seemingly reflects the course taken by economics, it is likely the case that the rational choice subject of law was constituted by different processes than was true for liberal economic and political theory, and to a distinctive result. To begin with, it appears that the rational choice actor and the abstract contractual relationship emerged out of understandings that were brought to court by lawyers and, by implication, their clients – especially those in business. Rather than being deduced or formulated

---

2 In quoting Bernoulli's conclusion, formulated in the late 1730s, Daston (1988, pp 70–73) stresses that this, in its turn, was clearly influenced by such sources as Mandeville's *Fable of the Bees* and related debates that distinguished between the consequences of actions (such as the purchase and enjoyment of luxuries) for individuals and for collectivities.

3 This does credit neither to the sophistication of Bernoulli's argument nor to Daston's brilliant account of it and its subsequent development. However, such complexities are beyond the scope of the current argument.

theoretically, the key influences seem to have been situational, arising from the specific and pragmatic issues that drove people to legal action. It is also the case that law's rational choice subject was more hedged around with moralised principles and considerations than its economic parallel. The courts, after all, made moral decisions about what kinds of activity it would protect and facilitate, to whom it would give – and to whom it would refuse – remedy. One form of moralisation of the rational choice actor was carried out under the rubric of the reasonable man.

Economic theory, as noted, dispensed with the reasonable man, or alternatively, collapsed this figure into *homo economicus*: reasonableness was rationality and vice versa. For law this was never the case. Concerned with the moral dimension of rationality, the common law courts took reasonableness to be a much more problematic category, for central to its concerns were questions about how legal subjects should treat others. In the emerging contract law, where relationships were imagined as formed between abstract rational choice individuals who came together only for specific purposes, a new array of questions came to be posed that focused on what could and should have been taken into account as contingent obligations by the contracting parties. It is in this context that the reasonable man of classical probability was transformed in order to provide new criteria of judgment for the courts. While the reasonable man of the 18th century had been unusually wise, this could not be assumed of contract's rational choice subjects – who had no characteristics other than those that qualified them as rational. In a double sense, the reasonable man was reinvented as a subject who had an ordinary – 'reasonable' – capacity to anticipate the future. He was to be calculative and rational, not statistical. Like the wisdom of the original reasonable men of the 1700s, this capacity for 'reasonable foresight' was based in the idea that 'judgment and past experience guided practice'. Like the understandings of the theorists of uncertainty, such uncertain judgment was expected because the situation was sufficiently unique that expectations could be formed only through analogy – with respect to situations that appeared similar. Statistical calculations of probability were thus inappropriate: they were part of the knowledge expected of expertise rather than of the abstract subject; part of the mathematical discourses associated with aggregate futures rather than with the pragmatic person confronting a particular business relationship; and were associated with the discredited legacy of classical probabilism – the route taken by economics but not law.

This transmogrification of the didactic vision of the classical probabilists, thus, does not have its origins in the rise of liberal theory as articulated by Smith, Bentham and their colleagues. Rather, I argue, it appears out of the process, influenced much by the practical concerns of people – especially those in business – who brought their concerns to court. These protagonists, and their jurisprudential interpreters, forged their own route toward creating contractual parties as legal 'equals' who were understood to be the appropriate judges both for calculating their own interests, and for formulating their own expectations. The reasonable man was no longer the exemplary wise man, for the courts were moving away from any 'ideal' outcome other than that defined by the parties; but neither was he a statistical abstraction. In a strong sense, I suggest, the reasonable man is a subject of uncertainty rather than risk: confronting particular situations; armed with experience and rules of thumb; able to estimate possibilities – and held to account for his failure to estimate them 'reasonably'. In this way, the common law of contract continued the didactic project of the classical probabilists, but not by proposing a regime of rational conduct (which was assumed) so much as through developing a regime of moral conduct in terms of which the rational, contractual subject should 'reasonably' practise autonomy. It is to a more detailed account of this genealogy in law that our attention now turns.

On the genealogy of contract

While contract law obviously is only one institution through which economic life has been governed, its apparent closeness to the conceptual heartland of liberalism places it as one of the more definitive and generalised bodies of law governing enterprising activity. So much is this the case, that it has been taken for granted until recently that, in Atiyah's (1979, p 294) terms, 'the fact is that freedom of contract was at the very heart of classical economics, and there is good ground for thinking that the common lawyers may have taken over the concept from the economists in the early part of the nineteenth century' (see also Horwitz, 1977). This assertion would make for a convenient argument, for then it might be a simple matter to trace the ways in which common law judges took on board a knowledge of the classical economists and translated calculative rationality, and perhaps liberal economists' models in particular, into contract law. However, as Gordley makes clear, one of the startling features of the genealogy of contract law is that in the writing of the jurists who developed contractual 'will' theory:

> we find little direct borrowing from philosophers, economists or political theorists. Only rarely do we find any sign of a commitment to liberal values of freedom or individualism. We find almost the opposite: an insistence that the jurist can do his job without taking account of economics, philosophy, politics, or values such as freedom. In England and the United States, contract theory never became truly systematic until the time of Pollock [ie the late 1800s]. Jurists earlier in the century had groped toward system amid a clutter of borrowed continental expressions and ad hoc modifications. They said almost nothing about any larger principles on which they were building. (Gordley, 1991, pp 215–16)

The accounts piecing together this story, while differing in detail, concur that the formation of the modern law of contract occurred through the 'creative plagiarism' of the works of civil law jurists, in particular, Pothier's *Law of Obligations* (published in French in 1761).[4] These accounts argue that because this process began well before the publication of the works of Smith, Ricardo and Bentham, there is something odd about tracing law to these sources.[5] Instead, they seek to

---

4   See in particular Simpson, 1975 and 1979; Hamburger, 1989; Gordley, 1991; and Wightman, 1996. Pothier is referred to extensively by Hamburger and Gordley. It should be said from the outset that there are various disagreements between these authors, although few are of much concern to the arguments being made here.

5   As noted by Atiyah (1979, p 428), this is despite some surprisingly 'modern' sounding arguments of Bentham's that complain about jurists' refusal to consider expectations. For Bentham the 'idea of property consists in an established expectation – in the persuasion of power to derive certain advantages from the object according to the nature of the case. But this expectation, this persuasion, can only be the work of the law ... it is from the law alone that I can enclose a field and give myself to its cultivation, in the distant hope of the harvest' (Bentham, 1962, p 308).

constitute the emergence of contract in terms of processes internal to the common law rather than one rendering it a reflex of developments in political science, 'liberal ideology' or economic interests. The shared answer they arrive at is that the law governing exchange (which cannot accurately be referred to as 'contract' law before this time) did undergo a major change around the late 18th and early 19th centuries, but the source of the change was to be found in the rationalising work of jurisprudents. In this reading, European civilian jurists stretching from Grotius to Pothier, by the mid-18th century, had produced a coherent synthesis out of a number of sources, especially the doctrines of Roman law and the Christian juridical writings of Thomas Aquinas. The critical part of this synthesis, especially as it appeared in Pothier's writings (which probably had most impact on the common law), was the importance of will – particularly as expressed in the actions of offer and acceptance. It was assumed in these civilian works that, as was later to become a foundation of the 'will theory' of liberal contractualism, offer and acceptance are the visible manifestation of two free wills coming together in a consensus that each voluntary subject must have regarded overall as beneficial.

Yet this civilian, jurisprudential core of contract was embedded in a rich and complex set of doctrines, including, for example, those concerned with equality, assent and fairness, as derived from Thomist principles. In these moral claims, offer and acceptance were hedged around with an array of requirements: that a just contract be founded on full knowledge and understanding by all parties of the terms and conditions; that there was complete openness and fairness in bargaining; that there be a just price and that a just price created a warranty on the soundness of the goods. In addition, many different types of contract and promise were envisaged, such as loan, hire, barter and so on, for which specific conditions were to apply. However, all these specific, substantive and moral considerations were omitted when this continental, civilian law of contract was received into common law (Wightman, 1996, p 67). What was taken on board were only those parts of the theory concerned with the parties' wills, and categories that were held to be the expression of their agreement, such as offer and acceptance. This, as Gordley (1991) argues, was to create problems for the later development of contract law. For example, as a result of stripping away requirements for full understanding between parties, the common law of contract had no consistent way to deal with the implied lack of consent where a party made a mistake about facts associated with the contract. In this sense, it is suggested, contract law in the first half of the 19th century and even beyond, was far from the logical and complete doctrine imagined in discourses on liberalism. It was a patchwork with major gaps and omissions that later would need to be filled in an *ad hoc* way, and did not simply reflect the elegant theories worked out in the tomes of Smith, Ricardo and Bentham.

There is much in this account that is appealing to a governmental analysis, particularly the vision of so central a legal institution as contract being assembled in a more or less *ad hoc* fashion from available resources. But a key question not posed at all clearly in the new legal historiography concerns why the complex doctrines of the civilian lawyers were sloughed off in favour of a stripped-down will theory. Most of the commentaries are strangely silent on the question, perhaps because a principal item on their agenda is the denial of propositions concerning the impact of capitalist economic interests and liberal political theory on common law.[6] The effect, seemingly, is to leave their analysis having to accept as a rather strange coincidence the overlapping of law with political and economic theory. The one study that carefully examines this issue (Hamburger, 1989, pp 265–68) comes to two conclusions that cast light on this. On the one hand, beginning in the mid-1700s and continuing through the early 1800s, is a process in which 'the need to treat civil law as jurisprudence and the irrelevance of the details of civil law of contract' led common lawyers to simplify the civilian doctrine to a few generalised jurisprudential ideas. In turn, Hamburger argues, these 'details' appeared 'irrelevant' because both the existing remedies and the civilian elaborations were 'so distinct from the consensual reality' – that is, from the ways in which jurisprudents and lawyers understood pragmatic business relationships. As a result, 'lawyers ... developed the consensus analysis unfettered by practical concerns about remedies' (Hamburger, 1989, p 311). As Hamburger is arguing, the old law of exchange had become problematic precisely because in the lawyers' eyes their clients' problems and demands were an expression of changes in the nature of law. Thus, for example, the immediate cause for the reception of offer and acceptance into common law was that the courts were increasingly dealing with long-range trade in which contracts were formed by mail and the two elements of agreement were not transacted simultaneously (*Adams v Lindsell* (1818) 1 B & Ald 681). Other changes along the same lines had a longer lineage. Hamburger argues that doctrines of common law that paralleled the 'details' of the civilian law – such as equality of knowledge (that is, relating to defects in goods), just price and fairness – were already under siege in the courts by the late 18th century. This was, in his view, due to what he refers to as 'economic practice and non-theoretical economic sympathies' (1989, p 268). More precisely, following Simpson (1979), he concludes that the civilian model of offer and acceptance 'attracted common lawyers beginning in the later 18th century because it provided them with what had long been absent from common law, a description of the consensual reality of contract'. It is perhaps less important to ask the

---

6 The key work in this respect is Horwitz's (1977) *The Transformation of American Law* which argued that judges ushered in revolutionary changes in contract and tort law, reflecting the interests and demands of the new capitalist entrepreneurs. Horwitz's account included claims that the judicial legislation of the new will theory of contract eroded the principles of fairness that had characterised the pre-capitalist moral economy, and thus created a situation in which the economic negotiating power of merchants and employers could be used more oppressively and with far fewer legal checks. In addition, the law of torts effectively dismantled strict liability law governing recovery for harms outside of contract. As the doctrine of negligence was developed in its place (requiring plaintiffs to establish that harms had been suffered though the negligence of the defendant), Horwitz claimed that many harms now would no longer be actionable. This, he claimed, represented a massive subsidy to those who created most injury and harm in an industrial economy – the capitalists. To rub salt into the legal historians' wounds, he also claimed that such changes came about by the judges creating a sort of interregnum, in which precedent was overridden while changes were put in place through judicial innovation. Once this process had ensured that the law basically reflected bourgeois interests, new and more restrictive rules of precedent were imposed, in order to cement things in place. The considerable and outraged response that followed, led by Simpson (1979), sought to re-establish the received wisdom of the autonomy of common law. The appearance of Atiyah's (1979) *Rise and Fall of the Freedom of Contract* – which displaced Horwitz's Marxism with a eulogising of the lost world of *laissez faire* capitalism – allowed many liberals to come to terms with the idea that common law had been shaped from without, by liberal philosophy. The debate has continued, however. See most recently, Gordley, 1991; Kercher, 1996; Wightman, 1996; and Collins, 1997.

question of whether or not contract was actually changing in practice, and whether this 'really' reflected consensual bargaining, than to note the fact that lawyers and jurists were problematising the issue in this fashion. Contract law, it is being argued in these analyses, changed in a direction shaped by lawyers', judges' and jurists' estimations of current 'economic practice' – a point that emerges with particular clarity in later discussions of 'uncertain subjects' in case law.

If this is so, then it helps to answer a broader question in the genealogy of contract. If there is no discussion of the general principles of liberalism as formulated by Smith, Bentham and Ricardo, then how was it that the common law still had sufficient coherence at the end of the 19th century that Pollock and other systematisers were able to produce a consistent *rationality* of contract law? Part of this answer is provided by the acceptance of the 'stripped down' will theory of contract – the underlying assumption of voluntary subjects freely contracting to their rationally calculated advantage. But this, by itself, will not account for the particular ways in which the courts formulated solutions to many problems that were sufficiently specific that nothing as general as offer and acceptance or 'the will theory' could by itself provide answers capable of later rationalisation into the 'elegant theory' of contract. A more complete answer, I suggest, needs to recognise that throughout this period, and continuing into the present, the common law was adopting the stance of the uncertain subject. Such subjects were, and still are, assumed to operate with a form of common sense rationality and reasonable foresight that common law read into the activities of those engaged in commerce, and by means of which in turn it governed and sought to shape them. As this implies, and the discussion that follows illustrates, it is neither possible nor necessary to engage in a chicken or egg debate – the obsession of common law lawyers and their critics (for example, Horwitz, 1977; Collins, 1997; Ferguson, 1983; Gabel and Feinman, 1982; Simpson, 1979; Hamburger, 1989) – over whether law or 'political' liberalism comes first in the shaping of the rationalities of contract law. Liberal political and economic 'theory', jurists' readings of civilian law, the constitution of business rationality in the common law of contract, the 'realities' of economic practice, the mentalities of capitalists, and any number of other specific sites of governance were no doubt *simultaneously* engaged in the formulation of the related but distinctive problematisations, categories and techniques that were eventually rationalised into the coherent fabric that we now think of as classical liberalism.

Will theory and the invention of expectation damages

It is generally accepted that prior to the 19th century there was no law of contract in the modern sense of the process of offer and acceptance. The significance of this is not immediately obvious until we consider contract's precursors, primary among which were debt and assumpsit. With some simplification, debt concerned the fulfilment of promises where an exchange, in part performance of an agreement, had already occurred. Its legal remedy involved the completion of a process already in train. This required either the payment of money for the completed or part-performed delivery of a title or service, or conversely, the remedy of 'specific performance' (that is, exact completion) of the agreement for which one party has paid. Assumpsit was founded on the notion of reliance – essentially, that as a result of acting on a promise or undertaking made by another, the plaintiff had suffered a loss. Built into this, from an early point, was that any pleading of assumpsit had to demonstrate 'consideration'. In other words, if a plaintiff was making a plea on the basis of a promise, the courts wanted to know why the promise was made, and it was assumed that a promise should not be enforced where it was gratuitous – that is, where the promisor stood to gain nothing from making the offer. Each of these pre-contract law forms of redress governs in a sense through the past: a debt to be paid for prior provision of some good or service; goods or services to be delivered when already paid for; and so on. There was no consistent idea that a purely executory promise – one made but not yet acted upon by any party – should be enforced.[7]

What was selectively plagiarised from Pothier and other civilian jurists changed much of this. First, as offer and acceptance was a bilateral consensus, the content of the promise ceased to be of concern to the court. The focus on this bilateral quality of contract, which may, as Hamburger suggests, have been developing all along in the background of 'real' contracts, provided grounds for eliminating much of the legal concern with fairness associated with the idea of the 'moral economy' (Thompson, 1977).[8] Thus the content of the promise was evacuated from law. Secondly, as noted, the old doctrine of consideration implied that a gratuitous promise may create a moral obligation, but without some demonstrable benefit accruing to the promisor, no legal responsibility was established. As will readily be perceived, this construction of consideration focuses on the motive, and thus would throw the court back into a position that required it to investigate the issues of retrospective government that concerned collection of debt and enforcement of part completed exchange under assumpsit. In none of this could risk or uncertainty have a place, for these both look to the calculation or expectation of a future state of affairs. The old law reflected and formed economic exchange which was oriented to an instantaneous present and to the past that informed it. In almost every respect this was revolutionised during the course of the 19th century. Legal recognition of the bilateral promise made possible contracts based merely upon expectations, imagined to be in the mind of the contracting parties at the time of the agreement.

Consider the sequence of early New South Wales cases discussed by Kercher (1996).[9] In 1806 an action was brought before the Court of Civil Jurisdiction by John McArthur, seeking payment of a promissory note (*McArthur v Thompson*). The note promised to pay 99 bushels of wheat in exchange for monetary

---

7   As Wightman (1996) indicates, while there are earlier instances where fully executory promises had been enforced, it is not until after the turn of the 19th century that any consistency appeared in this respect.

8   There has been considerable debate over this point. At present, the most robust position is that fairness had been an accepted principle in exchange, but was progressively being eroded during the 18th century, in law and in practice (Hamburger, 1989). Horwitz's (1977) view of a sudden and revolutionary change in the 19th century now appears anachronistic and overstated. The fact that this process in law occurred more or less gradually in the last half of the 18th century and the early part of the 19th, is consistent with the conclusions reached earlier in this book about the emergence of the diversity of 'liberal' practices of government.

9   The following cases are unreported, and presented as discussed by Kercher. For this reason no case references are provided.

consideration. But between the date the note was issued and the date set for payment, flooding caused wheat prices to rise sharply. The defendant, a farmer who had already lost much in the floods, sought to pay only the value of the wheat at the earlier price. The court decided that as the rise in the price of wheat had been the effect of a flood that adversely affected the defendant, it would not be *fair* to award damages to the plaintiff. In most respects this was a traditional case, in which a part-performed exchange was adjudicated on the principle of a fair price, in which the vicissitudes of market uncertainty should not determine the right to recover. Certainty, the order of things past, and fairness, were being enforced. Later in 1806, the same court deliberating the case of *McArthur v Badgery* decided that a promissory note should be paid to the value of the goods on the date the note was payable. In addition, the court ruled that if the defendant failed to pay on that date and if the market value of the goods increased, he would be liable to pay this higher price. As Kercher notes (1996, p 152), the court effectively recognised that by delaying payment, the note holder had agreed to take on the risk of further, unpredictable or uncertain price changes. Yet this action still had one foot in the past. It did not involve a fully executory contract but a part-performed contract, for consideration had already been provided (presumably a loan) in exchange for the promissory note. Six years later, in the case of *Murray v Hook*, the court took a major step. A buyer of wine had refused to accept delivery, it is assumed because the price of wine had fallen since the contract was made. As no exchange had yet occurred an earlier court would have been unlikely to entertain the action and, at best, might have provided specific relief by enforcing the sale. However, the court advised the plaintiff to sell the wine on the open market, and sue the defendant for the difference between the market price and the contract price. Likewise, in the action of *Kelly v Clarkson* in 1813, when the court dealt with a similar case of refusal to accept delivery of wheat at an agreed upon price, it awarded damages of £80 to the wheat seller, even though no exchange had occurred. Damages were set on the principle that the seller would have to dispose of the wheat on a falling market – and thus suffer an avoidable loss. The quantum of damages would be set by the difference between the price contracted and the price of wheat at time of sale.

Two obvious features of *Murray v Hook* and *Kelly v Clarkson* are that they concern a market in which prices were expected to be variable, rather than fixed by custom, and the courts were not concerned with how parties settled on prices. In focusing on the contract and market prices, it avoided any issue of a fair price. Instead, it assumed each party had taken possible market fluctuations into account and determined that the agreed price was in their own interest. The court was expressing its acceptance of the idea that legal subjects who are parties to an exchange are calculating actors who act rationally and, as such, take full responsibility for the future consequences of their decisions. It was not the court's concern whether or not the outcomes were fair according to any other criterion. This emerging 'will theory' of contract assumed there was no way to assess the value of a commodity other than by the subjective estimations of the contracting parties. In the absence of relevant evidence vitiating consent (for example relating to fraud, unconscionability or coercion), even a contract which varies greatly from prevailing market prices must be presumed by the court to represent the outcome of calculations taken by both parties who estimated that they would benefit in some valued way. If subsequently it proved otherwise for one of the parties, then this was the product of an erroneous expectation, and not the business of the court. In *Murray v Hook* and *Kelly v Clarkson*, the clear implication is that the court regarded the decline in market price as a possibility the defendants should take into account, and thus they would have to suffer – just as they would have reaped benefits had the market price risen. As far as the court is concerned, in this emergent model, the legal subject who is party to a contract is a speculator, and is to be protected, or not protected, as such. The courts were beginning to govern uncertainty through contract law and, conversely, to govern exchange in terms of uncertainty. But how exactly was this uncertainty governmentally understood and given expression?

In *Murray v Hook* and *Kelly v Clarkson*, the court was promoting the category of an 'expectation interest' – that is, the posited interest of the plaintiffs in the value they reasonably expect to be delivered by the market if the contract is fulfilled. Whereas previously the law would be concerned to see the contract performed, or the parties put back into the state they were in prior to the agreement, now the court concerned itself to see the parties put into the position *they would have come to be in*. As Baron Park's classic statement in *Robinson v Harman* (1848) 1 Ex D 850 later expressed it, '[the] rule of the common law is, that where a party sustains a loss by reason of a breach of contract, he is, so far as money can do it, to be placed in the same situation, with respect to damages, as if the contract had been performed'. From now on, courts would recommend not the return of the parties to the *status quo* or to the *status quo ante*, as under earlier law, but their advancement to the consequent *status quo*. Indeed, this advancement may be to a hypothetical consequent *status quo*, a situation that never came into being because the contract was not performed and thus must be speculated about by the court.[10]

Henceforward, contract law was to be about governing through the future and futurities; it no longer operated primarily in terms of an instantaneous transfer of property, or required the specific performance of a promise, but increasingly became oriented toward the transfer of the profit potential. For this reason, simple return of money paid would not provide remedy for lost profits that could have been earned. Likewise, monetary expectation damages displaced the old remedy as of right, that is, specific performance of the terms of the contract. It can readily be understood that specific performance (say, the delivery of goods) may be worse than useless to the plaintiff as entrepreneur, who may no longer have access to profitable opportunities related to the commodity concerned, may have new and more profitable avenues for their capital, or who may be being delivered a commodity whose market value is a fraction of what it was at the contracted time of delivery. Rather, the category of expectation interests and the remedy of expectation damages normally involve the court using hindsight to calculate the value of a lost opportunity – for example, using knowledge of changes in market prices between the formation of the contract and its breach. However, there is no expectation that the defendants should have calculated this change, for the direction or volume of changes in market prices are never discussed as predictable. Rather, what is expected is that they should have taken account of the

---

10 See the later discussion of *Howard v Teefy* (1927) 27 SR (NSW) 301.

fact that the market behaves uncertainly, have recognised that an adverse shift in prices was a reasonably foreseeable possibility, and are thus held accountable and responsible for the consequences.[11] The genealogy of contract law, I am suggesting here, stems not simply from the fact of the 'will theory', but rather from the forms of subjectivity that contract law imagines. These assume and sanction particular processes of reasoning about the uncertain future. As such, it is also an important part of the genealogy of uncertainty, and its further development, particularly with respect to the category of reasonable foreseeability, bears closer scrutiny.

Uncertainty and foreseeability

The early development of expectation interest in contract, which had become established law by the mid-19th century, left open the possibility of compensation to a plaintiff for an array of outcomes that were to be determined as *not* 'reasonably foreseeable' at the time of the contract. For example, it is quite possible that one of the parties had a special interest in the contract which was not known to the other, with the implication that non-completion of the contract would involve costs unforeseen by the other party subsequently in breach. In a line of decisions, beginning in 1854, that focused on the issue of 'remoteness of damage', the common law moved toward a fairly comprehensive definition of what constitutes foreseeability in such issues affecting contracts:

> Where two parties have made a contract which one of them has broken, the damages which the other party ought to receive in respect of such a breach of contract should be such as may fairly and reasonably be considered as arising naturally, that is, according to the usual course of things, from such breach of contract itself, or such as may reasonably be supposed to have been in the contemplation of both parties at the time they made the contract, as the probable result of the breach of it. (*Hadley v Baxendale* (1854) 156 ER 145)

This famous ruling brings together two concerns with uncertainty: the 'subjective' act of the contractors in contemplating or calculating the future, and the 'objective' process whereby loss was understood to be 'naturally' consequent upon the breach. In both respects, the decision in *Hadley v Baxendale* sets in place certain ground rules for reasonable (in both senses of the word) dealings with uncertainty which, through the guarantee of law and its sanctions, are to provide an enforceable regime for its government. *Inter alia*, the court's ruling meant that in the event that one party stood to gain or lose in some unusual fashion from the contract, unknown to the other, or as the result of some possibility the other party 'reasonably' did not consider as bearing on the contract, then the award of damages would be restricted to what the court decided was reasonably foreseeable. The court reasoned that 'had the special circumstances been known, the parties might have specially provided for the breach of contract by special terms as to the damages in that case' (*Hadley v Baxendale* (1854) 156 ER 150). The significance of this may not be immediately apparent. Evidently this sets up a model for governing in which it is expected that contracting subjects should take into account the foreseeable ramifications of their contract. It also means that,

---

11 A significant point noted by Heimer and Staffen (1988, p 9) is that the word 'responsibility' only came into use in the late 1700s, and combines the earlier distinct notions of imputation and accountability.

henceforward, contractors may negotiate between themselves the conditions of their future legal liability with respect to any agreed upon 'special terms'. For Patrick Atiyah and other legal historians this is regarded as a 'triumph of the entrepreneurial ideal' because 'the idea of responsibility [as] being based on the foreseeable consequences of one's action was central to utilitarian philosophy' (Kercher and Noone, 1990, p 128). Yet, as we have seen, this interpretation appears more as an act of historiographic hindsight than any explicit gloss placed upon it by the judiciary. Indeed, once again, the court did not mention any such ideal, nor any texts of liberal philosophy or government.

What, then, *was* on the court's mind? While it could be claimed to be obvious that it was influenced by what had become politically commonplace by 1854, such speculative imputations may be avoided by examining the second rule in *Hadley v Baxendale*, concerned with the estimation of what 'naturally arises out of the breach'. In Kercher and Noone's (1990, p 129) view, the 'first or normal rule assumes that business people contemplate the possibility of liability for breach in setting their prices, those calculations accounting only for normal losses'. They continue by saying that what 'little evidence exists as to their actual conduct in entering into contracts suggests that business people do not make neat calculations about liability at that time'. While Kercher and Noone regard this as a criticism of the decision, what they unintentionally highlight is that the court is not describing what actually happens. It is, rather, providing a blueprint for governance in which a certain kind of subjectivity is being formulated, and in which certain rules are provided for the conduct of business under conditions of uncertainty. But through the enforcement of these rules, and particularly via the award of expectation damages, the court is not simply making assumptions about subjects. In an echoing of the classical probabilists' project, it is also establishing a didactic technology for *creating* such 'free' subjects of uncertainty.

The implications of these rules were made abundantly clear by the elaboration provided nearly a century later in *Victoria Laundry (Windsor) Ltd v Newman Industries Ltd* [1949] 2 KB 528. Here it was decided, in accordance with the two rules in *Hadley v Baxendale*, that the plaintiff is entitled to recover only 'such part of the loss resulting as was at the time of the contract reasonably foreseeable as liable to result from the breach' (p 539). The court went on to stress that what is 'reasonably foreseeable' will depend on the two kinds of knowledge possessed by the parties at the time of the contract. The first is the special knowledge passed on in the contractual negotiations and which is assumed (by virtue of the contract) to have be been accepted as a 'risk' by the plaintiff. The second, and more generally significant, is imputed knowledge. This assumes that 'everyone, as a reasonable person, is taken to know "the ordinary course of things", and consequently what loss is liable to result from a breach of contract in that ordinary course' (1949, p 539). In other words, the defendant need not have made this calculation. But had they done so, as would a reasonable (legal) person, then they would have taken into account that the loss was indeed liable to have occurred.[12]

---

12 Again, it is important to note that the court was not expecting the defendant to have *calculated* the vicissitudes of the market. In *Hadley v Baxendale*, what was at issue was the late delivery of a part required for the operation of a mill, and whether it was reasonable to expect that the defendant should have recognised that this part was essential to the profitability of the mill.

In all of this, it may appear that we are just examining the 'reasonable person' in law, already endlessly subjected to critique. However, the point being made is that the standard of the reasonable person is being deployed to require a certain kind of calculation of all contractual subjects. In addition, it is quite explicit that this standard is not that of statistical probability nor theoretically-based prognostication by expertise. Rather, to borrow Hamburger's phrase, it involves 'non-theoretical economic sympathies'. Uncertainty is regarded as employing foreseeability as a technology of everyday life, as deploying the categories of practical experience. In consequence, searching the common law rarely, if ever, reveals any estimation of likely outcomes expressed in terms of statistical probability.[13] Thus, the court in *Victoria Laundry (Windsor) Ltd v Newman Industries Ltd* [1949] 2 KB 540 required that a reasonable person should have regarded the outcome of loss as 'a serious possibility', 'a real danger' or 'on the cards'. That this was no passing semantic foible of the court is indicated by the fact that subsequent elaborations and disagreements have followed the same linguistic discourse of possibility or probability, even though this has clearly caused many difficulties. Thus, 20 years later in *Koufos v C Czarnikow Ltd* [1969] 1 AC 350, the House of Lords tried to refine the definition further. Lord Reid used 'the words "not unlikely" as denoting a degree of probability considerably less than an even chance but nevertheless not very unusual and easily foreseeable' (pp 382–83). Other judges' formulations in the same case included 'not unlikely to result' and 'liable to result'.

Such analysis of everyday forms of foresight by the courts could be extended almost indefinitely, both in terms of the detail of calculation expected, and in terms of its generalisation in law.[14] For example, the question of 'certainty' in contract law has been explored in depth. Courts will not award damages if the

---

13 An apparent exception to this exists in the well-known American example of Judge Learnedhand's risk calculus as laid out in *United States v Carroll Towing Co* 159 F2d 169 (2d Cir) (1947). In this he provided an algebraic formula: 'If the probability be called P; the injury L; and the burden (the cost of avoiding the harm) B; liability depends upon whether B is less than L multiplied by P; ie, whether $B<PL$.' While this appears impressively mathematical, probability remains a linguistic expression. Thus in this case, involving a barge breaking loose and damaging other vessels, the probability was described as 'substantial' and the burden 'minor'.

14 Almost identical exercises have been carried out with respect to the issues of foreseeability and of certainty of loss in the law of torts. (More generally see Tilbury, Noone and Kercher, 1993; Hart and Honoré, 1987.) Thus we find the following musings of the court with respect to an action involving a passer-by being injured by a cricket ball:

   If the test whether there has been a breach of duty were to depend merely on the answer to the question whether this accident was a reasonably foreseeable risk, I think that there would have been a breach of duty, for that such an accident might take place some time or other might very reasonably have been present to the minds of the appellants. It was quite foreseeable, and there would have been nothing unreasonable in allowing the imagination to dwell on the possibility of its occurring. But there was only a remote, perhaps I ought to say only a very remote, chance of the accident taking place at any particular time. (*Bolton v Stone* [1951] AC 850 at 868, *per* Lord Radcliffe)

   This example is interesting because it seems reasonable to suggest that the statistical calculation of such a risk is virtually impossible. The closest to a statement of statistical probability that I have been able to find is in Australian commercial law, where the Full Federal Court referred to '[a] real or not remote chance of possibility regardless of whether it is less or more than 50 per cent' (*Taco Company of Australia Inc v Taco Bell Pty Ltd* (1982) 42 ALR 202).

loss of an opportunity for profit is so uncertain as to be entirely speculative, but they may award damages where there is a 'reasonable' chance of loss having been sustained (*Davies v Taylor* [1972] 3 All ER 840). The general rule, as Kercher and Noone (1990, p 135) indicate, is that 'where a loss of opportunity is established, damages will be calculated by assessing the likely sum to have been gained, and reducing it by the chance of the money not being gained ... until eventually the possibility becomes "fanciful" or "speculative" and substantial damages are refused'. This may take us very far away from the familiar forms of calculating expert assessment, toward what Kercher and Noone refer to as a 'need to guess the future'. Where an opportunity to profit is established, but difficulties in estimating the profit are deemed too difficult to assess even in hindsight, other solutions can still be found. For example, in *Howe v Teefy* (1927) 27 SR (NSW) 307, an action over loss of opportunity suffered when a contract to lease a racehorse was breached, it was ruled that the calculation involved was not how much the plaintiff 'would probably have made in the shape of profit out of his use of the horse'. It was reasoned that it was impossible to decipher this; after all, how could this be known, as it was dependent on races that were never run, wagers that were never made, and so on? Instead, the court decided that damages were to be calculated in terms of 'how much his chance of making this profit, by having use of the horse, was worth in money'.

Many such solutions are ingenious inventions, but as Lord Denman has remarked, some people find the situation distressingly imprecise. So much so that, with respect to such issues as the subtle differences between 'not unlikely to result' and 'liable to result', he found himself unable to 'swim in this sea of semantic exercises' (*Koufos v C Czarnikow Ltd* [1969] 1 AC 802). Despite this, at no stage did he contemplate the abandonment of uncertainty. Nor, especially, did he resort to a statistical model of risk, or to the calling in of experts to provide more precise specification of likelihood of diverse outcomes. Rather, the assumption accepted by him and generations of his peers is that outlined by Hart and Honoré (1987, p 68) – the first edition of which Lord Denman had turned to for help in his deliberations. They conclude that 'in theory' such matters 'might be decided by statistics, but in practice we make use of rough notions of the likelihood of defined events and so can decide from a common sense point of view'. Hart and Honoré go on to say:

> Our moral or legal judgements of the actions of others depend not on the foreseeability of harm considered in isolation, but always in foresight in relation to a practical decision; foresight of harm such that in all the circumstances a reasonable man would adopt or refrain from a particular course of action. Reasonable foresight, in relation to culpability, is therefore a practical notion, and we may term the harm, the risk of which is sufficient to influence the conduct of a prudent man, 'foreseeable in the practical sense'. (Hart and Honoré, 1987, p 263)

Uncertainty, expertise and responsibility

Uncertainty proves to be a venerable, resilient and foundational modality through which liberal subjects are expected to govern themselves as rational and responsible agents. In legal governance, uncertainty is formulated as a set of rules derived from an imagery of entrepreneurial calculation that is pragmatic and situated, rather than abstract or quantifiable. It formulates in terms of a problematic of 'foreseeability' in a domain of 'expectation', rather than precise calculation in a domain of stable predictability. With respect to the government of harms generated out of enterprise – not only in breach of contract but also in much of the law of tort – 'reasonable foresight', that imprecise or 'vague' form of governing through the future, appears as an appropriate adjunct to the vision of the creative innovation of the entrepreneur: an intelligible way of problematising the uncertain and unformed future that this creates.

In all of this, expertise has been the silent party, and it is perhaps the absence of the calculable precision associated with expertise that Lord Denman found so frustrating. Things probably have become worse for this manner of thinking. As we have seen, current discourses of neo-liberal business enterprise, especially those that propose the extension of its models of creative uncertainty to the government of most areas of activity, not only gravitate away from statistical models, but maintain a jaundiced view of the role of expertise in government. This despite the fact that the apostles of enterprise culture portray themselves as experts in such skills as 'thriving on chaos', 'teaching elephants to dance' and 'managing crazy organisations' – for *these* expertises appear as grounded not in the arcane domains of the human sciences, or in actuarial tables, but in the practical forms of indigenous governance that are imagined by these writers as the hallmark of the entrepreneur. They defy systematisation into arcane 'mathematical dramas', and represent themselves, as Reddy (1996) perceives, as democratic in their will to empower, and forthright in their suspicion or even hostility to the expertises of the sciences and authoritative professions.[15] However, this tension between 'elitist' expertise and 'democratic' everyday practicality is not a new innovation of neo-liberalism, important though its reformulation is. Rather, it is drawn from a deep well of assumptions about common sense reasoning and uncertainty as fundamental conditions of the autonomy of the rationally calculating, free subjects of liberalism. Once again this appears in law. If contract law, especially, has vigorously pursued the ways of uncertainty 'reasonably', this is by no means peculiar to it. Common law has been, and remains, decidedly ambivalent about the status of expert knowledge, and the law of evidence makes very clear that expert evidence is only admissible where the lay person cannot be expected to have their own form of knowledge about the matters in question. This 'common knowledge rule' (Palmer, 1998) provides that:

> Admission of [expert] evidence carries with it the implication that the jury are not equipped to decide the relevant issues without the aid of expert opinion and thus, if it is wrongly admitted, it is likely to divert them from their proper task which is to decide the matter for themselves using their own common sense. (*per* Dawson J in *Murphy v R* (1989) 167 CLR 94, pp 130–31)

Thus while, as Rose (1996a) suggests, liberalism forms a special relationship with expertise and knowledge, this relationship is a fraught one. In part, this is because the place of expertise and its knowledge is created by the recognition that the self-governing subjects of liberalism – population, economy, and individuals especially –

---

15 As Rose (1996a) notes with respect to the human sciences, but with equal application to professions such as law and medicine, this is more often expressed in efforts to bring them to heel through the techniques of the entrepreneurial market, than to undermine their knowledges.

must be understood in order that good government align its various autonomous capacities to the outcomes which it seeks (cf Foucault, 1991). At the same time, government should not interfere with these autonomous forms of 'indigenous governance' for it cannot achieve its ends without their operation. The result, as Foucault indicated with respect to governmentality more generally, is that the field of liberal government is swept by an ongoing tension not just between the allocation of governance to 'the state' and 'civil society', but over the place and role of expertise in good government. With respect to the self-governance of the autonomous subjects of liberalism, this appears in many ways in the distinction between statistical and professionally estimated risk, as a field of expert scientific governance, and uncertainty, as the mode of self government required of the liberal, reasonable, free and calculating subject. Uncertainty appears crucial to liberal freedom and enterprise. For this reason, rather than anything much to do with technical difficulties in extending the calculable technologies of risk, the domain of uncertainty will continue to occupy a pre-eminent place in the heartland of liberal government.

Chapter 5
Risky Contracts: Gambling, Speculation and Insurance

> In modern times, lawyers and economists are accustomed to think of contracts – executory contracts for future performance – as devices for allocating the risks of future events. So prevalent is this viewpoint that it is commonly assumed that this is the sole function of contracts, and that every contract must necessarily allocate the risk of future events affecting its performance. Now, in the eighteenth century it is probable that a contract expressly designed to allocate the risk of future events would have been thought to be akin to a wagering contract. In the early eighteenth century there was also much hostility over new dealings in stocks since many of them plainly partook of wagering ... The idea that it was an acceptable and useful function of contracts to allocate future risks was not at all an obvious one at this time. (Atiyah, 1979, p 176)

In the light of Atiyah's comments, it is hardly surprising that, since the middle of the 18th century, courts have spent considerable energy and time differentiating gambling contracts from legitimate financial contracts. Indeed, it is not stretching things very far to say that contracts in insurance and stock market speculation have been defined in terms of their Other of gambling. Gambling is the absent presence that not only haunts the margins of contract law, but by its very existence has done much to create them. What is surprising is the degree of difficulty courts have experienced in making this distinction practicable. It might be assumed that, given the widespread moral condemnation of gambling, it would be relatively easy to distinguish what constitutes a hedonistic vice from reputable and socially vital exchanges. After all, Blackstone (1767, IV c 13) famously remarked that:

> Taken in any light it [gambling] is an offence of the most alarming nature tending by necessary consequence to promote idleness, theft and debauchery among those of a lower class, and among persons of a superior rank it hath frequently been attended by the sudden ruin and desolation of ancient and opulent families and abandoned prostitution of every principle of honour and virtue, and too often hath ended in self murder.

Any monograph on gambling will give an extensive list of similar grounds upon which moral condemnation of this sort has rested (for example, Dixon, 1991). Yet the courts have found it difficult to differentiate this morally degraded category from the rationally calculative activity foundational of bourgeois industry and accumulation. How can this be? Part of the answer is that, as Atiyah suggests, the distinction had to be invented. As a result it has often been argued that there is no 'real' difference between 'legitimate' contracts enforceable at law, and gambling – or wagering and gaming – contracts which are not actionable as such. Ann Fabian, for example, has suggested that the disreputability of gambling acted as a brake on the activities of the rising bourgeoisie. If their own speculative activities were regarded as identical to a vice, these would be condemned and even proscribed. In addition, from the point of view of bourgeois sensibilities, the comparison between admirable speculative investment and degenerate gambling was distasteful and outrageous. In Fabian's view the outcome reflected the power and morality of the rising bourgeoisie. While there is no 'real' difference between the two activities, '[for] ... the speculation to stay the gambling had to go' (Fabian, 1990, p 160). Somewhat less conspiratorially, Brenner and Brenner (1990, p 63) suggest that gambling's association with 'the reallocation of property by chance ... went against a main feature of the Protestant ethic'. Making gambling contracts legally unenforceable played to 19th century moral tastes and reflected middle-class concerns about gambling's effects on thrift and diligence among the working classes. Thus the legal subordination of gaming and wagering contracts reflected 'the continuing expansion of the entrepreneurial middle classes'. Recently, Kreitner (2000, p 1,097) has argued more comprehensively that the nexus between gambling and contract law is part of a:

> ... complex story of Americans' love/hate relationship with risk. The background to the doctrinal analysis and policy discussion is the shifting morality and religious world view that were dominant in the United States until late in the nineteenth century. This world view contained a strong opposition to speculation and gambling, and therefore, life insurance and commodities trading, which were viewed as difficult to distinguish from gambling, were targeted as immoral. The attempt to establish a firm distinction between speculation and gambling was not primarily a legal question, but rather a cultural conflict about the role of the individual person. Distinguishing between gambling and its cousins in the realm of legitimate speculation was part of a process of socializing individuals.

Kreitner reiterates the thesis that no 'technical' difference exists between the various forms of financial contract – whether the insurance, gambling or speculative variety – for all are about the allocation of financial risk and all occur as exchange relations. The difference between them, he insists, arises from the valorisation of normative behaviour associated with prudent and self-reliant individualism, and the condemnation of those who relied on fortune to get rich quick.

This is familiar enough territory. But the consequence of this fact, Kreitner suggests, is that as the 'moral aversion to gambling has dissipated', the nature of the problem for government and law has been transformed from concern with the differentiation of risk, insurance and speculation into a question of 'the proper way to regulate a market in risk' (Kreitner, 2000, p 1,122). It is difficult to disagree that the distinctions between insurance, gambling and speculation are invented, for the invention of distinctions is surely the kind of work law generally performs. The question, rather, is whether the moral condemnation of gambling as a vice was the lever used to create the legal differences. I think that there are some significant problems with this argument.

First, it does not explain why in the present era, despite the fact that gambling has been reconciled with bourgeois interests and reinvented as an industry, gambling contracts *per se* remain unenforceable at common law. This problem is all the more puzzling in the light of numerous and strong complaints about the nullifying impact of the courts' interpretation of 'genuine' commercial transactions as mere wagers (Ciro, 1999; 2002b). By and large, only certain kinds of gambling contracts, involving gambling 'industries', have become enforceable – through the intervention of legislation. Were moral condemnation of a certain style of individual conduct as critical an issue as is made out, then insofar as Kreitner and others are correct about its abatement we might have expected a more general shift in common law and not this very particular pattern. After all, as Dixon (1991) has indicated, this shift in moral and legislative acceptance of gaming 'industries' has been underway for the best part of a century.

Secondly, as Kreitner would be aware, the focus on American moralities is too particularistic, for the legal issues to which he refers arise in similar form in England and extend across other common law countries such as Australia and New Zealand. This is no quibble, for the relevant 'moral' histories in these contexts are rather distinct from that of the USA. For example, Kreitner raises the relevance of intense hostility to life insurance in the USA, through the vision of it as gambling with god or with the actuaries. As Zelizer (1979, pp 68–94) has documented, this did much to slow the growth of life insurance in the United States, which remained illegal or unenforceable in some jurisdictions until the last quarter of the 19th century. If this is intended to indicate the identity of gambling and insurance, how is it reconciled with the fact that life insurance in Britain was officially and popularly approved of from the late 18th century onward? Once the distinction between gambling and insurance had been invented in the late 1700s, at least legislatively, governments bent over backwards to facilitate the formation of life insurance. This despite concerns with the similarity of fraternal insurance to working class industrial 'combinations' that were outlawed at the time. While there were significant political struggles over working class life insurance (to be discussed in the following chapter), these never brought into question the moral and governmental approval of life insurance even for those sectors of the populace where gambling was regarded as rife. Much the same is true for the operation of futures markets, for the furious American political condemnation of these as fostering 'gambling' was almost entirely missing in England.

Moreover, as Downes (1976, pp 29–32) and his colleagues have argued, debates leading up to most of the significant English legislation soft-pedalled and often ignored the question of the immorality of gambling. While the foundational legislation and cases separating insurance from gambling were settled in the last half of the 18th century, only by the 1820s did legislation (banning state lotteries) adopt an overtly moralistic tone in the sense implied by the 'bourgeois morality' thesis. Prior to this period, anti-gambling legislation was focused on issues of disorder, excessive gambling and cheating rather than the morality of gambling *per se*. Even so, the 1820s legislation was not a watershed in this respect. The Gambling Act of 1845 (8 & 9 Vict c 109), which finally excluded wagering contacts from enforcement by the courts, was little concerned with the immorality of gambling. Downes and his colleagues (1976, pp 31–32) argue strongly that no such conclusion could be deduced from the deliberations leading up to its enactment:

> The 1844 Committee expressly *denied* any intention of interfering with betting and sought only to suppress gaming houses, not gaming as such. They saw betting as on the decline from the excesses of the eighteenth century, and sought to rid the courts of the burden of settling gambling disputes, rather than seeking to suppress gambling by the removal of the legal context. Indeed, the main purpose of the 1845 Act seems to have been a clean sweep systematization of the law on gambling along classical *laissez faire* principles, rather than an onslaught on gambling *per se* ... The Committee went on to recommend that wagering should be freed of such penalties as had become attached to

it in the previous century … [which] brought English gaming law into line with that in Scotland and on the continent, and was justified by the Committee in terms of saving the courts' time from disputes which called for 'private settlement' rather than legal adjudication.

Having said this, their argument nevertheless continues that this Act was an exercise in 'boundary maintenance' cordoning off gambling from 'legitimate speculation'. But if any conclusion is to be drawn from Downes' analysis it is that gambling contracts were regarded as too insignificant for the courts to waste their time on. It is not that the burning issue is the moral whitewashing of 'legitimate' speculation and insurance in contrast to the *vice* of gambling. Likewise, as will be seen, in later years English and Commonwealth courts' attempts to distinguish gambling from other financial contracts do not seem to have been very concerned with gambling as morally reprehensible.

Yet this observation in its turn appears to confront a difficulty. If gambling contracts were regarded as trivial and beneath the gaze of the courts, why is it that the Commonwealth common law courts were – in ways almost identical to their American counterparts – so exercised about the boundaries between insurance, speculation and gambling? And in this context, why did the courts show only occasional signs that they feared opening the floodgates to trivial gambling contracts? If there was a single matter that was prominent in legislatures and courts it was neither the triviality nor the viciousness of gambling: rather it was about the impact of such contracts on 'commerce'. Analysis that focuses on this point makes rather better sense of many of the developments at issue than does that focusing on the morality question. Starting with the Acts of 1743 and 1774 that established the legal distinction between insurance and gambling, the underlying assumption has formed that gambling is bad for the economy, or is at best irrelevant to it. Conversely, legitimate contracts are those understood to be good for the economy. From this standpoint it is possible to recognise the (limited) truth in the morality theories. The law of financial contracts has occasionally been concerned with issues of the personal vice of gambling, but only as part of a broader concern with what is good for the economy. Where the former has been invoked, it is usually in subordinate relation to the latter. The effect of this, I want to suggest, is that the process has been rather the reverse of that promoted by Fabian, Kreitner and their colleagues. It is not that gambling was thrown to the dogs to make speculation and insurance respectable. It is much more the case that forms of speculation – ultimately including commercial forms of gambling – have been lifted clear of the disabilities inflicted in 'gambling contacts' to the extent that they have been defined as of 'advantage to commerce'. One way of looking at this is that the question law posed for itself is thus not intrinsically one of form, but more one of function.

This, of course, raises the question of how to distinguish exchanges that are good for the economy from those that are not – that is, how to identify the positive economic function of particular fiscal bargains. This has been the source of great trouble for the courts. More tentatively, I want to suggest that the difficulties they have experienced in distinguishing insurance, speculation and gambling register the effects of certain assumptions about commerce underlying the courts' evaluations of what is good for the economy. These are based not so much on the individualist idea that gambling renders workers idle and thriftless, although this is not irrelevant. Rather, they focus on a distinction between 'empty' or 'fictitious' exchanges, and those that involve 'substance' or 'value'. Gambling contracts are those financial contracts that relate to 'empty' or 'fictional' exchanges, while legitimate contracts involve 'real' value. This question makes the problem of verifying the status of gambling contracts a matter of public policy importance, and may thus explain why – in the face of so much difficulty in distinguishing gambling from legitimate financial contracts – courts for so long pursued the question as though the distinction was nevertheless real and important.

The legal solution to the problem of economic functionality, perhaps not surprisingly, has been in terms of tests that can be applied to the form taken by contracts. Indeed, more speculatively, I will argue that the tests imposed – such as 'insurable interest' or the 'intent to exchange title' – reflect an assumption that wealth is created through the exchange of titles or material values. One result, I suggest, is that as the theory and practice of financial capital changed and became more abstract, it collided specifically with this 'materialist' theory of commerce which the common law of contract has found difficult or impossible to abandon. This collision is registered in several features of the legal struggles over gambling, speculation and insurance that this chapter examines. For example, even in the USA, efforts to legitimise speculative trading in futures focused not on the issue of individual industriousness, but specifically on whether 'fictive exchange' (in which there was no exchange of title) was good for the economy. The collision is also registered in common law's tenacious hold on a requirement for an exchange of title – even in the face of long-held economic 'knowledge' that such limitation would be economically disastrous.

Finally, I will suggest that insofar as this confrontation has been resolved, it has not been by common law caving-in in the face of the truth that there is no 'real' difference between the invented categories of insurance, speculation and gambling. *All* legal categories are invented, including contract itself. In this sense, the 'individualist morality' theorists are slightly disingenuous, for it is not that the distinctions were created out of a previously unified position. Rather, the previously existing situation operated with a different invented distinction (perhaps reflecting class or status differences) between 'illegitimate' gaming contracts and 'legitimate' wagering and other contracts. The Gambling Act 1845 resolved this distinction by collapsing wagering into gaming contracts, and disbarring both as empty and trivial. By and large, the courts have stuck to this position. Changes in the legal status of gambling contracts have come about through two processes that highlight the place of concerns with 'the good of the economy' rather than with questions of individual morality. First, legislation and policy has redefined some forms of gambling as an industry and therefore as 'productive', leaving 'unproductive' forms of gambling still without access to the law. Such contracts have become enforceable. Secondly, legislation increasingly is placing troublesome forms of futures speculation and insurance out of reach of gambling laws. It is highly significant that this has been carried out not by reference to issues of individual morality, but by defining them as 'financial products' and 'financial services' – and thus as economically beneficial. This is, in its turn, a morality of sorts, but it is based on a new understanding of what is good for the economy.

Inventing insurance

By the 18th century, marine insurance had become the focus of considerable economic activity. But as Daston (1988, pp 134–38) indicates, this was as yet little affected by actuarial calculation and quite distinct from the industrial applications of statistical manipulation that have come to be associated with it. Nicholas Bernoulli had performed some theoretical estimations, but the data that would allow calculations to cover such issues as the proportion of ships that navigated a certain route safely did not exist. As late as 1839, marine underwriters were still concerned about the 'total lack of data' on which to base their calculations (Zelizer, 1979, p 31). There is no issue here, therefore, about insurance being demonstrably functional because of statistical guarantees for risk-spreading. Marine insurance was carried through on the uncertain practices of applying past knowledge and rules of thumb about the condition of a ship, the cargo carried, the skill of the captain, the ports to be visited and so on. Insurance practice conformed with the *uncertain* techniques of business judgment routinely practised by all speculators. In Daston's words:

> It is clear from the method that what was being insured was a business investment contingent on the merchant's survival ... Since such policies could be envisaged as a kind of bet on the merchant's survival, they were not easily distinguished from pure 'wager' policies on the short term survival of a third party, further confusing the categories of gambling and insurance already identified under the rubric of aleatory contracts in legal treatises like Bernoulli's. (1988, p 137)

To suggest that the categories of gambling, insurance and business were 'confused', of course makes the assumption that 20th century understandings of their mutual distinctiveness are the benchmark of clarity against which things can be seen as 'confused'. Instead, it appears that the distinctions between business speculation, gambling and insurance had not yet governmentally been invented. Thus the legality of wagers at common law was accepted in insurance law until the middle of the 18th century. As Merkin argues, '[up] to this period the courts were laying down general contractual principles and it seems never to have occurred that wagers were anything other than ordinary contracts ... [and moreover] important concepts have their origins in decisions on wagers' (Merkin, 1980, p 333). As suggested already, in terms of technology, too, such distinctions were not made. Thus insurance on the life of another, to which Daston refers, was soon to be defined as a form of gambling, and often appears to have revolved around everyday forms of calculation relating to those conditions likely to affect longevity and mortality. Like any other 'business transaction', it was a case of one party making a business assessment on the outcome of an event, and 'investing', or 'betting', their money in an 'insurance' contract.[1] Such was the case until the English parliament passed the Marine Insurance Act in 1743.

---

1   As Daston argues, the rise of mathematical probability 'did very little to sever the connections between gambling and other forms of aleatory contracts like annuities and insurance'. More to the point, she suggests, while '[j]urists and their clients had looked to experience and judgement; the mathematicians looked to tables and calculation. This was the theoretical legacy of mathematical probability to institutionalised risk taking in the eighteenth century; what was its contribution to practice? ... The short answer to the above question is, nil' (1988, p 138).

The Marine Insurance Act (19 Geo II, c 37), in the words of its preamble, concerned itself with the practice of taking out insurance policies 'interest or no interest without further proof of interest than the policy'. In other words, it was concerned that insurance policies were being issued, on a ship or its cargo, to parties who had no economic interest in the property insured. A second variant of this kind of speculation, also attended to by the Act, was the practice of taking out several insurance policies each to the value of the economic interest in the voyage. In both variants, the insured party sought to make a profit should any accident befall the vessel and/or cargo. It is clear the Act had two concerns. The first was the belief that these 'wagering' practices created a temptation to fraud, so that 'great numbers of ships with their cargoes' had been destroyed, presumably in order to collect on and profit by such policies. Its second concern was that insurance interest or no interest had 'introduced a mischievous kind of gaming' that 'perverted the institution and laudable design of making insurances' (19 Geo II, c 37). In other words, if the separation of insurance from gaming had not yet occurred, there was certainly recognition of economically functional differences on which such a separation should be based. In relation to this, the preamble to the Act stated that 'both [variants] were a species of gaming without any advantage to commerce'. In this, the legislation reflected earlier laws that had already rendered unenforceable 'all notes, bills, bonds, judgments, mortgages or other securities or conveyances whatsoever' that were transferred in relation to gaming debts (1710, 5 & 6 Wm IV, c 41). These, in their turn, were regarded as matters too inconsequential for the courts to enforce, for the critical issue was the nature of 'games' and 'pastimes' that were of no 'consequence' (*Jeffreys v Walter* (1748) 1 Wils KB 220). While it is nowhere stated that this inconsequentiality was specifically economic in character, in the context of insurance, this was to be the content with which it was invested.

The key question, then, was how to differentiate 'gaming' policies (which were now to have their historical ties with betting on games loosened) from 'laudable' insurances that performed a valued economic function. The solution was to create the category of 'insurable interest'. All marine insurance policies would become legal and enforceable only where the insured party could demonstrate an independent financial interest in the ship and/or cargo insured equivalent to (and not exceeding) the value of the policy. What appeared to be a clear line of demarcation was now established between marine insurance and inconsequential and disorderly financial gaming. The view was, as Robert Jerry (1996, p 235) still expresses it, 'that insurance, an economically valuable transaction, should not be used as a subterfuge for gambling. A gambling transaction merely transfers wealth; to the extent that anything is produced by a gambling transaction, it is merely the possibility of fortuitous gains'. The critical difference then is that for insurance, elements assumed to be of financial value are exchanged, whereas in gaming only a fiction of such exchange occurs. It is thus in the act of exchanging 'real' value rather than 'fictional' value that the advantage to commerce – in this case, spreading financial risk – exists. This theory of value, I suggest, remains prominent throughout subsequent legal attempts to differentiate gambling, insurance and speculation, even to the present day.

Thirty years after the passage of the Marine Insurance Act, parallel legislation was passed dealing with life insurance. The principal target of the Life Assurance Act 1774 (14 Geo III c 48) was an array of insurance forms that focused on the life of another or others. At the time, insurance policies could be taken out on the life of any person, including politicians, the elderly, the famous or notorious. Premiums and benefits were usually set on the basis of common sense calculations about the insured party's age, health, occupation and so on. In addition tontines were targeted. In this practice a number of persons formed their own risk pool, calculated individuals' premiums using the usual rule of thumb techniques, and allocated a lump sum benefit arising to the last surviving member. All these factors would be subject to actuarial calculation over the next century. But in the late 18th century the technology was basically identical to that which applied to marine insurance: pragmatic, experience-based estimations of uncertainty. There was thus again no possibility of making a case that insurance was a form of statistically guaranteed 'investment', as later insurance ideologues (see Zelizer, 1979) and theorists (for example Ewald, 1991) would come to understand and even define it. Rather, a prominent issue concerned a temptation to crime and disorder, most specifically with respect to bringing about the death of insured parties or surviving members of the tontine.[2] At the same time, such contracts performed no risk-spreading function and were thus recognised as a form of gaming. Indeed, the second of these issues loomed the larger at the time (Brenner and Brenner, 1990). To counter both problems, the statute nullified any contract issued with respect to 'the life or lives of any person or any other event or events whatsoever, wherein the person or persons for whose use, benefit, or on whose account such policy or policies shall be made, shall have no interest, or by way of gaming or wagering'.[3]

Following in the steps of the Marine Insurance Act, the key criterion defining *all* insurance (by virtue of the provision relating to 'any other event or events whatsoever') thus came to be possession by the policy holder of an insurable

---

2 It is of course the case that the second aspect of gaming – its association with the temptation to crime in order to profit from insurance – persists. Within the insurance domain, this falls under the category of moral hazards. The common law courts, too, have been considerably exercised over this issue with respect to insuring the life of another. But the issue here no longer is strictly relevant to the question of distinguishing gambling from insurance, and is no longer even necessarily related to the question of insurable interest. Parents, for example, usually cannot insure the lives of their children even where they may suffer an economic loss in the event of the child's death.

3 The Life Insurance Act 1774 (14 Geo III c 48) renders illegal all insurances on any event in which a person or persons assured have no interest. The key provisions of the Act are:

   1 No insurance shall be made ... wherein the person or persons for whose use, benefit or on whose account the policy or policies shall be made, shall have no interest, or by way of gaming or wagering. And every assurance made contrary to the true intent and meaning thereof, shall be null and void ...

   2 It shall not be lawful to make any policy or policies on the life or lives of any person or persons or other event or events without inserting in such policy or policies the person or persons' name or names interested therein, for whose use or benefit or on whose account such policy is made or under-wrote.

   3 In all cases where the insured hath interest in such life or lives, event or events, no greater sum shall be recovered or received from the insurer or insurers than the amount or value of the interest of the insured in such life or lives, or other events or events.

interest of no lesser value than the benefits specified in the contract. The absence of this interest transformed the 'insurance' contract into (a legally unenforceable) 'gambling' contract. Thus, as it was later to be observed, '[a] contract which would otherwise be a mere wager may become an insurance by reason of the insured having an interest in the subject matter – that is to say, the uncertain event ... must be an event which is *prima facie* adverse to the interest of the assured' (*Prudential Insurance Co v Commissioner of Inland Revenue* [1904] 2 KB 663, *per* Channell J).[4] In short, the payment of premiums spreads the risk of loss to the insured party for some specified value. Thus, in the 18th century invention of the distinction between insurance and gambling, the key problem had little or nothing to do with gambling itself as a *vice* of individual character. Nor was the concern with whitewashing bourgeois speculation at the expense of gambling. Rather, it focused on the net harmful effects to commerce believed to be the product of those forms of insurance that were founded on 'economically fictive' exchanges of value rather than on exchange of a value deemed to be economically 'real' as indexed by the presence of insurable interest.[5] The invention of insurance in common law was an act of considerable and constructive inventiveness, not simply a matter of throwing gambling to the dogs.

Distinguishing speculation and gambling

Perhaps it is no coincidence that the passage of the Marine Insurance Act occurred within a few years of that of Sir John Barnard's Act of 1734 (10 Geo II c 8). This earlier legislation had prohibited the buying and selling of stocks not in the seller's possession at the time of the contract. The 'evil practice of compounding or making up differences' was stated in the Act's preamble as operating 'to the great discouragement of industry, and to the manifest detriment of trade and commerce'. Although Sir John Barnard's Act does not focus on gambling, its target was soon to be referred to in common law along such lines, for 'making up differences' – or 'difference contracts' – soon came to be defined as 'gaming and wagering'. A difference contract is, in short, where no exchange of titles or goods is intended, but rather that on the day of settlement an amount of money will change hands depending on whether the market price of a specified commodity has fallen or risen (that is, modern financial derivatives). The language and the underlying theory of the Act foreshadow those embodied in the insurance legislation of 1743 and 1774, and reflect an 18th century perception of exchange as involving property or title

---

4 This could certainly be made to fit the thesis, as part of the aim of consideration is to distinguish 'genuine' economic transactions from mere gifts – which would occupy a similar space to gambling in this respect. But the interpretation would be anachronistic, for it is not until the 1840s that consideration takes the form of a requirement for value. Prior to this time, consideration was not a question of a requirement for the exchange of value but of providing evidence that a promise existed (Greig, 1987, p 18).

5 In this respect it is noteworthy that, rather than relying on the justifications provided by the foundational 18th century Acts and cases, Kreitner links the twin issues of inducement to crime and wagering policies to the moralities of 'industrious exertion' by invoking Ashton's 1898 history of gambling. Governmentally this is problematic simply because Ashton's late 19th century American concerns were not those of the 18th century legislators, nor were they governmental: they were a popular gloss rather than a legal justification or foundation.

rather than more abstract forms of value that were later to become economically central. At the time of their enactment, all three items of legislation appear to have envisaged a relatively straightforward understanding of financial value as involving existing title or property. But within a very few years they clashed with the increasingly future-oriented theory and practice of the economy.

The insurable interest requirement was the first to come under scrutiny, and by the early 19th century the question of expectation interests was already emerging in an elementary way. In *Lucena v Caufurd* (1805) 127 ER 630 the question was raised as to whether an expectation provided an insurable interest and the court had some difficulty in agreeing. Lord Eldon's view accorded with the spirit of the previous century, arguing that insurable interest required 'a right in the property' insured, and that 'expectation, though founded upon the highest probability was not interest ... whatever might have been the chances in favour of the expectation' (127 ER, pp 650–51). On the other hand, his fellow judge took the line that was to become characteristic of the 19th century and beyond. Lawrence J determined that an economic expectation that would be realised 'in the ordinary and probable course of things' constituted such an interest. He reasoned that a person with such an expectation would have an interest in the success of the venture, not on the outcome of a wager or the destruction of property: 'That a man somehow or other be interested in the preservation of the subject-matter exposed to perils, follows from the nature of this contract when not used as a mode of wager, but as applicable to the purpose: but to confine it to the protection of the interest which arises out of property, is adding a restriction to the contract which does not arise out of its nature' (127 ER 643).[6] The dynamic market to which Lawrence J was oriented created some problems concerning what degree of probability would be adequate to satisfy the law – a matter that was to become general in contract law. But concerning the issues raised with respect to speculation, the problem was to become more complex.

The rise of executory contracts already meant that contracts could be legally binding even through mere statements of intention to exchange rather than through the instantaneous exchanges of title more characteristic of the previous century. The development of futures markets during the middle of the 19th century rendered the difficulty doubly acute, for now title was passed to commodities that did not yet exist and might not exist for months or even years. This created major problems, for 'genuine investors' could legitimately speculate through agreements to exchange titles at some time in the future, whereas the titles themselves related to commodities that would not exist until some future time. Capital was in this sense becoming more abstract than was envisaged in the 18th century. But as the century progressed, it became possible to raise a new and even more revolutionary problem. If the enforceable aim of contracts is the creation of profit, and if remedy can be given in the form of expectation damages that take account only of profits – and

---

6 In addition, as Jerry (1996, p 249) has argued, '[i]t is the insured's factual expectations – not the presence of a technical legal interest – that provides the deterrent to wagering and to the destruction of property and lives'.

often hypothetical profits at that – then why should the exchange of rights or titles to property be required to occur at all? The problem for law soon started to become clear.

In an action involving the transfer of shares (*Grizewood v Blane* (1851) 11 CB 526), the court determined that if the jury believed that neither party *intended* to purchase or sell the shares the contract constituted a gambling contract and was thus void. A few years later in *Ashton v Dakin* [1859] 7 WLR 385 Pollock argued that:

> ... if no actual purchase had been made, but the object merely was to speculate, without buying or selling, upon the price on a future day that would be by way of gaming and wagering. But I see no objection to a man, confiding in his own judgment, saying to a broker 'Will you buy corn (or anything else) for me and let the bargain be so as to the day of payment that you may have an opportunity of re-selling it for me by such a day, when I expect the market will have risen, and then you will pay the seller for me with the money you receive from the purchaser, and I shall receive the gain from you, if any, or pay you the loss ... That is not gaming.[7]

That is, there must exist an intent to exchange titles. Where such an intention exists, then even if the parties did not intend to take possession of (that is, materially exchange) the *things* and even if the only reason for exchanging titles was to profit from the difference in prices, the contract is valid and not gambling. Where the parties did not intend to exchange titles but only to pay price differences at some future date (a 'difference contract' of the sort condemned in Sir John Barnard's Act) the contract became a wager. Consequently, if in the contemplation of only *one* of the parties the exchange represents a *bona fide* sale, then the fact that the other party never intended to complete the exchange will not vitiate the contract. The reason for this being that as long as one party is so intended, then an exchange could be enforced.[8] Speculation was now *defined* by the absence of *intent* to gamble, and gambling again appears as an 'empty' transaction because there is no exchange of value.[9] Thus it became possible for the court to assert that '[it] must be made clear that speculation does not necessarily involve a contract by way of a wager, and to constitute such a contract *a common intention to wager is essential*. A contract may be speculative and yet a perfectly good contract. It would be disastrous to hold otherwise' (*See v Cohen* (1923) 33 CLR 182, *per* Isaacs J; emphasis added). In short, common law had adapted to the abstraction of capital by retaining a material sense

---

7   In a masterpiece of understatement, Windeyer (1929, p 20) concludes that it 'is often not easy to say whether a particular agreement is a wager or not'.

8   This was confirmed in *Carlill v Carbolic Smoke Ball Co* [1892] 2 QB 491):

> If the evidence is such as to make the intentions of the parties material in the consideration of the question whether a contract is a wagering one or not, and those intentions are at variance, those of one party being such as, if agreed in by the other would make the contract a wagering one whilst those of the other would prevent it from becoming so, this want of mutuality would destroy the wagering element of the contract and leave it enforceable by law as in an ordinary one. (*Per* Hawkins J)

9   This concern with the intent to gamble, while still valid law, created its own new breed of difficulties. To begin with, how was this intent to be known? Perhaps uncharacteristically in contract law, it was determined as early as 1860 that the court should go behind the contract itself and consider all of the evidence relating to the exchange in deciding whether or not the parties intended delivery (*Ex parte Phillips and Marnham, Re Morgan* (1860) 2 De GF & J 634).

of value but abstracting the moment of exchange – this had to occur, as Marxists might say, 'in the last instance'.[10]

For those who argue for the 'real' identity of gambling, insurance and speculation, the fine distinction here being relied upon may be (and is) taken as evidence that the distinction between speculation and gambling, at least, is an unworkable fabrication performing an ideological function. All the more so because, as will be seen shortly, the courts could rarely carry this distinction through in practice. Even commissions of enquiry in the late 19th century suggested that courts were not the site in which such a distinction could be made, and (ironically) stock exchanges positively rejected its significance. However, I argue that – far from illustrating the real identity of all risky financial contracts – these are indications that the 'commercial' theory and practice of common law and that of the institutions of financial capitalism were drifting apart.

The whole question of futures trading and the closeness of its relationship with gambling became a major issue in the final quarter of the 19th century, in large measure because of the rapid growth in this kind of activity. In Britain, a Commission of Inquiry (LSEC, 1878) set up to examine the operation of stock exchanges concluded that gambling did go on under the cover of futures trading, and pointed out that it was normally impossible to identify whether or not

---

10 Based on this view it was later reasoned that even if the security given by A to B in a gaming contract was then passed to a third party C, it still had no value and could not be enforced at law. However, if in that exchange, consideration (eg, money) was given by C to B for the security, the third party did have a right of recovery from B: the 'worthless' gambling property of B has achieved economic or commercial value by the fact of C's investment in it regardless of whether C knew or did not know that the security was based on a gaming debt. (*Fitch v Jones* (1855) 5 E & B 238). It is not that the security was eternally worthless or unenforceable because of its association with gambling. Once consideration (value) is given any disability is removed: it has become a matter imagined as one of material commerce. *Fitch v Jones* may be interpreted differently. Instead of a theory of material value, it could be that this is simply the concept of consideration being applied. In other words, for a contract to be a contract, there must be an element of consideration in the form of value promised or delivered, otherwise the exchange is merely a one-sided, gratuitous understanding. For most interpretations, this differentiates contracts from gifts, but it could be seen here to differentiate contracts from gambling. Yet the point at issue is that this understanding of consideration may not be distinct from the same theory to which is owed the legal definition of insurance. In the 18th century, consideration referred to evidence of *causa* or motive for entering a contract. Thus Simpson (1975, p 321) has argued that at this time 'the essence of the doctrine of consideration, then, is the adoption by the common law of the idea that the legal effect of a promise should depend upon the factor or factors which motivated the promise. To decide whether a promise ... is binding, you need to know why the promise was made'. In this sense, however, the promise constituted the consideration. Even by the 1760s, Lord Mansfield (*Pillans v Van Mierop* (1765) 97 ER 1038) was still able to argue that 'consideration was for the sake of evidence only'. But the law during this period was undergoing a shift from the 18th century model of *causa* and reliance to exchange and expectation (Greig, 1987, p 18). Thus by 1842, it was possible for the court to argue that '[m]otive is not the same thing with consideration. Consideration, means something which is of some value in the eye of the law, moving from the plaintiff: it may be some benefit to the plaintiff, or some detriment to the defendant' (*Thomas v Thomas* (1842) 114 ER 333, *per* Patteson J). By 1875 this was elaborated so that 'valuable consideration, in the sense of the law may consist either in some right, interest, profit, or benefit accruing to one party, or some forbearance, detriment, loss or responsibility, given, suffered, or undertaken by the other' (*Currie v Misa* (1875) LR 10 Exchequer Division 162, *per* Coleridge CJ). In Grieg's view, this focused on 'the giving of value, or exchange or bargain. This notion was the epitome of the legal doctrine of the time' (1987, p 21).

particular contracts were gambles rather than legitimate 'investments'. While finding this regrettable – although it did not indicate why – it pragmatically concluded that legislation and the courts were not the most effective avenues for dealing with the problem since they would only be concerned with individual contracts, and investigation would, therefore, often prove inconclusive. Rather, since members of the stock exchanges would recognise gamblers from the fact that they *repeatedly* failed to exchange titles, it was best to leave it to these organisations and their experts to regulate the problem. It does not appear to have struck the Commissioners that, if they found it impossible to tell the difference between a gamble and an investment, the difference might not be 'real' or of consequence in any economic sense. Nor does it seem to have appeared to them that there was no difference between gambling and futures speculation. Rather, they perceived that regulation rather than common law was the appropriate mode of governance. Except in egregious cases, their observation was that regulatory bodies capable of continuous monitoring, and provided with expertise appropriate to the industry, provided a more effective mode of governance than did the courts.

Nevertheless, there was a considerable irony – perhaps even disingenuousness – in this decision, for the leaders of stock exchanges in both Britain and the USA believed that difference contracts were economically vital. But they also recognised that difference contracts were not enforceable at law and relied on 'gentlemen's understandings' to make these contracts work. Indeed, to attempt to enforce a futures contract in court was to invite exclusion. It seems clear the Commissioners must have known this, for in addressing the Parliamentary Committee that led to the establishment of the Commission a representative of the Stock Exchange noted, '[t]here is not a gentleman in the Stock Exchange who could stand on the boards one day which refused to carry out the contract he has made ... he would be obliged to walk out; he would be expelled; simply because it would be dishonourable' (quoted by Ferguson, 1984, p 196). The same was true in the United States. In principle a purchaser of a futures contract could demand delivery of the material product. Yet as Cowing (1965, p 14) points out, '[i]n practice, however, the distinction was meaningless, because futures contracts were settled just as simple options were – by the payment of differences. In only three per cent of the futures trades was there actual delivery; in fact to demand delivery was to brand oneself a miscreant and led to ostracism by the brokers'.

In Britain, at least, governance of the problem largely had been passed over to the economic 'sector' and its expertise. Even the courts softened their position somewhat. In the same year, Lord Bramwell argued pragmatically that it 'may be a sad thing that there should be gambling upon the Stock Exchange, but that is not the point which we have to consider; and I am not sure that it is a disadvantage that there should be a market where speculation may go on, for it is owing to a market of that kind that we now have so many railways and other useful undertakings' (*Thacker v Hardy* (1878) 4 QBD 692). Perhaps for this reason, in England the issue remained relatively dormant, although still problematic from time to time.[11] No such peaceable conclusion was reached in the United States, where moral concerns over

---

11 For a review of some 20th century cases, see, eg, Ciro, 1999; 2002a; 2002b.

gambling wound up to a considerable pitch in the late 19th century. For this reason, it is worthwhile taking a slight detour back to the United States. This is home soil for the 'individual morality' thesis, for the critiques of speculation as 'gambling' were very influential, and it is not my aim to reject the salience or the moralistic tenor of these struggles. However, with both the accusations and the defences, the charge of gambling overwhelmingly focused on its impact on the economy and on economic players (such as farmers). In the debates and analyses surrounding the 'Hatch Bill' (US Congress, 1892a; 1892b) and several reports to governments over the subsequent 20 years, accusations typically took the following form:

> Those who deal in 'options' and 'futures' contracts, which is mere gambling, no matter what less offensive name such transactions be designated, neither add to the supply nor increase the demand for consumption, nor do they accomplish any useful purpose by their calling, but on the contrary they speculate in fictitious products. (Representative before the Hatch Committee, quoted by Brenner and Brenner, 1990, p 108)

Certainly futures speculators were frequently depicted as morally corrupt and physically degenerate gamblers, especially in the populist press. But the central issue they were accused of was selling commodities they did not own – thus creating surplus supply – thereby driving prices down so they could then buy low.[12] It was argued that this made prices unstable, interfered with the normal processes of supply and demand, and most significantly, along with all forms of futures trading, exploited the commodity producers, particularly farmers (Cowing, 1965). In short, futures contracts were bad for the economy. And it was in terms of this assault that they were defended.

While some of their opponents sought to ban futures trading outright, the most influential arguments were those that sought to impose a tax which would ensure that such trading would be carried out only by those who owned and possessed the commodity at the time of the transaction, thus resolving the practical ambiguities opened up by the issue of intent to deliver – and in the process effectively reverted to the 18th century ideal of property exchange.[13] In their own lights at least, they sought on both moral and economic grounds to resolve the problem of 'gambling on the stock exchange' by undoing the 'fiction' of intent into which it had been transformed.[14] In practice, the dice were heavily loaded against these critics. As in England, the emphasis in courts was on the intent to deliver, and the onus of proof of intent to wager was invariably placed on the challenger. In this sense, at least, the courts thought the distinction real and important; but it meant that few attempts at litigation were made against speculators. As Lurie (1979, p 61) points out, 'it was very easy for a commission merchant and broker to "intend" delivery, make a contract, change their minds, and settle between themselves'. The question arises then of whether this reveals a 'fictional' distinction between gambling and

---

12 Such concerns with short selling echoed Sir John Barnard's Act – which had been repealed in Britain in 1860 on the grounds that it 'imposed unnecessary restrictions on the making of contracts for sale and transfer of public stocks and securities' (Van Antwerp, 1913, p 227).

13 This was the aim of the 'Hatch Bill', for example. While this passed narrowly in the lower house, delays in the Senate meant that it was not enacted and subsequent political developments prevented its reappearance in legislation.

14 Sir John Barnard's Act was rescinded in 1860, on the grounds that it created unnecessary impediments to commerce!

speculation, or whether it reveals that neither law nor economy have a mortgage on truth. Rather, the theory and practice of key institutions of the economy and of law had diverged, yet increasingly the courts found themselves unable (or perhaps unwilling) to govern the issue with the blunt tools available to them. The future of such governance – as had happened *de facto* in England well before this – lay with regulatory agencies.

Before passing from this issue, it is critical to recognise that those seeking to defend futures trading – largely brokers and other representatives of the stock exchanges – sought to establish their own, distinct theory of the economy. In the legislative enquiries and depositions it was strongly argued that any attempt to proscribe and hinder futures trading would undo the major benefits it bestowed upon the economy. Even more significantly, it was urged that such benefits were created *even where there was no intent to exchange title, to deliver or accept delivery of real commodities*. In a strong sense, they sought to play the abstract principle underlying the distinction between gambling contracts and business contracts – the 'advantage to commerce' test – *against* the materialist version of it on which the distinction between gambling and insurance, and gambling speculation, had been based. Put another way, they recognised that the issue at hand was not the immorality of gambling as such, but a question to be answered in terms of a theory of economy. Consequently, their arguments focused on the positive functions of futures trading, and in this they coalesced on three matters.

Income and cost spreading. For primary producers, a continuing problem has been that crops and animals do not spread their maturation evenly through the year. Harvests, shearing and culling come usually once or a few times per year, whereas costs associated with production spread themselves more evenly throughout. Primary producers thus bear considerable carrying costs – the transaction costs created by the length of the production process. Futures trading was argued to spread these costs more efficiently. As the commodity was sold in advance, the farmer was able to realise and use capital otherwise tied up in the production process. This meant that it was possible for producers to spread their expenditures throughout the year without incurring interest charges, and thus create a more efficient distribution of market exchanges (for equipment, seeding, harvesting, etc) over time rather than in concentrated peaks. Suppliers also were said to experience these 'smoothing' benefits, as were others down the line. The costs of effecting such increased efficiencies were regarded as being borne by the speculator. In this way, claims were made that speculators were moral agents who provided *gratis* benefits to the economy (for example, US Congress, 1892a, pp 40–41, 156–81; 1892b, pp 75–85).

Risk-spreading. Primary producers experience poor harvests and gluts, unanticipated competition from other markets, unanticipated costs caused by the weather, and so on. Futures markets were argued to allow producers to spread these risks, passing them on in some degree to the speculators as they saw fit. Commodity producers could thus take the same speculative chances as any other participant in the market, choosing to take the certain prices on offer against the possibility of lower prices later, but running the risk that prices would rise. Producers were thus regarded as using futures markets as a form of risk management, for they could spread risk by prior selling of part of their product according to their estimates of market opportunities in the uncertain future. Once again, the speculators appeared as providing a service to the economy by providing producers with the means of risk-spreading, and thus effectively offering the benefits of a highly flexible crop insurance scheme (for example, US Congress, 1892a, pp 71–79; 1892b, pp 78–85). As Cowing (1965, pp 12–13) has argued, such practices were akin to 'hedging' bets or investments, but '[b]y using the respectable word "insurance" instead of "hedging" brokers felt they strengthened their case; in fact this whole line of argument made it possible to view the speculator not only as the incidental benefactor of the farmer ... but also as an indispensable cog in a system of agricultural insurance'. While sophisticated statistical techniques eventually were to govern futures exchanges in terms of risk, this form of 'insurance' was governed by speculators backing their own 'uncertain' judgments about the markets' future trend.

Stabilisation. In both of these 'spreading' techniques, futures trading was claimed to stabilise markets. To begin with, the spreading of purchases over time evened out the price fluctuations driven by short-term considerations such as poor harvests or increased costs. In addition, because futures markets are national, local variations are likewise reduced. Price fluctuations over both time and space would thus tend to be ironed out. Indeed, it was argued that the more exchanges that occurred, the greater this stabilising spreading effect would tend to be: for the overall fluctuation of prices would be divided up into more and more transactions thus reducing the risk to any party (for example, US Congress, 1892a, pp 156–68).

In short – as Cowing (1965, p 13) paraphrases it – their claim was that 'if trading were confined to actual products, prosperity would disappear'. These arguments generated largely by brokers and their representatives were subsequently translated into economic theory, notably in Emery's *Speculation on the Stock and Produce Exchanges* (1896), to become an orthodox position of liberal economists; but Cowing's expression serves to indicate something of considerable importance. The world of futures contracts represents an area of commerce in which capital has become almost completely abstracted or virtual, as 'monetized time-space' (Pryke and Allen, 2000). However, contract law – through which financial speculation is legally governed – remained, and largely remains, tethered to its foundation in the law of real property. Without exchange of title there could be no enforceable financial transaction – a virtual exchange does not represent an advantage to commerce but a gamble. In this respect the theories of law and capital have rather parted company.

Convergence, regulation and 'commercial gambling'

Gaming and wagering legislation should never have been allowed to apply to genuine financial transactions. The legislation was intended only to prohibit gaming in recreational activities. It was never the intention of the legislature to prohibit trading in financial instruments and to impugn the validity of genuine financial contracts through the gaming and wagering laws. Notwithstanding this, the reality is that gaming legislation has been allowed to apply and affect the validity of a number of financial transactions. This in turn has lead to a great deal of uncertainty, especially in the OTC [Options Trading Commission]. (Ciro, 1999, p 186)

Tony Ciro's cry of outrage and frustration of course oversimplifies matters and may be wrong in terms of the relevant legal history. It also begs the all-important question of how to distinguish 'genuine' financial contracts from those of a gaming and wagering sort. But it indicates very clearly that while the move over much of the last century has been to transfer governance of financial speculation to regulatory bodies, this has not meant that the common law of contract has resolved the issue of legitimate speculation versus gaming and wagering contracts. Quite to the contrary, as Ciro maps out, contemporary courts have continued to struggle with the distinction, notably because so many cases brought before them have involved debtors attempting to have their losing contracts nullified on the grounds that they are difference contracts and thus 'mere' wagers. Nevertheless, the 'mutual intent to wager' test (that is, requiring intent to enforce delivery) continued its disruptive influence, and it was legislative fiat that resolved this problem. For example, the passage of the Financial Services Act 1986 (FSA) in England removed futures contracts and difference contracts, as well as investments in shares and options, from the ambit of the constraints suffered by wagering and gaming contracts. More specifically, it rendered any contract made or traded in a recognised investment exchange an *investment*. The effect of the Act has been to change the meaning of what is a gamble and what is a 'genuine commercial transaction'. Interpreting the FSA, in *Richardson Greenfields* [1989] 1 HKLR 482, the court ruled:

> Although dealing in commodities may involve the delivery of the commodity because it is of a type where property may pass, eg soy beans, the Hang Seng Index commodity authorised by the legislature specifically envisages that no property passes. The legal obligation is to make a money payment. Even if these transactions can be called 'differences', which I doubt, they are *bona fide* commercial transactions and as such are not gambling.[15]

What renders this a '*bona fide* commercial transaction' is not any form of words, or statement of intent in the contract itself, but that the dealing occurs in a forum designated as a recognised place of business. As the same court determined, this is not a wager in the sense of a game, '[i]t is a commercial activity. The striking of a bargain for the purchase and sale of the index on the floor of the Exchange is clearly not a game'; and again 'uninformed persons might describe the activity of the exchange as a "casino" because there is a risk of losing as well as an opportunity of winning, but that does not mean what is actually occurring at the Exchange is gambling' ([1989] 1 HKLR 482).

Certainly this could be read as demonstrating that, after all, the law has finally conceded that there is no difference between speculative contracts and gambling, since the only way of telling them apart is where they occur. In which case, the stigma of gambling is all that stands between the collapse of the distinction altogether. I think this wrong for two reasons. The first is that unless we accept an essentialist view of gambling or of financial contracts 'as a whole', all that has happened is that there has been a change in the sign by which (according to legal theory) contracts of 'advantage to commerce' are to be identified. The function is paramount, the form merely the visible way in which the courts can identify the presence of the function. The second is that we would still need to explain why more recent legislation has not overturned the legislation nullifying gambling

---

15 Quoted by Ciro (1999, p 180). Several issues discussed immediately below draw on Ciro's analysis.

contracts, that is, why the legislature has not assigned *all* gambling contracts to the status of enforceable contracts. Why should not all gambling contracts merely become another 'financial product' as recent Australian legislation terms all manner of financially speculative and insurance forms?[16] The answer is, I think, instructive. That is, certain gambling contracts have been selectively salvaged from their ignominious status. This has occurred in several ways.

In Britain, the FSA legalised financial spread betting by which, since at least 1996, it is possible to bet on price fluctuations on the share market. These activities, regulated by the Financial Services Board and dealt with through licensed betting agencies, provide a form of difference contract. Under the FSA, as long as the contract occurs in a recognised place of business, the difference between a bet and an investment has, for all practical purposes, disappeared. Yet this is only one aspect of a far broader shift in which certain 'ordinary' gambling contracts have become enforceable over the last few decades. In Australia, for example, legislation has exempted a range of gambling contracts from nullification, specifically bets made with registered bookmakers, holders of a licence under the Gaming and Betting Act 1994, and bets made with a casino or gaming operators licensed under various control acts (Lotteries Gaming and Betting Act 1966 (Vic), as amended). This reflects the fact that, as Dixon (1991) has documented, a sector of gambling activity has been redefined as an industry and in that sense as 'productive'. Thus the Australian Productivity Commission has stressed that '[g]ambling is a big and rapidly growing business in Australia, with the industry currently accounting for an estimated 1.5 per cent of GDP, and employing over 100,000 people in more than 7000 businesses throughout the country' (Productivity Commission, 1999, p 2). Gambling, in a nutshell, is now defined as providing an 'advantage to commerce'.

In every sense, Kreitner is correct to argue that increasingly the differences between gambling, insurance and speculation are being collapsed, and that the area of financial risk is being regulated by a wide array of regulatory bodies.[17] This is a

---

16 Thus by the passage of the Futures Markets Act 1979 (NSW), the New South Wales Government gave immunity from gaming and wagering legislation to currencies futures contracts, and in 1982 amended this to include futures contracts generally. The Financial Services Reform Act 2001 (s 763A(1)) defines a financial product as 'a facility through which, or through the acquisition of which, a person does one or more of the following: (a) makes a financial investment ...; (b) manages financial risk ...; (c) makes non-cash payments'. In turn, a person manages a financial risk when they 'manage the financial consequences to them of particular circumstances happening; or avoid or limit the financial consequences of fluctuations in, or in the value of, receipts or costs. Examples of managing financial risks include 'taking out insurance' or 'hedging a liability' (s 763c). The distinction between insurance, futures and some forms of gambling is thereby collapsed for the purposes of the Act.

17 With respect to futures, the first significant legislation in this respect was the Grain Futures Act 1922, which restricted trading to supervised exchanges, thus effectively reproducing the strategy recommended by the English commission in 1878. This was extended and revised in the Securities Exchange Act 1934 that subjected securities markets to regulation by the Commodities Exchange Commission, and the Commodity Exchange Act 1936 that required the registration of futures brokers. The latter was related to providing protection to small investors – a matter discussed in Chapter 2. Amendments in 1974 set up a regulatory body – the Commodity Futures Trading Commission (CFTC) '... to have exclusive jurisdiction over commodities futures and options trading' (Ciro, 2002b, p 19). Perhaps the most important from the point of view of the present discussion is the Futures Trading Practices Act 1992 which exempted sophisticated participants ('appropriate persons') from regulation by the CFTC.

process that, effectively, began in the 1870s in Britain. It is not so much that this simply reflects a diminishing moral prejudice against gambling. Rather, this diminution reflects a linked, but much broader, change that has been occurring for many years – that is, gambling is being progressively defined and regulated as commercially valuable. As an effect of this, gambling probably has lost most of its moral taint – but it does not appear that this moral taint is what has been relevant to legally distinguishing it from 'legitimate' speculation and insurance. Thus only those aspects of gambling that are 'commercial' are being legitimated. As Ciro's complaint makes clear, outside this new perimeter set up by legislation, the courts still police the boundaries of gambling and legitimate speculation – it's just that commercial forms of gambling have been escorted into the protected domain of contract law.

One of the broader conclusions to emerge from this analysis is that it may be quite misleading to imagine that during the 18th century gambling became the scapegoat that was sacrificed in order to make previously undifferentiated or 'identical' forms of bourgeois speculation acceptable. It would be far nearer the truth, as Atiyah (1979, pp 176–77) hinted quite a few years ago, to say that the reverse is true. On the basis of their identified advantage to commerce, speculative contracts have gradually, selectively and with some difficulty, been lifted clear of the handicap that traditionally applied to gaming laws. The exception to this rule – the 1845 excision of wagers from the charmed circle of common law enforcement – is in one sense no exception at all. Rather it was that by the middle of the 19th century the principle of commercial benefit and its implied criterion of 'real' value-based exchange had emerged as the norm – and was at about this time built into consideration to become a principle of contract more generally.[18] As Downes argues, by this time it made perfect sense to regard wagers as trivial, for they were without commercial substance: it was not that they were evil or were to be moral scapegoats; they were simply not worth the courts' time.

The enterprise society and responsible gambling

There is, nevertheless, an important difference between commercial gambling and other forms of financial speculation. In the words of Australia's Productivity Commission (1999, p 6):

> Gambling has been formally defined as 'staking money on uncertain events driven by chance'… this can encompass many activities, including the more speculative areas of commodity and financial markets. Nevertheless, gambling retains the distinguishing feature that as a group, gamblers inevitably lose money over time – it is more like a consumption expenditure that investment.

Of course, in many respects this was one of the arguments traditionally raised against gambling. So the question remains: how could the rise of a gambling industry be justified as commercially advantageous when its net commercial cost to society may be seen to exceed its net commercial benefit – something even the

---

18 The process was, as Atiyah has argued (1979, pp 463, 776–77), rather more rapid and consistent in American than it was in English law.

Productivity Commission recognises? A key part of the answer is that the debit side of the equation is largely cancelled out, for gambling has been redefined: no longer is it a vice; it is now a leisure activity. Thus for the Productivity Commission (1999, p 1) the 'main source of national benefit from the liberalisation of gambling has been the consumer gains from access to a service that gives people enjoyment'. The net losses of gamblers appear as the collective cost paid for 'normal' commercial service, akin to a theatre ticket. In this respect, such 'leisure' gambling – as opposed, say, to financial spread betting – ceases to be a form of financial speculation.

In the leisure industry, as Collins argues (1996), there is a form of consumer protection at work, for gambling can be viewed as a market in which there are bound to be casualties, some of whom are regarded as vulnerable and in need of care or protection. Whereas once upon a time such casualties were seen to be the victims of vice who might have deserved their fate but fell below the lofty gaze of contract law, the last quarter of a century has witnessed the emergence of the 'pathological' or 'problem' gambler. These subjects, unable to govern themselves, become the target for a new market in psychological therapeutics, not dissimilar to those developed with respect to other forms of compulsive behaviour. As Collins rightly notes, the appearance of such a subject corresponds with the rise of an enterprise culture: a neo-liberal emphasis on financial risk-taking as good and on government paternalism as bad. Thus the Productivity Commission made the point that consumers 'should be just as free to exercise choice in this area of their lives as any other' (1999, p 5). In this account, the casualties of risk-taking are held responsible for their own problems, for by implication the problem gamblers – like the problem investors of the early 20th century – are those who gamble beyond their ability to absorb losses.[19] The point is made that they are thus morally reprehensible in some degree, especially insofar as this impinges on their family obligations. Certainly there are signs that such a revised morality is emerging. In the Australian state of New South Wales, for example, the Gambling Legislation Amendment (Responsible Gambling) Act 1999 now provides for the legal exclusion from gambling venues of persons defined as problem gamblers. Should a person under such an order violate its provisions they will have committed a criminal offence. However, the court may decide that it will not impose a penalty providing the persons 'undergo such gambling counselling, for such a period not exceeding 12 months, as is specified by the courts'.

It is perhaps fitting that the legal 'normalisation' of commercial gambling should be associated with the resurgence of a moral discourse on the irrationality of *certain* gamblers. Of course this development does not morally judge gambling, only the gambling behaviour of those who are unable to manage their own consumption of this risky commodity. However, the form of the problem nevertheless echoes the fears of the 19th century, focused on the fecklessness and lack of prudence of those who gamble. Isolation of the 'problem' gambler corresponds to the transformation

---

19 Thus in the Productivity Commission's report, problem gambling is defined by 'a lack of control by the gambler over his or her gambling behaviour; and/or adverse personal, economic and social impacts which result from a gambler's actions – particularly the financial losses (relative to the gambler's means)' (1999, p 17).

of gambling into an industry – for these legal provisions, of course, are applicable only to those who pursue their compulsions through commercial gambling services. If it is still the case that 'private' gambling is beneath the gaze of the law, this would seem equally true of those whose gambling 'pathology' is outside the commercial arena!

In all the legal struggles to develop a governable category of insurance, there is not a word about insurance (or for that matter gambling or speculation) being defined by its deployment of actuarial or statistical methods. The legislators and the courts appear rather uninterested in the ways in which the insurance industry renders the future calculable. Yet insurance is taken by many theorists as emblematic of the technology of risk. For Beck (1992) the question of whether an insurer will agree to insure is indicative of whether the issue 'really' concerns a technology of risk or a technology of uncertainty. Disagreements between scientists who make claims about low levels of risk and insurers who refuse to insure these risks are held to be symptomatic of the currently problematic status of risk-calculative expertise. In turn, this is taken to demonstrate the arrival of risk society. For governmental analysts likewise, risk technology is usually taken to be the principal defining point of insurance:

> *Risk is calculable.* This is the essential point, whereby insurance is distinct from a bet or a lottery. For an event to be a risk, it must be possible to evaluate its probability. Insurance has a dual basis; the statistical table which establishes the regularity of certain events, and the calculus of probabilities applied to that statistic, which yields an evaluation of that class of events actually occurring ... When put in the context of a population, the accident which taken on its own seems both random and unavoidable (given a little prudence) can be treated as predictable and calculable. One can predict that during the next year there will be a certain number of accidents, the only unknown being who will have the accident, who will draw one of existence's unlucky numbers. (Ewald, 1991, p 202; emphasis in original)[1]

From this basis, Ewald builds up a framework for analysing insurance. The abstract 'technology of risk' is distanced from the specific institutions of insurance (for example marine insurance, life insurance, socialised unemployment insurance) by the fact that '[i]nsurance institutions are not *the* application of a technology of risk; they are always just *one* of its possible applications' (Ewald, 1991, p 198). Because economic, moral and political environments are always changing, insurance is always developing new 'forms', such as public liability insurance or house contents insurance. In their turn, these are the specific products of the 'insurance imaginary' – that is, ways of inventing useful purposes to which insurance technology may be put. Different forms of insurance are the specific ways in which the insurance

---

1 See also Simon, 1987; Knights and Verdubakis, 1993. Knights and Verdubakis (1993, p 739) point out that '[t]he relation then between actuarial calculations was not one of a straightforward application of mathematical formulae to insurance problems. Until halfway through the eighteenth century insurance premiums shared with gambling stakes, tontines and annuity rates a similar representation of risk based on a diversity of mathematical and non mathematical criteria'. See also Daston, 1988, p 240. However, Knights and Verdubakis move on more problematically to suggest that since that time insurance can analytically be defined in terms of actuarial technologies.

institutions 'utilise' the technique of risk. Because the social, political and economic environment is ever changing, the resulting vision of insurance is of a contingently changing, adaptable and diverse field.

The net effect of this analytical framework is a useful way of approaching the question of the emergence and development of insurance. However, as seen already in the example of catastrophe insurance, some insurance forms and institutions are difficult to define as 'applications' of statistical or actuarial technique because risk technology is attenuated or even absent. As Ericson, Doyle and Barry have shown (2003), even where it is assumed that actuarial calculations are thought to be fundamental to insurance, they are often ignored or unavailable.[2] However, while this does imply that actuarialism should be regarded as only one possible technique for creating and operating insurance, this does not lessen its significance for understanding the genealogy of insurance. Rather, I wish to argue that the deployment of actuarial technique itself is linked with certain visions of insurance, and that these in their turn may be linked with broader political rationalities. In the 18th century insurance was imagined as a speculative venture involving little or no application of actuarial technique even where – as in life insurance – some progress had been made with this technology (Clark, 1999). The legislative curbing of insurance by the requirement of insurable interest had a major impact not simply on those forms that thereby were consigned to the category of gaming, but also on insurance as it became after 1774. As seen already, as a result of the legislative reformulation, *insurance in this period became a form of compensation or indemnification*. In turn, this shaped the course for the deployment of actuarial techniques in the 19th century. For example, it will be seen in this chapter that as life insurance and insurance against unemployment and injury came to be defined governmentally as a way of providing security, especially for the working classes, the state began to *expect* that such insurance be subject to actuarial governance. This was by no means accepted as an unqualified good by working people who valued other, fraternal techniques for governing insurance. The superior calculability of actuarialism was valued by governments because it provided a more certain way of keeping people from requiring public relief. Nonetheless, it was disliked by many working people because it passed control to a class of experts and weakened the social bonds that were both intrinsically valued and provided a source of security that extended beyond that provided by insurance alone. Indeed, in many ways it was the governmental preference for appointment of actuaries which kick-started the generation of actuarial data on which reliable tables of mortality could be constructed.

Looked at in this way, it is not simply that insurance need not be actuarial, but that its actuarial character may reflect a genealogy of state government 'insurance imaginaries' (visions of what insurance is or can be) that generated these insurance forms. This is quite different to the way things are represented elsewhere in the

---

2 It can quickly be seen that Ewald's distinction between insurance and gambling is problematic for a similar reason. Many forms of gambling, such as lotteries, rely on chance, but others – for example poker and backgammon – frequently are subject to statistical calculation.

governmentality literature. For example, Ewald's work in insurance and government makes the point that insurance has as its object indemnification, while its form is that of capital. However, he strives to derive this not from a genealogy of insurance, but from mathematical probability itself. Thus in a direct reversal of what occurred in common law, he argues that:

> Insurance is not initially a practice of compensation or reparation. It is the practice of a certain type of rationality: one formalised by the calculus of probabilities. This is why one never insures oneself except against risks, and why the latter can include such different things as death, an accident, hailstorms, a disease, a birth, military conscription, bankruptcy and litigation. (Ewald, 1991, p 199)

In other words, for Ewald and others following this logic, it is the development of actuarial technique which accounts for why insurance becomes a practice of compensation or reparation, rather than the reverse. In common law, however, insurance is first defined as compensatory. Only later, and then partially, does it become actuarial as a result of political policy. This chapter will examine the history of British working class life insurance (and especially the type known as Industrial Life Assurance) through such a lens.[3] In this genealogy, the category of 'thrift' takes a central role. In the 19th century thrift appears as a moral attribute of the individual, associated with what would now be thought of as risk-avoidance and risk-spreading. Thrift was thought to be indispensable for working people, for governing their autonomy and security. This shaped the early development of insurance for the poor not only through the struggles over actuarial techniques, as noted above, but also by linking these with disciplinary practices that enforced thrift. Regular collection of premiums at the home of the insured came to be regarded as an essential practice, simply because the poor were regarded as unable or unwilling to manage their own financial affairs in this respect. With the rise of social or welfare liberalism, however, 'thrift' was re-imaged, and new insurance techniques were developed in line with this change. Distinguished into two forms – 'compulsory' thrift and 'voluntary' thrift – it provided the conceptual basis for a bifurcated insurance apparatus: socially ('compulsory') and individually ('voluntary') based. Later still, and paradoxically under the umbrella of restoring the Victorian virtues, thrift was turned on its head. In the 1980s, people came to be imagined as too cautious and risk averse, rather than insufficiently so. In this environment working class life insurance was reinvented and marketed as a fully commodified 'investment product' with a *risk-taking* element. Under this political rationality, the social and individual actuarial techniques were supplemented with the uncertain techniques of market investment so that superannuation became, for many, a speculative venture on the stock market.

As this suggests, risk, uncertainty and insurance are governmental constructs whose nature and form vary through time, but which exist in a triangular relationship – so that variations in each has implications for how the others are imagined and practised. These processes, in turn, are strongly influenced by the prevailing political rationality, in such a manner that rethinking the meaning, nature

---

3 The term 'assurance' here is synonymous with 'insurance'. While the former is strictly the correct term in this history, for ease of comprehension I will refer throughout to 'industrial life insurance' – except of course in direct quotations using the original term. 'Industrial Life Insurance' is the American name for the equivalent institution.

and place of risk and uncertainty in terms of changing political rationalities has been central to the ongoing process of rethinking the nature of insurance.

Classical liberalism: policing thrift

In Britain insurance for the working classes emerged during the late 18th century with the activities of the Friendly Societies – fraternal and benevolent insurance arrangements formed among skilled artisans. Despite some liberal suspicion of the Friendly Societies, during the early part of the 19th century, as a form of combination in restraint of market relations, successive political administrations legislated to encourage the Societies' role in providing life, burial and sickness insurance for the working class. This was regarded not only as fostering self-help and industry but also as alleviating pressure on the poor rates.[4] Fraternal societies were characterised by 'intentionally organising themselves around notions of "friendship, brotherly-love, charity"' in which 'any self-understanding in terms of "risk" or "insurance" (was) largely absent' (Doran, 1994, p 134). It was clear at the time that the frequent failures of these funds followed from an inability of fund managers to predict liabilities and balance these against contributions and funds in hand. The reason for this lay in the benevolent principles of the early Societies, which distributed payment of benefits to members according to their need rather than in proportion to their premiums or levels of risk.

> [T]he nature of the societies, their emphasis on brotherhood, and their preoccupation with respectability and self-help, forbade them to cut adrift a brother so long as a penny of reserve was left to help him. Normally, there was no age limit to membership and older members could and did live on friendly society sick pay year after year. In doing so, they forced the society to provide for them what was in fact an old age pension, which the societies' reserves had never been calculated to carry. (Gilbert, 1965, p 556)[5]

In order to facilitate thrift and self-help, legislation 'encouraged' them to replace their traditional emphasis on fraternalism and benevolence with actuarially-based principles of fund management. From 1819 onward statutes required that the data tables and distribution guidelines of societies applying for registration be approved by 'two persons at least, known to be professional actuaries or persons skilled in calculation'. The uneven contest between the representatives of these competing principles – the workers on the one hand and the government and the actuaries on the other – resulted in the displacement of a horizontal, fraternally-based and essentially amateur organisation by a hierarchical, actuarial and managerial form of insurance which distanced the rank and file members from the professionals who operated the funds. Thereby, control of the business of insurance was taken from the hands of policyholders. (Select Committee, 1889, pp vi–vii). The monthly meeting in the local inn, which was simultaneously a convivial social gathering and a business committee, had largely disappeared by the middle years of the 19th century

---

4 For example, the Friendly Societies Act of 1819, and the Acts of 1793, 1829 and 1834 (33 Geo III, c 54, 10 Geo IV, c 56, and 5 Wm IV, c 40). The preamble of the Act of 1793 referred approvingly to the Societies' role in 'diminishing the public burdens'.

5 It should be noted that terms such as 'fraternal' usually need to be taken literally, at least in the sense that they refer to all-male organisations. There were few benevolent societies that allowed women as members, and the principal examples were those run by and for women – usually in relation to providing for the post-birth 'laying-in' month (Gosden, 1973, pp 26–27).

(Gosden, 1973, p 23). In its place there emerged the domination of this field by large-scale Fraternal Orders, who operated out of centralised offices and held annual meetings at which the membership was rarely able to wield effective power. More than that, the principles of actuarial methods that were set in place further eroded benevolent ideas and introduced a 'disciplinary element into membership' (Doran, 1994, p 175). In particular, graduated contributions were imposed, and members became divided and ordered according to their levels of contribution and risk categorisations. The solidarity that characterised the Fraternal Orders of old was thus fragmented and transformed. While the resulting insurance arrangements were still collective, this collectivity was increasingly abstract, individuated, fiscal and mediated by third parties.

Hand in hand with these shifts came new relationships that were involved in the collection of premiums. In the fraternally-organised Friendly Societies, premiums, as noted, had either been paid at the monthly meetings, or had been collected by members themselves in their spare time. The larger, actuarially-based societies (the Friendly Collecting, or more simply, the 'Collecting Societies' or 'Collecting Orders'), however, substituted a model based on the deployment of salaried or commission-funded collectors. By the 1870s, the Royal Commission into Friendly and Benefit Building Societies reported that full-time paid collectors were the 'pivot of the whole system' (Royal Commission, 1874, p 961).

In this arrangement, the working class insured were ordered increasingly around a regime of contributions which was subject to the pressures of collecting agents working to a formally actuarial, hierarchic and bureaucratic routine. The relation of actuarially-driven discipline in the Friendly Societies were magnified in scale and intensity by the rise of industrial life assurance companies, which made a commercial principle out of the emergent form of insurance relationship. Life insurance for the working class had changed dramatically under the impact of actuarial techniques, but the emergence of these collectors was not simply an outgrowth of actuarial science or technology. Rather, it reflected a way of doing business in a particular social and class context. As the Fabian critics Wilson and Levy (1937, p 25) lamented, what emerged was that a 'new class of intermediary strangers had come into existence, replacing the old bond of personal faith and friendship by commercial instincts scarcely hidden behind a veil of demonstrative humanity and friendliness'. Significantly, such disciplinary relations were extended to a much wider market by the rise of industrial life insurance companies, which made a commercial principle out of this form of insurance relationship. Industrial life insurance – dominated throughout the next hundred years by firms such as The Prudential – focused on the poorer sections of the working class, whereas the Friendly Societies had been providers for the 'aristocracy of labour' (Gilbert, 1965).[6] The development of the commercial industrial insurances thus extended the reach

6 Gilbert (1965, p 552) comments with respect to the fraternal associations that:

The grey, faceless, lower one-third of the British working population lay altogether outside their province. The dock worker, the railroad navvy, the carter, the hawker, the crossing sweeper, the casual city labourer of any sort, was shunned and distrusted. Friendly society membership was traditionally the badge of the artisan. It indicated that within his own social level he was clubbable.

of life insurance to the 'the poor'. By the early part of the 20th century, industrial life insurance had become the principal institution for governing working class thrift, and few households were not enlisted in this regime.[7]

Part of the success of these rising companies was that, while they retained endowment policies (which were to grow again in importance during the following century), they also increasingly emphasised burial insurance – exploiting the working class fear and shame associated with the pauper's funeral (Morrah, 1955; Johnson, 1985). Equally vital to their success was the *disciplinary* nature of the collecting strategies of industrial life insurance. Sale of policies and collection of premiums were characterised by the deployment of an army of agents who collected small weekly premiums, normally of only a few pence, at the home of the policyholder. Detailed reviews of the collectors' techniques, undertaken by a series of governmental inquiries and committees from the mid-19th to the mid-20th centuries, map out a strategy of infiltration into the fabric of working class domestic life, aimed at maximising the sale of insurance (Royal Commission, 1874; Passfield, 1915; Departmental Committee, 1920; Select Committee, 1933). The collector's regular call was timed to coincide with pay day, for it was recognised that the 'thriftlessness' of the poor and the unpredictable pressures on their vulnerable domestic economy meant that available cash may have been spent within 24 hours. Collectors were instructed to pay detailed attention to the state of the home and its contents, to look for additions to household furnishings which would indicate an ability to purchase increased insurance, or to watch for the disappearance of items of furniture – which would indicate sale or pawn to tide over hard times (Johnson, 1985; Wilson and Levy, 1937).

From the industry's point of view, this form and level of intrusion was not exploitative. Rather, it represented both a necessary way of doing business and a disciplinary strategy for ensuring the thrift and prudence of poor policyholders in their own interests. Without such interventions, it was argued, the poor would not take out life insurance or would grossly under-insure themselves. It was claimed that they did not have the social and moral resources to sustain, unassisted, the long-term commitment required to maintain insurance policies. The industry represented its activity in terms of providing a necessary discipline of thrift, in which its roles were said to include those of educating people about the need to insure for the future, ensuring payments, generating security for the family, and providing moral support when other temptations were more alluring or competing necessities more demanding. As one turn of the century advocate urged:

> The Industrial collector calls at the houses of the insured week after week for the premiums falling due. To anyone familiar with educational processes it must be clear that such a constant reminder of life insurance as a duty and of the necessity of foresight and self denial must needs have a considerable effect in other directions. As it has properly

7 By 1911, Lloyd George estimated that there existed in excess of 40 million industrial life insurance policies, and that '[t]here is scarcely a household in this country where there is not a policy of insurance against death' (HC Deb, 1911, vol 31, p 1,181). The Parmoor Committee estimated that close to three-quarters of the British population contributed to some form of industrial life insurance (Departmental Committee, 1920).

been said, one cannot develop thrift habits in one important direction without developing similar habits in other directions. (Dryden, 1909, p 53)[8]

Nevertheless, from an early date the question of their role in inculcating thrift among the poor became the centre of political contestation between the insurance industry and the government.

The state versus business: the critique of 'useless thrift'

While the moral role of insurance in promoting thrift and reducing reliance on the Poor Law had dominated early British debates on life insurance, by the 1860s new issues were arising, concerned with the efficiency and the justice of governing thrift through industrial life insurance. It was argued, most notably by government commissions and parliamentary leaders, that two major *systematic* problems involved in this model of insurance undermined its privileged status as a moral technology.

First, and most significant, was the problem of the *expense ratio*. For the middle classes, life insurance premiums were paid once or twice yearly at the office of the company. Making large individual outlays of this sort was beyond most working people, who relied instead on small but frequent payment patterns. Such frequent collection procedures were labour intensive and costly, and the payment of commissions to the army of collectors generated a drain of between 25% and 50% of the value of premiums collected. Accordingly, the rate of return for poor people's thrift was recognised by all to be much lower than for the middle classes and, effectively, involved 'useless thrift' on the part of the poor. This was linked to a criticism that because useless thrift represented a disincentive to thrift among the poor, and because the collectors were required to bear upon the poor in order to make them save, industrial life insurance did not in practice work to instill a moral virtue – a free-willed embracing of thrift.[9]

---

8   This was still being argued in the 1930s, when it was claimed:

> Ordinary methods of saving are often disappointing. But the man who deposits a specific sum periodically with the Equitable enters into a contract under which his deposits become obligatory. Although he is free to stop making them, he cannot do so without abrogating his agreement. Thus a steady and continuous pressure is brought to bear on him. And this pressure strengthens his purpose and aids him in fulfilling the obligation he has voluntarily assumed. In addition to this he is taught systematic *habits* of saving. His payments fall due at regular intervals, and whenever he is forgetful or dilatory he is reminded of his obligation. (Alexander, 1932, p 5)

9   The term 'useless thrift' was coined at the end of the 19th century by the anonymous author of *Useless Thrift or How People are Robbed* (see Wilson and Levy, 1937). It is worth noting that some contemporary critics regarded both the cost of collection and the mode of collection as working *against* the inculcation of thrift, rather than producing useless or even useful thrift – for thrift had to be undertaken as a result of the will rather than of the routine compulsion of collectors:

> Some men argue that the fact of such large sums of money being collected from the working classes, for the purposes of providing assistance in the hour of need, goes far to prove what a hold provident habits has [sic] taken upon them. This is an error. There is nothing that shows so much indifference, inconsideration, utter want of thought, reckless mode of wasting means, as the mode in which these contributions are generally paid. (Quoted by Johnson, 1983, p 32)

One implication is that not leaving prudence to the operation of the will destroys thrift, which must be achieved by the exercise of the will. As will be seen, William Beveridge's rethinking of thrift turned such ideas upon their head.

Second were the twinned problems of *lapses* and *overselling*. As the collectors benefited directly from the value of premiums collected, there was systematic pressure to increase sales. Overselling was held responsible for a high rate of lapsed policies among the poor. As early as the 1860s, the rate of lapses was seen by government officials as a *deterrent* to thrift among the poor, for holders of lapsing industrial insurance policies received nothing by way of return from their savings. Gladstone pointed out the specific injustice to the poor: 'among the higher classes the holder of a policy who is unable to continue his payments has a certain proportion, generally about one third of his premiums, repaid to him, but no such right is conceded in the case of the industrial classes ... If the poor man fails ... to pay one premium, the policy drops and he loses everything' (HC Debs, 1864, vol 173, p 1,575). Ten years later Northcote's Royal Commission made the claim that it was in the agents' and companies' interests to sell policies to people whom they knew were unlikely to be able to sustain them because the lapsing of policies amounted to windfall profits through 'confiscation of the premiums of its members' (Royal Commission, 1874, pp cx–cxxxiii). Thus, while the importance of thrift, as a means for governing the poor, was never brought into question and, indeed, was the driving concern of parliamentary critics, a contest emerged that focused on whether the lack of adequate provision for security was the result of the absence of thrift among the poor, or the unsatisfactory institutional means for instilling thrift or for converting any such thrift into security.

The government's concerns about the need to encourage habits of self-reliance and to make the poor less reliant on poor relief brought it to challenge the inadequacies of industrial insurance. In 1865 Prime Minister Gladstone set up a state-run, fully-contributory life insurance system, in order to drive the industrial insurance companies from the market. In the Government Annuities Act of that year a scheme was introduced which retained the practice of small premiums paid weekly, but dispensed with collectors. Instead, it required contributions to be made at the local Post Office. The expectation was that the thrifty poor would be attracted away from the industrial insurance companies because the Post Office scheme reduced collecting costs and would result in a much higher rate of return to the policyholder. Moreover, because the officials of the Post Office would have no financial interest in overselling policies, the plan would eliminate another of the evils afflicting life insurance for the poor.

Within a decade, however, Post Office insurance appeared to have failed, with few people entering the scheme or sustaining payment of their premiums. The Northcote Royal Commission concluded from such evidence that the insurance industry, after all, was correct in its view that the poor would not practice thrift unless 'specially invited and urged to do so by personal application from the collectors; nor will they keep up their payments unless the collector calls for them' (Royal Commission, 1874, p cxxi). Accordingly, the Commission recommended that for any scheme of life insurance directed at the poor, 'house to house collection will be required'. Otherwise, it supported the continued operation of the Post Office scheme. Because this model worked through the fair 'competition of the government' the Commission felt that insurance companies could not claim state interference in the market. Moreover, as the Post Office scheme was fully contributory, it 'did not carry with it something of the appearance of a relief system'

(Royal Commission, 1874). The unanimous recommendation of the Commissioners, therefore, was that the system of government insurance, newly armed with insurance collectors, should be extended to compete more effectively in the field of industrial insurance.

By implication, government collectors would now enter the field in direct competition with the companies and societies. However, this proposal was never enacted, not because of liberal fears about the state entering the market, but because it created an image of government postal agents – or 'special postmen' – acting inappropriately. In particular, it was felt unacceptable that officers of the state would be constrained to act like common commercial salesmen. As Brabrook, the Chief Registrar of Friendly Societies, noted, if the private insurance collector supports himself 'by the arts of persuasion which he uses upon poor mothers to induce them to effect insurances; [then] the special postman, if he is to be a success, would have to learn to use the same arts of persuasion, and would thus become as unlike the ordinary Government Officer as could be' (Brabrook, 1898, pp 78–79). There was also concern that the commercial nature of such 'special postmen' would blur the distinction between private and public, taking the government into private homes in a way that was still a concern to classical liberalism. Indeed, Gladstone had adverted to this very danger when setting up the Post Office scheme in 1864, stressing that 'the House of Commons is not going to vote money to enable us to go into every cottage in the country' (HC Debs, 1864, Vol 173, p 1,566). Finally, as Brabrook pressed, if an army of state collectors entered the field, then this would eliminate one of the main justifications for state involvement – the lowering of expense ratios.[10]

Available technologies of insurance for the poor thus appeared to be intrinsically compromised: first, because the volitional basis of moral virtues, such as thrift (which, under the regime of moral virtue, had to be exercised freely and habitually), was compromised by the necessity for some form of compulsion; and secondly, because the apparent impossibility of avoiding high collection costs meant that the institution of industrial life insurance generated wasted thrift. Thrift, as a moral virtue, was thus *problematically* embedded in specific institutional forms of insurance. The tensions set up were to transform thrift itself as a way of thinking about and governing working class security.

Welfare liberalism: social insurance and 'the consumer'

Into the 20th century, continuing critiques of industrial life insurance condemned its failures and injustices.[11] Despite this, Prime Minister Lloyd George decided against

---

10 Without collectors, the Post Office scheme continued to function in a marginal fashion. In 1920 it was again dismissed as ineffectual by a government inquiry – this time the Parmoor Report – largely on the basis of its inability to attract life insurance business without deploying collectors. It eventually closed in 1928.

11 This critique was unabated despite the fact that after the turn of the century there was, as Johnson notes, a marked change away from burial insurance (in the form of assurance maturing on the death of the nominated person) (Johnson, 1983, p 41). Beginning in the 1880s, industrial assurance offices began to offer endowment policies (ie, maturing after a set number of years rather than only on the death of the assured), and by the time of the Cohen Report of 1933, the latter represented over a quarter of industrial life insurance business. By the time of the Beveridge Report, endowment policies represented three-quarters of such business.

incorporating industrial life insurance into his nationalised insurance scheme in 1911. Ostensibly this was because 'there is hardly a household in this country where there is not a policy of insurance against death … [and] the ground has been very thoroughly covered' (HC Debs, 1911, vol 31, p 1,181). Almost certainly, this decision was made to minimise industry resistance to other developments (notably social health insurance) and reflected a pragmatic desire to deploy the insurance companies and their collectors as convenient agents for collecting state insurance contributions. The outcome, nevertheless, was that industrial insurance survived. As such, it was to remain the target of repeated and severe criticisms, first by Sydney Webb (Passfield, 1915) and later by further government reviews such as the Parmoor Report (Departmental Committee, 1920) and the Cohen Committee (Select Committee, 1933). None of these reports did very much more than reiterate and painstakingly document the problems already identified in the 19th century.[12] However, during the Second World War, developments that foreshadowed the formation of the post-war welfare state brought to bear new pressures on industrial life insurance.

The invention of 'socially desirable thrift'

The proposals of successive inquiries between 1879 and 1930 had more or less taken for granted the market-based delivery of life insurance. Northcote had recommended that the state enter as a competing supplier, Cohen urged that it expand its role as a competitor, and Parmoor had advised increased regulation of the industry. However, in his report on *Social Insurance and Allied Services* – in many ways the blueprint for post-war British welfare institutions – Beveridge shifted the debate into the realm of welfare liberalism. He argued, in short, that '[t]he criticisms made upon life assurance in the past have not been met, and cannot be met while the system remains, as at present, a competitive business' (1942, p 274). While the problems with industrial insurance, noted by Beveridge in this report, were virtually identical to those identified by each of the previous enquiries, Beveridge bypassed their inability to resolve the problems of industrial insurance by arguing:

> The proposal that life assurance among persons of limited means should be a public service rather than a competitive private business is based upon the special character of industrial assurance, as a business in which competition leads to overselling and as a business in which the seller's interest presents special danger to the consumer. Life assurance is not like other commodities because those who insure make their choice once and for all when they take out a policy. They cannot buy less insurance or another form of insurance the next day or change their assurance company without loss, as the next day they can substitute bacon for beef or change their grocer without loss. Industrial

---

12 The Cohen Report (Select Committee 1933, p 29) castigated alleged overselling (and consequent lapses) in the strongest terms:

> We do not see how it is possible for an all-pervading army of professional canvassers, paid to enrol the largest number of recruits, on a method of remuneration that makes loss of livelihood the penalty for every failure of persuasiveness, invariably to abstain from a magnification of the advantages and of slurring over of the shortcomings and of the cost of a policy which the public absolutely refuse to read, and which is couched in language not as clear as it might be, and certainly incomprehensible by the vast majority of those concerned. The system amounts, to say the least, to a standing temptation to deceit.

assurance, that is to say life assurance among people of limited means, is so different from most other commodities that it cannot be safely treated as an article of commerce. (Beveridge, 1942, p 275)

Beveridge achieved this position not by focusing on the moral problematic of thrift, but by imagining insurance in terms of the nature and behaviour of commodities and consumers. He then moved on to distinguish two kinds of insurance commodity, those that behave like normal commodities ('luxuries') and those that behave like exceptional commodities ('necessities', which were in their turn defined by the fact that people with less than the means of subsistence continue to purchase them). In the case of the latter, market distribution presents 'special dangers to the consumer'. For the moment, we must pass by the highly significant re-imaging of people as 'consumers', for at this point Beveridge reintroduces the idea of thrift; but it is a thrift transformed, for he argues that in the light of this analysis it is necessary for the state to create new 'socially desirable forms of insurance and thrift' (Beveridge, 1942, p 275).

The first of these forms, which Beveridge labelled 'compulsory thrift', referred to the provision of necessities. Necessities have a common characteristic, namely that they correspond to universal needs, and can thus be provided to all, in universal form. This being the case, the state could provide insurance for such commodities via compulsory premiums extracted at source, providing all subjects with the same level of benefit. In the case of such universal needs, Beveridge suggested, personal practices of thrift were inappropriate or inadequate, for where personal thrift could not provide, the public purse would have to compensate. Thereby, Beveridge took the element of compulsion that had always been mixed up in industrial life insurance, restricted it to provision for necessities, removed it from the 'voluntary' market sector (where it had ever been problematic) and assigned it to the state where – even according to the tenets of classical liberalism – coercive power belongs.

Having evacuated compulsion to the realm of necessities, Beveridge could now articulate a second novel category: 'voluntary thrift'. If compulsory thrift was to deal with 'necessities' that could become a charge on the public purse, voluntary thrift was assigned to the sphere of 'luxuries' – the provision of which, even if not provided for by the individual, could not legitimately become a responsibility of the state. Moreover, as luxuries related to needs 'less uniform and less universal', they were deemed by Beveridge to be appropriate subjects for 'voluntary action rather than compulsion' (1942, p 275). In this way, the creation of two socially desirable forms of thrift, especially of voluntary thrift, allowed elements of working class insurance to become fully commodified for the first time since the passage of the Gambling Act 1774. By 'fully commodified', I refer specifically to the removal of moral compulsion, and the voluntarisation of these aspects of insurance deemed not to relate to necessities. These would become the subject of a new kind of liberty through which people will be governed: 'freedom of choice'. The model was applied to burial insurance, once the mainstay of industrial life insurance (Beveridge, 1942, pp 271–75). Beveridge had been concerned that more of the income of the poor was allocated to this purpose than he believed necessary, and that this excess interfered with the purchase of other essentials. 'On the occurrence of a death, money may be paid and undoubtedly is in a large number of cases paid, for which there is no obvious need either in meeting direct funeral expenses ... or in meeting personal expenditure of relatives ... Insurance money for funeral expenses may fall due at a death in such amounts that there is no choice between extravagant spending and making a profit out of assurance on life-of-another' (1942, p 270). In addition, insurance money 'may be spent in other ways leaving the funeral unpaid for', still leaving the state to cover the essential expenses. The elimination of both these problems could be achieved by distinguishing between those aspects of the burial that could be seen as necessities and those deemed optional. Accordingly, Beveridge proposed the introduction of compulsory burial insurance for 'the essential universal need for direct funeral expenses'. Expenses for 'luxuries', that is, items over and above those needed for the provision of what he referred to as 'a decent burial', being less uniform and less universal, were assigned to the action of voluntary thrift.

Some of the old concerns upon which governing through the morality of thrift had focused, particularly those relating to the proper expenditure on necessities, were thus still to be governed; but they were to be governed 'scientifically' rather than 'morally' by state technocrats who would decide levels of need and determine the premiums required to fund these. In the process, Beveridge almost defined out of existence the 19th century moral virtue of thrift, together with its disciplinary regime enforcing habits of frugality and saving. 'Compulsory thrift', taking the form of contributions extracted at source, required no such moral compulsion. 'Voluntary thrift', on the other hand, clearly implied that saving and insurance were matters of personal choice and discretion rather than moral pressure (Beveridge, 1942, p 275).

Commodifying insurance under welfare liberalism

In analyses of insurance under welfare liberalism, the compulsory and state-based nature of social insurances has normally monopolised the attention of theorists of insurance (for example, Defert, 1991; Ewald, 1990; 1994). However, with respect to life insurance in the mid-20th century, Beveridge's focus on voluntarism and choice, and his analytical starting point of commodities and consumption, are equally fundamental issues. In subjecting thrift to a regime of social liberalism, Beveridge was by no means absolving individuals from the responsibility for self-help, even with respect to social insurance schemes. Thus he was clear that 'citizens as insured persons should realise that they cannot get more than certain benefits for certain contributions' and 'should not be taught to regard the state as the dispenser of gifts for which no one needs to pay' (1942, p 108). Moreover, he stressed that for the state 'to give by compulsory insurance more than is needed in subsistence is an unnecessary interference with individual responsibilities' (1942, p 118).

Nevertheless, by creating a domain of compulsory insurance, he simultaneously created the possibility of a new concept of thrift. Voluntary thrift was dislocated from necessity and, thus, disarticulated from the provision of security which could reasonably become a charge on the public purse. Forms of thrift among the poor could now be assigned to the sphere of personal discretion (Beveridge, 1942, p 275). Once it became possible to think of the thrift of the poor in this way, then the moral governance of 'voluntary thrift', at least, was attenuated. Certainly it could be removed from that domain of moral compulsion sustained by institutional reinforcement.[13] The question remaining was how, practicably, to achieve this. As long as the industrial assurance companies remained, then – as generations of enquiries had shown – collection and its attendant evils were impossible to eradicate. The solution was to nationalise the industry under an Industrial Insurance Board, which 'would work steadily to substitute direct payment of premiums for collection' (1942, p 275). But why should this work, when its precursor under Gladstone had failed?

Beveridge proposed to remove the grounds justifying the market forms of disciplinary compulsion by creating both a field of 'universal needs', in which state compulsion created security, and a field of 'personal needs', in which the moral grounds for compulsion were exhausted. If the term 'voluntary thrift' would have been a meaningless redundancy to Victorian moralists – for how could a moral virtue be other than voluntary – the term represented a precise and socially generated field for the programmers of the new insurance form (Beveridge, 1942, p 275). For the latter, *voluntary* no longer meant 'disciplined' and thus morally compelled. Rather, it took on connotations of choice. Indeed, and more precisely, the shift in Beveridge's language toward that of commodities and consumption informs the distinction between compulsion and volition. For Beveridge, the latter begins to imply a rather distinct model of the subject of liberal rule: the citizen as consumer, for whom technologies of negative discipline would no longer be necessary or fitting.

Beveridge's focus on consumption and commodities should not be seen as either totally contingent, or simply as an effect of the influence of economics 'in general'. The economic discourse that shaped and provided the foundation for Beveridge's thinking was that of John Maynard Keynes, which may be distinguished from the classical economics of the previous century by, *inter alia*, its focus on consumption rather than production (Cutler *et al*, 1986; Waine, 1991). Beveridge was quite clear about the fact that the reforms he was proposing were to be understood in this framework, as being an expression of this shift in focus away from a framework of production:

> Correct distribution does not mean what it has often been taken to mean in the past – distribution between the different agents of production, between land, capital, management and labour. Better distribution of *purchasing power* is required among wage earners themselves, as between times of earning and not earning and between times of heavy family responsibilities and times of light or no family responsibilities. (Beveridge, 1942, p 167; emphasis added)

The full implications of this observation only emerge when a second matter is considered. Beveridge had observed that compared with the situation prevailing at the turn of the century, real living standards had increased by 30% and, still more important, the surplus income of those workers above the poverty line was eight times as great as the deficiency of those below it. Viewing authoritative predictions of post-war growth, he was confident that this trend would continue for the foreseeable future (Harries, 1977). Beveridge's first conclusion was that poverty

---

13 The term 'voluntary thrift' was given formal political status in the Labour Party's post-war policy documents, *Labour Believes in Britain* (1949) and *The Future of Industrial Insurance* (1950).

could be eliminated by redistributing incomes within the working class – seemingly dispelling the lingering 'Poor Law' concern that support for the poor represented a charge on the wealthy. This was to be the role of compulsory insurance. His second conclusion was that industrial life insurance would become obsolete in this new environment. The real incomes of workers would be such that door-to-door collection of insurance premiums, together with the problem of the expense ratio it created, could be dispensed with. Workers would be able to pay insurance premiums in the same manner as the middle classes and reap the benefits of increased returns on investment.

This set of observations underlay his linking of voluntary thrift to the category of discretionary income, and to the notion that a sector of working class insurance could now be more completely commodified than had previously been thought possible.[14] As Zelizer (1994) notes, thinking of income as 'surplus' to necessities is a very specific way of thinking about money. If nothing necessary has to be gone without, personal expenditure is far less subject to moral constraint: it is rendered, as Beveridge termed it, 'voluntary' in a sense that could not readily be applied 50 years previously. More generally, the rethinking of insurance, thrift and surplus in this way took its place in what May and Cooper (1995) regard as part of a broader 'reconstitution of citizenship' in which individuals and groups increasingly are seen not as *citizens* but as *consumers*. As seen above, this rethinking of the subjects of insurance as consumers was quite explicit in Beveridge's work. While this is partly explained by his focus on Keynesian economics, it is also linked to the new ways of thinking about liberalism that Beveridge saw emerging. As Judy Brett (1993) has argued, in the liberal political discourses surviving into the 1940s, 'choice', 'freedom' and 'liberty' scarcely appeared, while concepts such as 'frugality', 'thrift' and 'savings' held centre stage. Accordingly, individualism 'took its primary meaning from Protestantism and its ethic of hard work, personal responsibility, thrift and community service'. By contrast, in the coming years, the key characteristic of the individual shifted from this image of *independence*, so that 'today it is *freedom*, most generally understood as freedom of choice in everything ranging from the colour of a new stove to sexuality' (Brett, 1993, p A1; emphasis in original. See also Rose, 1989).

Neo-liberalism: putting the risk back into insurance

Beveridge proposed that the only way to rid the life insurance industry of its coercive and expensive collectors was to nationalise industrial life insurance and displace it with a state Industrial Insurance Board that 'would work steadily to substitute direct payment of premiums for collection' (1942, p 275). However, while social insurance on this model subsequently absorbed areas such as burial insurance soon after the war (in 1948), the political muscle of the insurance industry and failures of political will in the Labour Party resulted in little change over insuring voluntary thrift. Nevertheless, writing in 1955, still in the shadow of Beveridge's threat of nationalisation of industrial life insurance, one of the last apologists of industrial life insurance foresaw the conditions of its demise. It was

---

14 However, it needs to be noted that many critics challenged Beveridge's views on the 'reality' of this surplus. See, for example, Abel-Smith and Townsend, 1965.

possible, but unlikely, Morrah argued, that industrial life insurance could be ousted by the victory of a more determined socialist regime. In practice, however, a:

> slighter revolution than that would suffice to make it superfluous. If the great mass of the people possessed bank accounts, and could habitually maintain credit balances substantially exceeding the annual amount they thought reasonable to set aside for future needs, then they could provide against emergency by the methods of ordinary life assurance with its premiums paid at long intervals, and industrial assurance (paid) by weekly or monthly contributions, which is necessarily less economical, could not compete. (Morrah, 1955, p 171)

In Morrah's view, however, the survival of industrial life insurance was assured because it was still the case that the mass of the populace 'have neither bank accounts nor substantial capital resources', and that 'weekly wages ... so little exceed the necessary domestic outgoings of the week that thrift is always an effort'. In such a setting, echoing his Victorian predecessors, Morrah (1955, p 174) saw that 'pressure and even strong pressure is therefore essential' to effect adequate insurance against emergencies. Yet within a decade, the 19th century form of industrial life assurance – involving frequent collections of small premiums by insurance agents – had become only a minor aspect of the life insurance industry (Dunning, 1971), and it continued to decline by degrees until by the late 1980s it accounted for less than 3% of new life insurance business. As far as the insurance industry and its commentators are concerned, Beveridge and Morrah made correct predictions: the long boom of the 1950s and 1960s created the surplus income that made ordinary life insurance feasible for the working class, and the better return this offered attracted the market away (Dunning, 1971).

In these years of post-war consumer prosperity, the mass of the population came to be viewed as *positively enlisted* rather than needing to be *morally coerced* into the institutions of fiscal security. Insurance is no longer imagined to be about preventing poverty through regular little acts of sacrifice. Rather, it is envisioned by governments and the industry as the creation of wealth through the active ('voluntary') investment of disposable ('surplus') income – a vision of life insurance as fully commodified. This insurance language now speaks of 'investment and pension products'. Life insurance is 'viewed as an alternative investment vehicle' which 'no longer sits alone but forms part of the retail services sector' (Price Waterhouse, 1990). Current discourses of 'freedom of service' – that contrast so vividly with the 19th century imagery of moral compulsion – reflect a valorisation of the sovereign consumer that is associated with neo-liberalism and the 'enterprise culture' (Keat, 1991). As Clayton (1985) indicates, the insurance commodity now is provided, in its own understanding at least, not in terms of what 'is good for' the insured party, but in terms of 'what the consumer wants'.

If 'thrift' gives way to 'investment', it is in part because risk itself is being more positively evaluated in contemporary liberal political rationality. Previous generations of classical liberals and welfare liberals regarded the minimisation of future risk as essential for the security of working people. The former fostered thrift and frugality, and the latter established social insurances to achieve this end. To neo-liberals, however, risk is not only a negative thing related to harms and to be minimised, but also has its positive side that must be valued and made salient, as the source of profit, at the root of enterprise and self-reliance. It is also, as discussed in earlier chapters, in the post-welfare era seen as a potent weapon against the 'welfare dependency' that Beveridge's social insurances are now believed to have created.[15]

This positive vision of risk is now beginning to generate a further restructuring of insurance regimes for the working classes. Increasingly, the 'voluntary', commodified sector of insurance is being expanded into the 'compulsory' field of social insurances. Successive regimes of government in Britain have been involved in a programme of restricting access to, and diminishing the attractiveness of, welfare and compulsory social insurances, and of regulating and encouraging their substitution by 'private welfare' (Alcock, 1989). In this environment, life insurance takes on a changing role. 'Encouraged' by legislation such as the Social Security Act 1986, consumers are exhorted to purchase 'investment products which allow the public to gain additional benefits to supplement those gained from the state' or to 'contract out of the state scheme altogether in exchange for incentives'. Rather than being thought of as a contraction of social insurances and welfare, this process is represented as an 'expanding market for pension products' (Price Waterhouse, 1990).

In practice, the development of the 'personal pension' scheme in the wake of the 1986 legislation represents an even more far-reaching development than these commentaries imply. In many respects the commodification of insurance for workers that occurred during the 1960s and 1970s was no more than the extension of Beveridge's and Labour's version of consumerism, in which consumers exercised freedom of choice among the offerings of the market. Thatcher's neo-liberalism, however, attempted to establish a programme of 'worker capitalism' in which it was imagined that '[m]aking every adult a shareholder would serve as a specific antidote to the passivity and lassitude that overcome dependents of a welfare state' (Letwin and Letwin, 1986, p 11). The 'activated' worker thus moves beyond being a passive consumer to become an entrepreneur.

> The vast majority of British adults own investments in bank accounts, life insurance, unit trusts, and pension funds; and they thereby, though unknowingly, possess indirect claims on shares owned by such financial intermediaries. But ... however rewarding such investments are financially, they do not and cannot give their owners a sense of enjoying a rightful and potentially active voice in determining the policies of the nation's enterprises. (Letwin and Letwin, 1986)

In the personal pension schemes this 'defect' is remedied. While the contribution levels are still set at the time of the contract, instead of this delivering a fixed and actuarially calculated benefit upon realisation, the final amount of the benefit will depend upon the performance of the individual investment portfolio or the preferred level-of-risk (high, medium or low risk) policy package selected by the investor. This insurance, then, is not about 'the taming of chance', the term that has come to be so familiar in risk-minimising or risk-spreading readings of insurance.

---

15 For the most recent political expression of such a view, see former Prime Minister John Major's eulogising of 'the risk takers of Great Britain', whom he contrasts with those who take the prudent, cautious line. The latter, by implication, are at the root of any instances of economic underperformance (reported in *The Guardian*, 21–25 October 1995). Earlier views of a similar nature have been expressed throughout the literature of the New Right.

Rather, risk is to be given its head. Insurances now are to exploit risk and to expose the policyholder to the risk imagined to be the source of enterprise and gain. Ironically, the Prudential Corporation, formerly the doyen of industrial life insurance, is now the leading company in the personal pensions market (Waine, 1992).

Transforming Insurance?

For Francois Ewald, risk is understood as having two elements:

> Rather than with the notions of danger and peril, the notion of risk goes together with those of chance, hazard, probability, eventuality or randomness on the one hand, and those of loss or damage on the other – the two series coming together in the notion of accident. One insures against accident, against the probability of loss of some good. Insurance, through the category of risk, objectifies every event as an accident. Insurance's general model is the game of chance: a risk, an accident, comes up like a roulette number, a card pulled out of the pack. With insurance, gaming becomes the symbol of the world. (Ewald, 1991, p 199)

What is remarkable about this passage is that insurance is defined as risk related to loss or damage, while simultaneously it is defined as a game of chance, with its clear connotations of the possibility of speculative gain. This latter imagery, of course, was precisely that potential element of insurance that successive generations of industry and government had attempted to stifle since the foundational insurance legislation of 1774. While endowment policies certainly came to represent an investment for the future, it was always the solid security of actuarially known and guaranteed levels of benefit that were emphasised: investment devoid of speculation (Zelizer, 1979). Life insurance thus retained its faith with the Victorian virtues of thrift and frugality into the last quarter of the 20th century.

Ironically, despite the fact that welfarism is often assailed for eroding these virtues, the welfare-liberal reforms developed by Beveridge preserved them, albeit in a transformed state. Beveridge adhered to the idea that saving to cover future risks with respect to life's necessities, and for insurance to provide assured benefits, was absolutely crucial. So much so that it could not be left to inefficient mechanisms such as industrial life assurance, and certainly not to the vagaries of the market, but would be assigned to the scientific governance of state technocrats: experts in risk-spreading and risk minimisation. Viewed in this way, the welfare state can be seen to be a profoundly conservative institution. While transforming thrift from a personal moral virtue to an administrative procedure of the state (by making saving for individual security compulsory and rigorously predictable), it moved poles apart from the gaming model that was the skeleton-in-the-closet of life insurance. Neo-liberals, however, by encouraging insurance policyholders to expose their investments to the speculative hazards of the stock market, effectively restored this old sense of gaming to insurance – just as they were simultaneously transforming gambling itself into an acceptable 'industry' (Dixon, 1991).

Thus, while leaders such as Margaret Thatcher (1993) have made much of the idea that neo-liberals are restoring such Victorian virtues as thrift, in some ways nothing could be further from the truth. Thrift and financial speculation, at least in the lives of working class people, were at polar ends of the Victorian moral spectrum. There is, thus, little that is Victorian, albeit much held to be 'virtuous', about current promotion of the speculative life insurance market, mass participation in stock and futures markets, and generalised acceptance of 'responsible' gambling. If these are now the institutions of thrift, then indeed the meaning of this term has changed radically since Victorian times.

Chapter 7
Risk, Crime Control and Criminal Justice

The advent of 1984 led to a great deal of speculation and introspection about how far the West (as it then was) had moved down to road to Orwell's dystopian world of Big Brother and the surveillance society. In one of the most perceptive commentaries on the implications of 1984 for criminology, Stan Cohen remarked that the Orwellian drama had not been realised in the way imagined. The individual had ceased to be the concern of an emerging generation of criminology, criminal justice and social control. Rather:

> [w]hat is being monitored is behaviour (or the physiological correlates of emotion and behaviour). No one is interested in inner thoughts ... 'the game is up' for all policies directed to the criminal as an individual, either in terms of detection (blaming and punishing) or causation (finding motivational or causal chains) ... The talk now is about 'spatial' and 'temporal' aspects of crime, about systems, behaviour sequences, ecology, defensible space ... target hardening ... (1985, pp 146–48)

In his view we were on the cusp of a new wave of what Cohen described as 'actuarial' or risk-based control. Retrospectively, actuarial justice and penology have not emerged as the sole alternatives to modernist crime control and corrections (Simon and Feeley, 1995, p 166; Garland, 1995). Cohen himself regarded it as only one trend among several others, including retributive and restitutional justice, and it is clear that these alternative trends have become very influential in the succeeding decades. Yet there can be no doubt that in most jurisdictions, and in diverse areas of practice, risk-based justice has become a presence.

While accurate in his general assessment, Cohen could do no more than reflect upon his times. The mid-1980s were a period in which 'nothing works' was still an influential philosophy of corrections. A conservative New Right politics strongly influenced the shape of neo-liberal governance, and was hostile to 'welfare' interventions for offenders and explanations that attributed crime to criminogenic social conditions. Punishment and 'just deserts' were promoted. Victims began to reappear as the wronged party, and government increasingly accepted what Floud and Young (1982), in their influential report, saw as a need for offenders, rather than victims, to bear the burden of crime risks. Criminology began to reflect such changes, as with the emergence of disciplines such as victimology and perspectives such as Left Realist criminology (for example, Kinsey and Young, 1986) that centred victims rather than offenders. State agencies such as the British Home Office began investigating the potential for 'environmental criminology' and 'defensible spaces' (Mayhew et al, 1979). Other arriviste approaches that focused on situations and opportunities, such as routine activity theory (Cohen and Felson, 1979), provided a foundation for analysis that removed the 'caused' offender and social pathology even from the domain of criminological theory.

In this environment, Cohen's vision rightly identified risk-based governance of crime with approaches that were behaviourist and spatial, that rejected social analysis and therapeutic interventions, that were increasingly uninterested in offenders *per se*. Still widely influential 20 years later, such approaches and techniques are the focus of the first part of this chapter – particularly actuarial justice, risk-based policing and situational crime prevention. Outside Britain and the USA, such shifts in crime control were often registered less strongly. Perhaps this was because in such countries as Canada, Australia and France a social democratic politics was not as effectively marginalised by New Right mobilisations of neo-liberal strategies. But even in such countries, the last few years have witnessed a certain turning back of the tide in the direction of 'social' interventions in the governance of crime. With respect to risk techniques, actuarial approaches have melded with, and in some instances been overtaken by, approaches concerned with social risk factors such as poor housing, educational disadvantage and chronic unemployment. As Clarke (1992, p 29) has noted, even the situational crime-prevention brief of the Home Office had begun, by the early 1990s, to expand to incorporate 'an agenda of "softer" social measures' such as youth services, family intervention and community development. As I will suggest later, one of the consequences of this has been a change in the political significance of welfare politics and the strategies of risk. Whereas critical scholars have been concerned that risk-based government is displacing modernist 'welfare' and therapeutic responses to crime (for example, Garland, 2001), the signs now point to risk and welfare techniques being melded together into new assemblages. The distinction that now becomes more critical is not that between welfare versus risk. Rather it is between those risk-based strategies that are inclusive in their aims and effects (which would include most of the welfare-risk hybrids), and those which are exclusionary and seek to reduce risk by merely isolating and incapacitating those identified as risk creators.

Situational crime prevention, neo-liberalism and the New Right

As Cohen suggests, situational crime prevention may be understood as almost quintessentially 'actuarial'. It deals hardly at all with individual offenders, is uninterested in the causes of crime, and generally is agnostic toward correctional policies and practices. Its concern is entirely with opportunity reduction as crime prevention. In the 1980s this identified it with a variety of approaches hostile to the 'welfare sanction' and social crime prevention. Thus, in a fairly aggressive self-description, the National Crime Prevention Institute (1986, p 18) outlined the following basic assumptions of what it grandly called 'the contemporary perspective' in criminology:

- prevention (and not rehabilitation) should be the major concern of criminologists;
- no one is sure how to rehabilitate offenders;
- punishment and/or imprisonment may be relevant in controlling certain offenders;
- criminal behaviour can be controlled primarily through the direct alteration of the environment of potential victims;

- crime control programs must focus on crime before it occurs rather than afterward;
- as criminal opportunity is reduced, so too will be the number of criminals.

By the mid-1980s situational crime prevention had achieved considerable acceptance in Britain, the United States, Australia and elsewhere (Bottoms, 1990; Tilley, 2002). Its promoters claimed that this reflected its superiority over social (sociological and psychological) approaches to crime control; but the rapidity of its rise to prominence can scarcely be attributed to demonstrated evidence of its superiority over correctional penology, causal criminology and 'social' crime prevention (in the form of community development and so on). Were this so, then it is difficult to understand the retention of such social approaches, as in France and parts of Australia, and Canada. Rather, what emerged was a political struggle over the definitions and the criteria of failure and success.

This may be seen in several ways. First, advocates of situational crime prevention took rising crime rates as evidence of the failure of traditional sociological and psychological criminology (for example, Geason and Wilson, 1988; 1989).[1] Yet while this proved to be a politically persuasive argument, it was scarcely an indisputable fact. Between the 1960s and 1980s sociological criminology had fundamentally challenged the validity of crime rates in this respect, and there was little agreement on the issue. The meaning and validity of crime rates was, in other words, part of the politics of failure rather than a neutral gauge for measuring efficiency.[2] Secondly, the assault on social criminology's effectiveness, even where telling, could readily be blunted by the argument that at no point were its insights translated properly into practice. 'Failure' is always attributable to the mode of implementation rather than to the policy itself (Miller and Rose, 1990). Thirdly, situational crime prevention's own claims to success were undermined by counterclaims that it achieved merely the displacement of crime to less secure targets (for example, Cornish and Clarke, 1986). Years later, debate continues over the adequacy of assessing its costs and benefits (Welsh and Farrington, 1999). Perhaps more vitally, it was countered that it reacts only to symptoms and thus fails to address the enduring social problems that crime merely manifests (King, 1991; Bottoms, 1990). Tellingly, this critique has been revived and subsequently has been accepted by many current post-New Right programs including that of New Labour in Britain (Matthews and Pitts, 2001). What is clear is

---

1 Such a view, for example, was promoted by the Australian Institute of Criminology:

   The traditional approach to crime prevention has been to try to identify the social and psychological causes of crime and to attempt to remedy these deficiencies by treating the individual offender and/or designing special educational, recreational and employment services for groups regarded as being at risk. The escalating crime rate suggests that this approach is not working. (Geason and Wilson, 1989, p 1)

   An alternative is 'situational crime prevention'. It rests on two assumptions: that the criminal is a rational decision-maker who only goes ahead with a crime where the benefits outweigh the costs or risks; and the opportunity for crime must be there (Geason and Wilson, 1988, p 1).

2 Such debates are extremely complex. The position on the Left was confused by the infusion of a qualified respect for crime rates as understood by Left Realists (Maclean, 1991). More orthodox criminologists could not agree even as to whether crime rates were rising or falling (Steffensmeier and Harer, 1987) and many other commentators from social criminology retained their very critical stance toward the entire exercise (Greenberg, 1990).

that in the 1980s, the two approaches rather ceased to converse – for the goals of each appeared misguided to the other, and the already disputed criteria of success therefore lost the semblance of shared standards.

Such debates are endless, and continue to the present (for example, Garland and Sparks, 2000). They reveal only that the politics of success and failure normally are struggles over the status of criteria, and can rarely be reduced to any universally-accepted scale of relative success. If this is the case, then the question of why situational crime prevention proved so influential a technique will need to be answered in terms of its relationship to political programmes and strategies, and especially to those then in ascendance. This suggests that we examine the affinity between New Right governance and the features of situational crime prevention as they were valorised at the time. The primary affinities would appear to reside in the general emphases of both an increased allocation of 'activity' and responsibility to citizens – in this case to victims and offenders – and the correlative erosion of 'welfare' style interventions. While it is not at all necessary for situational crime prevention to be set in hostile opposition to social forms of crime prevention and even welfare sanctions, this was certainly the way it was valorised by its key advocates in the 1980s.

Situational crime prevention destroys the biographical individual as a category of criminological knowledge – but the criminal does not disappear. Opportunities only exist in relation to potential criminals who convert open windows into windows of opportunity for crime. Approaching crime in this way, situational crime prevention replaces the biographical criminal with its polar opposite – the abstract and universal 'abiographical' individual – the 'rational choice' actor (see also Geason and Wilson, 1989; Heal and Laycock, 1986; National Crime Prevention Institute, 1986). This abstract entity thinks in cost-benefit terms – weighing up the risks, potential gains and potential costs – committing an offence only when the benefits are perceived to outweigh the losses. Indeed, when Clarke (1992, p 13) summarised the basic techniques of situational crime prevention, he drew these together under three headings related to offenders' decisions: 'increasing the effort'; 'increasing the risks'; and 'reducing the rewards'. Bentham's felicity calculus, and the notion of freedom that it embodies, is at the heart of situational crime prevention.

If crime is performed by free and rational agents, then the relevance of social and causal criminology is fundamentally curtailed – with two major consequences. First, it silences the implicit and explicit critique of social institutions and structure mounted by much social criminology, and scorned by the New Right. Thus as Tilley (2002, p 19) points out with respect to the Home Office Crime Prevention Unit in this period, there was a:

> ... political dimension to the conception of crime prevention that it embodied ... Several matters which could, in other circumstances, have played a large part in crime prevention were not considered. For example, questions of large-scale social structural change affecting the class, 'race' and gender distribution of power, the decriminalisation of some behaviour, and much crime committed by the powerful, did not find a place in the crime prevention agenda, in part because this is set by the political and bureaucratic context in which criminologists in the Home Office work.

Secondly, as Foucault made clear, the 'criminological labyrinth' was constructed around the assumption that if crime is caused, this reduces the personal responsibility of offenders (1977, p 252). Exactly this perception was, as Garland (1985) has noted, behind the opposition of many conservatives to the formation of welfare-based sanctions at the turn of the 20th century. Elimination of cause and social pathology from the discourse of crime obviously restores individual responsibility and has allied effects on punishment. The emergence of situational criminology as a major presence may thus be aligned with a wide array of more punitive and 'just deserts' penal stances that were also emerging or reviving at the time.

If situational crime prevention short-circuits the link between criminality, social causation, and discourses of social justice, then it might be expected that the 'victim' becomes the centre of concern. In some sense this is undoubtedly the case, as the rhetoric of 'protecting the public' then rang – and still rings – loudly (Floud and Young, 1982; Home Office, 1989; 1996). However, just as the offenders are disconnected from the political dimensions of their existence, so too are the victims, for victims like offenders appear as rational choice actors, as responsible and free individuals. Prevention increasingly became the responsibility of the victim and permeated crime prevention thinking at all levels, although it has moderated of late. At one level, this position emerged no doubt because it reduces pressure on police forces, which have not noticeably reduced crime victimisation and which are therefore vulnerable to political pressure. Thus, a senior official of the Australian Insurance Council noted that 'severely restricted police resources and the sheer frequency of crime, means that any improvement in the situation will rely heavily on property owners accepting responsibility for their own property and valuables' (Hall, 1986, p 243). At broader political levels similar arguments were being presented for much the same reasons. Responding to news that crime rates in Britain had reached record levels, 'the Prime Minister, Mrs Thatcher, blamed a large portion of the crimes on the victims' carelessness. "We have to be careful that we ourselves don't make it easy for the criminal" she said' (*The Age*, 28 September 1990).

In this discourse, not only does responsibility and thus critique shift, but so too do costs. Dispersal of security practice and costs – to be seen in the trend toward private security agencies, the market for home security devices, domestic security practices, neighbourhood watch schemes and insurance – generate the rudiments of a user-pays system of policing security, and fit well with the imagery of active citizenship.[3] It was assumed that such a citizenry would come to see the justice in this:

---

3 A further element in emergent crime prevention practices consistent with the New Right credo is the focus 'cost effectiveness' and 'cost-benefit' analysis. Thus, eg, *Young People and Crime* (Potas *et al*, 1989), produced by the Australian Institute of Criminology as part of its series of publications dealing with crime prevention, ultimately asserts that no programme of crime prevention should be established without a prior and rigorous cost-effectiveness assessment (for which it duly provides a model). Indeed, for the more aggressively entrepreneurial versions of crime prevention:

This does not mean merely that it is important to keep the costs of security as low as possible (consistent with good security), it also means that he [ie the crime prevention analyst] should apply his knowledge of risk-management in as creative a way as possible, looking for opportunities for profit or other benefit as well as other ways to minimise loss. (National Crime Prevention Institute, 1986, p 51)

The general public's apathy about self-protection arises mainly from ignorance of the means of protection, and a perception that somebody else – 'the Government' or insurance companies – bears most of the cost of theft and vandalism. The community is beginning to realise however that crime rates are rising despite increased penalties, that the judicial system cannot cope, and that it is the individual who eventually foots the bill for crime through increased taxes for expanded police forces and more jails, and through higher insurance premiums. (Geason and Wilson, 1989, p 9)[4]

In this process, security increasingly was to become the responsibility of private individuals who through the pursuit of self-interest, and liberated from enervating reliance on the state to provide for them, will participate in the creation of the new order. Even so, it was not simply assumed that citizens would be able to take on these roles by sheer effort of will. On the one hand, extensive programmes provided by state bureaucracies such as the Home Office, police forces, insurance organisations, schools and local government, educated and 'skilled' the public in the knowledge and practices of situational crime prevention (O'Malley, 1991). Organisations such as Neighbourhood Watch provided their members with local crime data so they could assess their level of risk and act accordingly. Police began to form a multitude of 'partnerships in policing' with local 'communities', and through these means to provide a stimulus to participation and self-help (Crawford, 1997). In the more optimistic visions, these partnerships and the new spirit of public responsibility they engendered were to reflect a vision that harked back to the Peelite model of 'preventative police'. Police, it was argued, should shed many of the roles that illegitimately had been shifted onto their shoulders. Increasingly they would liaise with the public in a seamless web of information flows that would allow the constabulary to perform the role for which it was originally founded: prevention (O'Malley and Palmer, 1996).

Policing the risk society

However fanciful some of these ideas from the 1980s appear, changes were already underway that reflected an increasing focus of police work on risk-related and preventative information. Writing at the same time as Cohen, Nancy Reichman argued that police and related security organisations (for example, the Inland Revenue Service) were changing in risk-related ways. For Reichman (1986, p 155) 'information is central to effective risk management. To better predict offences and to interdict them before they can occur, social control must be "front loaded". Greater and greater amounts of personal data need to be collected and analysed on the behaviour of all individuals not just those under suspicion'. Of course, the police had always been gatherers of security-related information, and certainly had passed such information to the insurance industry for some time (O'Malley, 1991). But the emphasis was changing. In Ericson and Haggerty's view (1997, p 41), by the 1990s the role of information broker had become the 'main task' of the police. Perhaps,

---

4 Of course, what this kind of argument tends to forget is that 'user pays' models generally disadvantage the poor. In keeping with the tendency to abandon social justice, crime prevention of this sort – through the progressive underdevelopment of public sector services – tends to leave the weak to fend for themselves (see O'Malley, 1989; Sparks, 2001).

more precisely, the police – together with the insurance industry – had become the key institutions in a security communications network.

This change places demands upon police forces that are no longer consistent with their former principal roles of law enforcement, social support and order maintenance. The bulk of police time is taken up with information gathering, form filling and processing. In turn, however, the humble bureaucratic nature of these activities disguises their importance. The demands for security information are reflected in the official coding of incidents and situations in terms of risk. The most vital mechanism for producing this transformation, as Ericson and Haggerty make clear, has been the development and increasingly mandated use of forms that meet the risk criteria set by centralised security institutions (1997, p 430). Rather than reflecting traditional police concerns, these forms categorise events in terms of 'tightly formatted, fixed choice risk classifications'. As such, they almost ensure that whatever the orientation of the police officer, and no matter what the other dimensions of an incident or outcomes of an investigation or inspection, information is inscribed and transmitted in the form of risk and security data.[5]

The ascendancy of situational crime prevention and the ongoing risk-transformation of police would appear to be closely related. In part this is simply because much police work is about situational security: much of what they do involves reporting on 'criminogenic situations' (Garland, 1996). As such, both reflect Cohen's vision of crime control characterised by 'spatial and temporal aspects of crime, systems, behaviour sequences, ecology, defensible space and target hardening'. Even so, the path-breaking research of Ericson and Haggerty focused on Canada, and while it is likely that their findings reflect developments elsewhere, this cannot be taken for granted. Instead, the prevalence of this shift can only be deduced from analyses of the course of crime prevention in other countries, where the same political and administrative imperatives do not seem to have gripped quite so effectively.

In France, as Crawford (2002) points out, crime prevention also expanded greatly in the 1980s, but it did so in a quite different fashion from that reviewed above. Rather than abandoning or ignoring causal approaches to crime it embraced them. It suggested that exclusion of certain groups – notably marginal youth and certain immigrant groups – was a fundamental criminogenic problem and that crime could only be tackled effectively by programmes of inclusion. Principles of integration and solidarity were mobilised, for example in the Bonnemaison programme. This asserted a distinctly social stance that completely contrasted with the Thatcher regime's project in Britain. Causal analysis was still regarded as central to understanding problems and guiding interventions in France. For Crawford, this divergence was partly a reflection of the socialist politics of the Mitterand government. But the persistence of social and inclusive concerns persisted beyond this socialist era into a period of neo-liberal governance. With the exception of the National Front, *all* political parties have remained committed to a problematic of

---

5   Nevertheless, as Kemshall's (1998) work indicates, staff may sabotage risk-based schedules by entering their subjective or professional assessments as if they had been decided upon in terms of risk criteria.

social solidarity and inclusion. Not only political concerns therefore, but also a different tradition of governance appears to have shaped these policies. In Crawford's view, such factors include a French vision of the state as a 'moral unifier' and as necessarily involved in integration and practices of social identity. It also incorporates a 'deep cultural attachment to their metropolitan centres' (2002, p 235). Together, these valorise a collectivist tradition that inhibits the neo-liberal tendency both to devolve responsibility to individuals and to valorise their role as 'active' and 'enterprising' individuals over their place as 'citizens'.

In such accounts it is difficult to untangle the relative contributions of broader causal explanations concerning national culture from prevailing political visions. But in the Australian state of Victoria, under a Labor government, the Bonnemaison scheme found a fertile soil to which to be transplanted. There, situational crime prevention was integrated quite explicitly with a Labor government focus on social justice, and was linked with approaches to crime prevention that addressed the problems of marginalised youth, poverty and gender (Sandon, 1991a; 1991b). Likewise, feminist critiques of the Home Office-inspired crime prevention programs (for example, Stanko, 1990; Walklate, 2002) – which stressed the failure to identify issues such as sexual assault by intimates – were rapidly taken up in this context.[6] The resulting policies have extended well beyond narrowly defensive and privatised risk practices and policies. Beginning in the early 1990s measures embedded preventative techniques in socialising reforms, concentrating on 'reducing violence against women by targeting the involvement of the community to change male behaviour and attitudes, empower women in unsafe situations and change community perceptions and understandings about violence toward women' (Thurgood, 1991).

Crawford (2002, p 234) has suggested, with respect to crime prevention policies, that the 'contrasts between the experiences of many mainland European countries, notably France, and those of the United States and the United Kingdom raise the question of the extent to which the latter represent atypical rather than typical political responses'. To this could be added contrasts with other countries, such as Australia, Canada and New Zealand. While embracing many elements of neo-liberalism, such nations retained a considerable element of the 'social' in their risk-based responses to crime. There is, in principle at least, no reason why situational crime prevention need be set against social forms of crime prevention. In all of these countries both forms of crime prevention were integrated into a compatible whole. Following from this, it appears that the shaping of risk-based techniques has much

---

6 Consider, eg, Lake, 1990, p 21:

In one sense women have gained a measure of freedom. A real measure of freedom. Yet ... everywhere we are confined and I mean physically, mentally, psychologically confined. We know because we are told often enough that we must not walk the streets at night. We must not now, it seems, travel on trains. Or public transport. Nor must we walk to dimly lit car parks. We must also every night securely lock ourselves up at home. And even then, of course, our security is illusory, for men force their way through windows into one's house or, they may already live in one's house ... most domestic violence is committed on women known to the men who assault them, that is, it is committed on their wives, friends, daughters, sisters.

to do with the character of political regimes and, perhaps no less, with the habits of governance and traditions of social integration or solidarity. The importance of this point becomes still clearer when we consider 'actuarial justice'.

Actuarial justice. Otherness and the neo-conservative colouring of risk

Actuarial justice has been identified as the ascendant strategy of 'risk-based' criminal justice (Feeley and Simon, 1992; 1994). In this form, risk-based justice is predictive and statistical, and is systematically and managerially arranged in terms of internal or system-focused criteria of efficiency rather than external measures (that is, speed of throughput versus reduction in recidivism). It also incorporates forms of knowledge and practice that reduce the interventions of justice to merely incapacitating techniques that displace punitive, re-integrative, correctional or deterrent strategies. Examples are said to include the reappearance of curfews as a technique to manage 'at risk' groups, times and places. Another is the emergence of 'three strikes' laws that abandon proportional sentencing and individual justice in favour of formula-based sentencing according to risk. Yet one more often cited is the massive expansion of prison warehousing and of home detention as purely incapacitating measures. All these, and more, have been examined as part of the formation of knowledge and power that is actuarial justice. Accordingly, most academic criminology has regarded the emergence of actuarial justice, and even of risk more generally, as a blight on criminal justice (Hudson, 2000; Baumann, 2000; Kempf-Leonard and Peterson, 2000; Miller, 2001). Risk appears, explicitly or implicitly, as a negative turn that undermines the modest advances made toward reconstructive, inclusive and re-integrative criminal justice during the middle ('welfare state') part of the 20th century. By centring insecurity and threat, the governmental grid of risk is seen to work though negation: certain persons are defined primarily in terms of their purely negative and dangerous status as threats to others (victims), and accordingly are merely neutralised and segregated in new gulags of incapacitation.

As is often the fate of major breakthroughs, Feeley and Simon's work on risk in criminal law and penology has been followed by a rush to identify confirming instances, and in the process the specificity of actuarial justice has become something of a casualty. Actuarial justice does not exhaust the play of risk in the field of criminal law and criminal justice, and significant distinctions among strategies of risk-based justice have tended to be overlooked. In this respect, Feeley and Simon themselves provide many insights and observations about the nature and genealogy of actuarial justice that should have merited greater caution and finer analytic investigation than subsequently has been accorded. Specifically, actuarial justice appears to be a categorical and exclusionary strategy of risk. In this it is quite distinct from inclusive and restorative risk technologies and strategies such as those developed in France, and from more therapeutic and clinical regimes such as drug harm minimisation (O'Malley, 1999a). Actuarial justice, it would appear, is profoundly shaped by, and allied with, a tradition of American political and moral conservatism – particularly via the medium of the political invention of the underclass as the primary problem to be governed through criminal justice.

Actuarial justice and the politics of exclusion

In their discussion of the context and shaping of actuarial justice, Feeley and Simon go to some lengths to emphasise that 'actuarial thinking represents a deeper "pre-political" thought that cannot easily be associated with conventional political labels' (1994, p 190). At best, they argue, politics has some impact in shaping actuarial justice, and different political perspectives will employ actuarial justice 'somewhat differently'. This runs counter to the opinion that relates actuarial justice to conservatism. Feeley and Simon point out that while conservatism is often associated with actuarial justice, traditionally it is associated with a deep-rooted juridical individualism that does not sit well with the statistical and categorical techniques of risk-based justice. The examples of political influence that Feeley and Simon do detect, perhaps in keeping with this sceptical stance, are thus rather indirect – the major instance being the possibility that conservative 'lock-em up' policies created penal population pressures that facilitated the institutionalisation of actuarial techniques.

In their analysis there is thus little or no constitutive role for politics. This seems surprising at first glance, because the rise of actuarial justice historically coincides with the rise of profoundly anti-correctional politics hostile to what Garland (1985) refers to as the 'welfare sanction'. It sought to empty prisons of social workers, reduce costs and introduce 'truth in sentencing' – but not because of promotion of a pre-political agenda of risk. Rather, it reflected a variety of reasons including a greater acceptance of deterrence as a valid penal philosophy, a hostility to the social sciences and the helping professions, and a concern with fiscal accountability and cost effectiveness (O'Malley, 1992; Rose, 1996a). At face value it would seem to many that such political pressures very likely contributed to the formation of tariff-based sentencing and the evacuation of correctional content from prisons, transforming them into 'cost effective' warehouses for incapacitation. In other words, these critical elements of actuarial justice might have been an explicitly political creation.

However, the weakness of this argument, in turn, is that conservative politics has also headed in other directions, more punitive than 'risk-based' in appearance – notably the current array of 'emotive and ostentatious' punishments such as chain gangs and 'tough' prisons (Pratt, 2000a; 2000b). Likewise, we could add that neo-liberalism would appear to have fostered potentially progressive forms of rehabilitation – including the delivery of 'risk-needs' based services in prisons (in which risk factors are used to shape correctional programmes for individual prisoners) and the development of 'enterprising prisoner' schemes (in which prisoners are given responsibility for managing their own reform). As this latter example suggests, in some ways mere incapacitation sits ill with the neo-liberal visions of the active subject and switched-on capitalism (O'Malley, 1999b). Hence, Feeley and Simon could be supported in their claim that politics are no more than a facilitating condition, rather than a major constitutive influence, in the formation of actuarial justice.

Such an argument certainly reveals weakness in the 'political' case, if by that term we mean – as do Feeley and Simon – that the 'pendulum swings' to the Right and the Left of the political field. Yet it reveals an equally difficult, indeed identical, problem for their case. That is: if the process is merely technical or pre-political, why does risk take the specific shape of actuarial justice when there are many other risk-based alternatives to warehousing, such as the identification and treatment of offenders' criminogenic 'risk-needs' in prison? To answer this question, we need to examine elements of the genealogy of actuarial justice proposed by Feeley and Simon.

In discussing the possible impact of the law and economics movement in this genealogy, Feeley and Simon differentiate 'economic' thinking from 'actuarial' thinking (1994, p 189). Both, they stress, emphasise the utilitarian purposes of punishment over the moral purpose. But an 'economic' approach treats the offender as a rational choice actor, whereas actuarial justice 'treats the offender as *inert*, from the point of view of influencing decision making' (1994, p 189; emphasis added). Economic reasoning thus is associated with deterrence rather than incapacitation, and incapacitation is identified as the 'pure' actuarial response. But what is 'pure' actuarialism? For example, if by-the-numbers risk reduction is its characteristic, then risk-needs and preventative interventions have been argued to generate superior results to incapacitation (see O'Malley, 2001). If it is cost-effective risk management, then does this not become an *economic* actuarial argument? And in any case, targeted long-term 'empowerment' has been claimed by some as more cost effective than incapacitation (Rand Corporation, 1998; Welsh and Farrington, 1999). In short, it is not clear on what criterion incapacitation can appear as pure or undiluted actuarialism. The point, rather, would appear to be that, as Ewald (1991, p 198) observes, the technology of risk is highly abstract, so that any applications in an institutional setting 'are not the application of a technology of risk; they are always just one of its possible applications'.

Further, it would be difficult to argue that other statistically oriented preventative technologies – such as situational crime prevention – are somehow not 'actuarial' or not fundamentally risk-based simply because they deploy a rational choice actor as their subject. This point is by no means trivial or marginal to our understanding of the character of actuarial justice. As David Garland has argued (1996; 2001), the rational choice actor is the subject of what he terms a 'criminology of the self'. This is a criminology that defines crime as 'normal' in the sense that anyone could be a criminal under the right conditions – the criminal is not a distinctive type of person. Thus Felson and Clarke stress, for situational crime prevention, that 'nobody is exempt from the temptation to commit crime since human weaknesses are widespread and not confined to any one segment of the population' (1997, p 200). Consequently, situational crime prevention and other rational choice-based approaches do not seek to exclude types or categories of persons, or sectors of the population. Rather, they seek to deter abstract and universal potential offenders by rendering the effort and risk of offending greater than the likely benefits. In this way they converge with judicial deterrence; but they do so, as Garland suggests, by seeking to govern 'criminogenic situations', that is (more generally) to focus on the risks associated with environmental conditions, rather than on categories or types of person (Garland, 1996).

What does this tell us about the specific risk-centred assemblage that is actuarial justice? The critical point again is made by Feeley and Simon (1994, p 189) when they note that 'the rise of incapacitation and the other instruments of Actuarial Justice [are] a reflection of social forces ... [that push] a large portion of the population out of the range of normal economic signals'. In short, deterrence will not work for this social category, and thus actuarial justice is to be distinguished from situational crime prevention and related technologies of risk that focus on universal and abstract subjects. In this way Feeley and Simon see the distinction between deterrent models and actuarial justice as critical to their case. For them, actuarial justice works on the social category comprising the largely Black and Hispanic 'underclass', seen as permanently excluded from upward social mobility and economic integration by the effects of a global restructuring of the economy (see also Baumann, 2000). Not only is deterrence imagined as unworkable for this category but reintegration and rehabilitation are also rendered irrelevant, for there is nothing to reintegrate into. The heavy industrial and related economic sector that once provided for this category's employment has – as a consequence of globalisation – disappeared from the local economy. What, therefore, is installed is a government strategy designed quite specifically to contain this irredeemable, irremediable and dangerous 'other' population.

Looked at in this way, in line with the general tenor of Feeley and Simon's own analysis, actuarial justice emerges not as a pure form of pre-political risk management. Rather, it is a specific actuarial strategy designed and assembled for a specific governmental – and in this sense, political – purpose. In contrast to the risk technologies that deploy the universal rational actor as their subject, the subjects of this strategy are neither abstract-universal, nor 'normal', nor subject to normalisation. To these others – that are not like us and cannot become like us – the specific strategies of categorically-exclusionary risk are applied.

Despite the realist dimensions of their underclass argument, equally strong is the stress Feeley and Simon place on the invented nature of this category. That is, the underclass is a governmental category originally created within a 'critical' sociology but appropriated subsequently by (largely conservative) politicians and commentators. Indeed, I would add to this argument the claim that the underclass appears as the product of a neo-liberal political rationality. The same strategies of global governance that are implicated in relocating the underclass members' means of employment to the Third World – in the name of competition and efficiency – are also responsible for inventing the spectre of welfare dependency, and of welfare as a fiscal crisis of the state. The underclass was invented and deployed in the US at the same time as welfare was being withdrawn as 'counterproductive and costly'. It was introduced in relation to a population that now could be defined as having become 'dependent', as having lost the will to work and the ability to make an enterprise of their lives.

A governmental invention that, on the other hand, defined members of this population as victims of global restructuring, as Baumann (2000) sees them, could well have rendered them candidates for welfare inclusion and 'empowerment' rather than exclusion and incapacitation. This, for example, seems to have been the response in France with respect to an analogous, high-crime immigrant population. This is also the case in states such as Britain where neo-liberal constructs of the 'excluded' mobilise discourses of welfare state 'poverty traps' and promote 'individual responsibility' (for example, Giddens, 2000, pp 102–06). While risk-based justice has a considerable purchase, especially at the 'deep end' of offending (Kemshall and Maguire, 2001), the formation of a Social Exclusion Unit in Britain reflects a response that identifies crime as linked with inadequate housing, structural unemployment and other fundamental social conditions. Whatever its inadequacies (Matthews and Pitts, 2001), the response reflects a fundamentally different approach to that of actuarialism, and may help to explain why, as Garland (1995) and Pratt (2000a) have pointed out, actuarial justice has scarcely spread outside the US. Even where some elements of this model have been adopted, key elements of the approach are distinct from its US counterpart. For example, in Australia's Northern Territory there was a brief flirtation with 'three strikes' legislation. While it was scrapped in 2001 following intense criticism for targeting Aborigines, the correctional stress was not on incapacitation but on 'culturally appropriate' interventions that provided educational and vocational courses, with specific goals of 'reducing recidivism by increasing employment prospects', reduction of alcohol and drug related harm, developing 'restorative justice' and the development of 'partnership' programs designed to reintegrate offenders into their communities (www.ourmessage.org.au). Likewise, risk-based sanctioning has been developed for repeat sex and violent offenders in many Australian states.[7] Whatever the emphasis on risk and its place in assigning extended terms of imprisonment, treatment and therapy programs remain critical elements of the correctional programs set up under this umbrella (Pratt, 1998).

Finally, it is critical to recognise that the strategy and techniques of categorically-exclusionary risk have subsequently broadened in the US since actuarial justice was first identified. They have been applied to other social categories that fall specifically under the umbrella of irremediable and dangerous otherness. Persistent violent and sexual offenders are the prime candidates. They have become subject to the array of 'Megan's laws', enacted in the majority of US states. These, in various ways, notify the community of the identity of former offenders, often making public their address, record and photos for purposes of identification. As Simon himself subsequently has noted, they represent the expression of 'an entitlement to cruelty' (2001). The veneer of technical 'neutrality' of actuarial justice is transformed, in risk-based Megan's laws, into a politics of vengeance:

> ... the development of modern institutions, particularly the prison, was aimed at displacing popular emotions from the centre of punishment by extending the control of state based professionals. From a spectacle of solidarity between state and the people against their common enemies, punishment became a vehicle for inculcating habits of order suitable to a democratic society. Megan's law is a shift away from this process of modernisation. Starting with its name, and with the central role given to local prosecutors in applying the risk classification, Megan's law advertises itself as a new hybrid of public and private vengeance. (Simon, 1998, p 464)

Thus, while Megan's laws are similar in some respects to such other risk strategies as situational crime prevention, and while certainly mobilised in the name of potential victims taking 'rational' and 'reasonable' steps to protect themselves (Levi, 2000), these risk strategies are distinct. They are aimed at a category of subjects who

---

7 In Victoria, the Sentencing Act 1991 (Vic) s 6A proscribes extended imprisonment for sex and violence offenders. This is also the case in Queensland (Penalties and Sentences Act 1992 (Qld) s 163); Western Australia (Sentencing Act 1995 (WA) Part 14); and Tasmania (Sentencing Act 1997 (Tas) s 19).

are politically and governmentally demonised and excluded. These people are not 'inert' – as Feeley and Simon characterise the subjects of actuarial justice. They are the 'other' and, in this case, are characterised governmentally as 'monstrous' (Simon, 1998). Significantly, Simon's reference to this movement away from modernist penology (represented in Megan's laws) indicates that these responses are like those directed at the underclass in a key respect: they abandon the modernist project of socially inclusive reform and adopt a technology of categorical exclusion. Perhaps, therefore, thinking in terms of a specifically US version of 'conservative neo-liberalism' makes sense of that country's greater acceptance of categorical exclusion in the form of actuarial justice and its enthusiastic embracing of Megan's laws. The moral authoritarianism of the War on Drugs may also link with this. So too may the fact that – within the 'developed world' at least – the majority of the more 'emotive and ostentatious' legal sanctions discussed in the literature, such as chain gangs, the death penalty, military boot camps and mass warehousing, *remain* largely or completely characteristics of American criminal justice (Pratt, 2000a).

'Socialised risk': survival and transformation

It was noted in earlier chapters that in many countries affected by neo-liberal politics the welfare apparatus was not so much abandoned or pared back to a rump as transformed to suit the contours of neo-liberal politics (Dean, 1995a). Thus the unemployed have not *in toto* been cut off from assistance, but linked with it by contracts of mutual obligation, as discussed in Chapter 3. Images of the 'death of the social' (Rose, 1996b), associated with 'commodification' and 'privatisation' of risk, in earlier accounts (for example, O'Malley, 1992) were thus overstated. Linked with this, a second significant blind spot in earlier accounts of the transition to neo-liberal risk governance was the overemphasis on understanding the welfare state as constituted by 'social actuarialism' – in the form of social insurance, social engineering, the social wage and so on. While undeniably fundamental, this was only one aspect of welfare government. Other key characteristics were associated with the triumph of the positive human sciences and their deployment in the government of individuals. The survival of the welfare apparatus, albeit in a transformed condition, was thus linked with the survival – also in an altered condition – of the 'welfare' professions and their knowledges: psychiatry, social work and psychology in particular.

It may thus be better to identify a 'revised social' governmental environment as the outcome of neo-liberal assaults on the welfare state. This provided a foundation for developments in the 1990s – as in strategies such as the Third Way – that have sought to redevelop and expand social infrastructure in countries. In such revised social environments, foundations are available for the emergence of risk-based interventions in criminal justice that are inclusive and resourcing rather than merely exclusionary and incapacitating. This is not to suggest that these new risk practices are merely welfare in disguise. In virtually all cases there will have been some transformations effected under neo-liberalism, and in some cases these have reduced welfare practitioners to risk managers. Rather, it is to argue that the terrain is likely to be relatively unstable. In an environment favouring risk-based governance there will be the potential for the revised welfare knowledges and professions – or others – to capture risk techniques or to adapt them to 'social' agendas. Equally there is the potential for welfare techniques to be hollowed out into risk-based techniques whose purpose may be merely incapacitating or risk-reducing. In the United States, where the welfare state was perhaps most meagrely established and savagely assaulted, this instability may still be a characteristic. Welfare professionals are numerous and articulate in that country, there is a history of innovation in crime control, and state and metropolitan politics are diverse. So even there we might expect a wide array of species of risk-based governance, and extensive hybridity of forms, rather than the universalising of a 'pure' actuarialism or incapacitation.

To begin with, it is important to register the conversion of significant aspects of the work of welfare professionals into risk managerial and risk reduction roles. Rose (1998a), for example, has noted that 'in forensic psychiatry there has been a widespread shift away from dangerousness toward the assessment and management of risk. For psychiatric practice more generally the assessment, prediction and management of risk has become central to the new logics of community psychiatry'. Indeed, Rose suggests that risk has reshaped the mental health system such that psychiatric institutions 'are defined not in terms of cure or care, but in terms of the secure containment of risk' (1998a, p 184). In the criminal justice field there is little doubt that this process has occurred with respect to the work of probation officers and social workers. As Kemshall has argued, 'within the probation service ... risk is now the key organising principle for both practice activities and resource allocation' (1998, p 41; see also Kemshall and Maguire, 2002). To this end, probation officers are increasingly required to make decisions – for example about whether or not to release an offender – in terms of batteries of risk assessment schedules rather than in terms of their professional or clinical skills. In this, of course, there are many echoes of Feeley and Simon's discussion of the actuarial sentencing process and its displacement of probation and judicial expertise. Likewise, the 'risk of recidivism' instruments deployed by these professionals 'seek to increase the efficiency and effectiveness of resource allocation', a key theme in actuarial justice (Kemshall, 1998, p 57). However, at this point it becomes clear that such changes are not linked to mere incapacitation, as in actuarial justice. Rather, the primary purpose of many risk schedules (formally at least) is to assign offenders to the programmes and activities that will most effectively deal with their needs. In turn, part of this process is the assessment of which programmes operate most effectively to reduce recidivism. Together, these purposes converge in the development of 'risk-needs'

Put most simply, risk-needs (or 'criminogenic needs') are those needs of offenders that are defined as convergent with crime prevention. In the revised social environment, attention simply to the needs of offenders might smack too much of welfare interventions – of the provision of 'crutches' rather than of 'empowering'. The invention of 'risk-needs' enables provision of empowering services but within a rationality of measurable, or at least evidence-led, crime reduction. Now, as Hannah-Moffat (1999; 2001) has suggested, the emergence of such strategies cannot be attributed to welfare influences or resonance alone. With respect to Canadian prisons, the impact of feminist critiques – as with crime prevention – has been significant. During the 1990s the Canadian government took on board a series of critiques focused on the failure to produce women's prisons oriented to the needs of women rather than of men. The extensive remodelling of the women's prison regimes, however, has produced an 'unintentional hybrid'. Hannah-Moffat argues that:

> [e]merging in the correctional logic of the new women's prisons is that the concept of 'need' shifts from a vindication of a claim for resources (the feminist view) to a calculation of criminal potential (the risk of recidivism). Thus correctional strategies and programs now 'govern at a distance' by regulating women through their needs. Unlike past feminist narratives on women's needs that stress entitlement, the Correctional Service uses the language of 'needs' to facilitate responsibilisation. The prisoner is expected to 'cure' herself and manage her own risk by satisfying her criminogenic needs. (1999, p 84)

It may be, as Matthews and Pitts (2001, p 20) suggest, that this exemplifies a process in which risk assessment is disconnected from therapeutic or welfare interventions. Elsewhere in her analysis, Hannah-Moffat (1999, pp 74–76) certainly points to other translations in which risk-needs become indicators of criminal risk and thus point to further or intensified leverage for punitive intervention. This is clearest perhaps where prisoners are defined as in need of psychiatric intervention, or who are defined as having drug-related needs. But this is not a necessary pattern. To recognise such instances should not lead us to revert to models of the omniscient and omnicompetent state, or of an irresistible logic of risk. It is to point to government programmes as multivocal – of the interaction of diverse 'governmentalities' – as well as of planned assemblage by a single entity.

To pursue this in more detail, take the example of developmental psychology. The characteristic approaches of this discipline in the era of social welfare were modelled primarily in terms of pathologies requiring authoritative expert intervention that took over responsibility for the problem (cf O'Malley and Palmer, 1996). In current formulations, however, governmental emphasis is on the danger of such interventions producing powerlessness, apathy and passivity in interactions with welfare agency personnel. Instead, the emphasis is to be on 'accessibility', 'assistance', 'help', 'support' and 'empowerment'. Thus, with respect to the 'crime risk factor' of abuse, it is stressed that '[t]he professional focus on the medical model popularised in the 60s' has changed; now, 'the notion of community and neighbourhood services to assist vulnerable families with child rearing in order to diminish abuse is gathering momentum ... The thrust of our work has been maximising the empowerment of families' (Tolley and Tregeagle, 1998, pp 6–8). Despite these rhetorical shifts, the 'empowering' practices of this born-again discipline bear a very strong family resemblance to the interventions of the welfare era. They involve, for example, 'family support, early intervention, and home visiting programs' (National Crime Prevention, 1999a, p 17). Likewise, developmental psychology's list of crime-risk factors – 'family isolation', 'inadequate parenting', 'single parents', 'attachment difficulties', 'low self-esteem', 'poor social skills', 'poor cognitive skills' and so on, is seemingly identical to the list of causes of crime with which it worked under the welfare state. The preventative and rehabilitative agendas of the former era are thus reintroduced, ironically, amidst much fanfare, as 'new' and 'revolutionary' approaches to crime prevention (for example, Homel, 1998).

In addition, much developmental crime prevention of late has begun explicitly to identify as risk factors the kinds of 'social conditions' identified under welfare programmes, or social justice and social criminology. Consider the following:

> Children experience different levels and combinations of risk. Social and economic disadvantage, however, bring a host of associated risk factors for children and families. Conditions of poverty contribute to poor health and nutrition and increased levels of family stress. Children born into poverty are also at greater risk of experiencing discrimination and victimisation ... While there is much that children and families can accomplish by working together, additional financial resources and supports from governments and communities are necessary to reduce poverty and create environments that promote safety, gender equality and freedom from discrimination. (Crime Prevention Council of Canada, 1997, p 10)

The report goes on to recommend that a comprehensive crime prevention strategy provides 'educational, social and health services', and urges that it 'is essential that this strategy address child poverty' (1997, p 11). Perhaps this example is unusual in that it specifically discounts self-help and community governance, but the general tenor of its argument is not at all uncommon. The Australian National Crime Prevention (1999b, p 13) lists 'socio-economic disadvantage', 'population density and housing conditions', 'lack of support services' and 'social or cultural discrimination' among its crime related 'cultural and community factors'. The agenda, although situated within a risk discourse, gives expression to welfare-social rationalities. In so doing it begins to hint at social justice and certainly of the kinds of socially – rather than individually – ameliorative programmes that were associated with the welfare state (cf Stenson and Watt, 1999). In Britain, on a broader scale, this is of course implied in the New Labour rhetoric of being 'tough on the causes of crime'.

Reflecting the neo-liberal concern with cost effectiveness, almost without exception the programmes mentioned above propose strict evaluation. As noted, this is a technique that – because of its demand for demonstrable results in relatively short time frames – strongly restricts the scope of socially-oriented projects (Crawford, 2002). But even this, too, begins to break down in the new context. Proposals begin to emerge that advocate the formation of long-term and large-scale programmes addressing social conditions by proposing that each step can be evaluated as part of a long-term chain. Others emphasise that as developmental programs deal with children from birth (or before), then the term of evaluation has to cover a minimum period of 10 years, and frequently longer (for example, Everingham, 1998; Rand Corporation, 1998). Driven by the risk discourses and agendas generated by the born-again welfare disciplines, long-term, large-scale and long-range projects reappear. As Welsh and Farrington (1999, p 3) have pointed out, 'arguments such as "for every dollar spent, seven dollars are saved in the long run" have proved very powerful'. Such evaluations support the development of long-term 'social' strategies for preventing recidivism by deploying the accounting tools of neo-liberalism and, ironically, open the door for the return of socially-oriented rehabilitative or redistributive programmes.

In sum, the terrain is a now good deal less stable than would be supposed from a reading of the model of 1980s New Right neo-liberalism. Each of the points concerned can be thought of as points of contestation or of ambiguity and dilemmas in government. They are points of possible translation in which seemingly discarded elements are brought back by persistent disciplines and resistant (or at least inertial) groups following their own governmental agendas to re-socialise risk.

The invention of the 'protective factor'

Alongside the transformation of causes of crime into risk factors has come the invention of (positive) 'protective factors' – indeed, the category has become almost the partner of risk in recent work in the crime prevention field (for example, Farrington, 1994; Homel, 1998; National Crime Prevention, 1999a; Crime Prevention Council of Canada, 1997). If risk factors 'refer to the conditions that predict adverse outcomes', protective factors 'reduce the risk of harm' (National Crime Prevention, 1997, p 4). Thus a current Australian analysis suggests that:

> [t]he significance of protective factors is underlined by the fact that predictions from risk factors are statements of probability. Although factors such as early troublesome behaviour are highly predictive of later offending, more that 50% of at risk individuals may not progress to such outcomes. It is especially important then to identify protective factors and mechanisms that are likely to inhibit the development of antisocial behaviour. Preventative action cannot be solely directed toward risk, especially when risk factors are difficult to modify. (National Crime Prevention, 1999a, pp 119–20)

The last sentence of this passage is something of a giveaway. In the Australian example noted earlier, socio-economic disadvantage appears as a risk factor while protective factors emerge as 'access to support services', 'community networking', 'participation in church or other community group' and so on. The emergence of the 'protective factor', in such instances, appears to be part of a process of risk sequencing that defines precise strategies for governing risk in ways that do not address the prime risk factor itself. Where this is the case, and it very often is, two kinds of explanation are given by advocates.

The first, seen already above, points out that certain risk factors are recognised, but that they are not amenable to minimisation, at least in practical and foreseeable terms. The second argument suggests that such risk factors somehow are inadequate predictors and may thus be, in some fashion, discounted as targets for intervention. Thus with respect to abuse prevention:

> ... poverty alone does not differentiate high from low risk families, as within poor neighbourhoods, families differ in their incidence of abuse ... [However] a high degree of social support is a prime protective factor. Such factors as interaction between families and social institutions, the presence of parents in the home on the return of children from school, cohesiveness within the family and community pride and involvement, differentiate high and low abuse neighbourhoods. (Tolley and Tregeagle, 1998, p 3)

Such arguments are familiar New Right responses to claims that 'poverty causes crime'. The appearance of such claims, in the current era where even 'causes of crime' have resurfaced and been turned into a political slogan, indicates that no matter how far the persistence of welfare disciplines is at work, nothing is immune to political consideration. This is not to suggest that the purveyors of 'protective factors' are in league with remnants of the New Right, although of course some are. Rather, it is to suggest that disciplines are politically polyvalent and pragmatic: some developmental psychologists may (as with the Canadian example) demand attention to poverty factors, others (as with the Australian example) may not.

Globalising risk?

Risk in the area of criminal justice and crime control has proven itself diverse in form and not especially predictable in its trajectory. Even 10 years ago (O'Malley, 1992; Feeley and Simon, 1992), it was possible to regard the trajectory of risk in this area to be roughly predictable with respect to nature and spread. Broadly speaking, there was a degree of confidence that actuarial justice would globalise, that professional interventions would be displaced by the managerially more efficient processing of risk schedules, that a criminology concerned with the causes of crime would become an academic irrelevancy, and that technically neutral regimes of security would displace punishment and correction. No real consistency of this sort has emerged. In part, this is because we have entered a period of contradictory and volatile crime control, in which conservative, neo-liberal and new age forms of social democratic political agendas form an unstable and geographically variable mosaic of governance (O'Malley, 1999b; Garland, 1996). In the United States, the exclusionary agenda of a moral conservatism has fostered actuarial justice and spawned populist vengeance in the form of Megan's laws. Elsewhere these have failed to take hold in anything but a much more benign form. With respect to serious sexual and violence offending, sentencing and parole are increasingly dominated by risk-based procedures, but at the more trivial end of the scale, this form of risk-based technique has rarely been adopted (for example, Kemshall and Maguire, 2001; Rose, 2000). While incapacitation has a major role in some jurisdictions, outside of North America rehabilitation is accepted as a necessary strategy for risk reduction. While rational choice forms of situational crime prevention have remained influential, they have been joined by therapeutic, rehabilitative and redistributive forms of social crime prevention that had been pronounced dead or mortally wounded. With respect to policing and probation work, risk-based approaches are at present growing, although with respect to these areas, and to the work of the judiciary, this generally is much less the case than it appears on paper (Kemshall, 1998; Freiberg, 2000).

At the same time, as Cohen (1985) might have predicted, alternative strategies are carving out their own diverse empires in the justice archipelago. The victim focus that supported situational crime prevention and risk-based sex and violent offender sanctions has also fostered retributive regimes unrelated to issues of risk. Victim-offender reconciliation, restitution penalties, and the growth of 'victim impact statements' are examples that strengthen patterns of individual, not risk-based, justice. The rise of 'emotive and ostentatious' punishment has certainly had an impact, especially in the United States. In countries such as Canada and Australia, while changes have been significant, it is not clear that the 'welfare sanction' ever suffered serious diminution in its role as the primary strategy of penal policy.

This is not, of course, to suggest either that risk is unimportant, or that it has not gained significant ground as a technique for governing crime, nor that all is chaos and there is no pattern. Risk has extended its sway considerably, if unevenly. We can point to clear parallels between the nature of risk-based technologies and governmental frameworks, for example with respect to the place of social intervention in broader political rationalities. This is so even if the changes have not been predictable. However, if the trajectory of risk is driven by global or technocratic forces, this tells us very little about how to understand the political and even technical nature and implications of the changes generated in specific fields of government. Perhaps it is not unreasonable to suggest that, in itself, the characterisation of a penal policy or sentencing strategy as 'risk-based' may not tell us as much as we once thought and/or feared. There is much less of consequence, I would argue, in the difference between the welfare sanction and risk-based rehabilitation than there is between exclusionary and inclusionary crime prevention strategies. In the following chapter, this will be explored further with respect to risk-centred, drug harm-minimisation programs.

The drug addict suffers from a peculiarly liberal affliction. It is liberal in the sense that it is a pathology of the subject's individual freedom – what Mariana Valverde (1998) has referred to as a 'disease of the will'. It is also liberal in that the emergence of concerns about the impact of drugs on free will – beginning with alcohol – coincides historically and in focal concerns with the ascendancy of liberal governance. As Levine demonstrates, addiction was invented at a time when the liberal values of inner discipline and self-control were becoming paramount. It was a time when 'given the structural requirements of daily life for self-reliant, self-making entrepreneurs and their families, and the assumptions of the individualistic middle class world view, it seemed completely reasonable that liquor, a substance believed to weaken inhibitions when consumed (intoxication), could also deprive people of the ability to control their behaviour over the long run (addiction)' (Levine, 1978, p 168). Indeed, such liberal concerns with self-control and individual freedom are reflected in an array of 'epidemics of the will' that periodically sweep modern societies, in which any substance or any activity – even the desire for individual freedom itself – may be interpreted as excessive and addictive (Sedgwick, 1992).

Of course, this is not to suggest that the effects of drugs are imaginary in the sense of being fallacious. Rather, the point is that at other times and in other contexts these effects are understood in other ways altogether, for example as mystical or euphoric states that alter consciousness but do not render the subject *unfree*. In discourses on addiction, the addict is imagined as experiencing the attrition of free will, which in turn is a symptom of what the United States Office of National Drug Control Policy (ONDCP, 2000, p v) now refers to as a 'chronic relapsing disorder'. Yet this medical imagery has never been very secure. Addiction is something of a hybrid that awkwardly melds the moral, philosophical and political entity of 'free will' with biochemical processes and medical pathology (Valverde, 1998). Resulting ambiguities and paradoxes create dilemmas for government, especially over whether coercion is justified because rationality and freedom are already compromised, and whether coercion only further weakens free will rather than restores it. Furthermore, treatment comes into tension with punishment, for while the addict suffers from a disease or pathology that should be treated as a medical problem, this condition was contracted voluntarily through an illegal act and thus is subject to penalty. For such reasons, even in the pronouncedly 'medical' approach of the British, the history of governing addictions has been one of ambivalence, ambiguity and dispute, in which medical and judicial regimes have sometimes co-operated and sometimes struggled with each other, each with an uneasy grasp (Stimson and Oppenheimer, 1982).

This mix of governmental rationales has persisted in the United States under the War on Drugs. There, the government view has been that drugs 'drain the physical, intellectual, spiritual and moral strength of America' (ONDCP, 2000, p 3), a vision understandably linked with zero tolerance as a basic strategy. By the late 1990s this strategy had translated into massive increases in imprisonment, so much so that 60% of inmates in federal prisons had been sentenced for drug-related offences, and the average length of such sentences had more than doubled since the early 1980s (ONDCP, 2000, p 62). On the other hand, despite the emphasis on actuarial justice, there also appeared a major emphasis at the federal level on the idea that '[a] zero tolerance drug programme that includes treatment for substance abuse, in lieu of incarceration' will assist many drug offenders, and that treatment regimes in the prison context need to be expanded (ONDCP, 2000, p 62). Especially when this is linked with the growth of dedicated drug courts and therapeutic jurisprudence, it indicates the persistence of an uneasy mix of punitive and treatment regimes traditionally associated with discourses of addiction and abuse. As a result, it is not at all clear whether actuarial justice – with its focus on incapacitation – is the automatically preferred strategy for dealing with drug offences.

This is not to say that risk-based justice and related interventions have no part in the War on Drugs. Quite to the contrary, major aspects of the US national drug strategy focus on the deployment of risk-based strategies and technologies. Workplace and school random drug testing, and educational and related interventions aimed at preventing young people from using illegal drugs, lend a markedly risk-focused character to this exercise in warfare (O'Malley and Mugford, 1991a). The primary goals of the National Drug Control Strategy are to 'educate and enable America's youth to reject illegal drugs as well as alcohol and tobacco'. In turn, the social and clinical conditions relevant to this end are mapped out in a familiar series of 'risk factors' (chaotic home environment, ineffective parenting, anti-social behaviour, etc) and 'protective factors' (strong bonds with family, school and religious organisations, parental involvement, etc) (ONDCP, 2000, p 5). Thus the War on Drugs strategies centre on discourses of addiction and abuse while retaining a vision of these conditions as simultaneously scientific and moral pathologies invested with a risk-based character. Risk techniques are shaped by their placement in the War on Drugs, and take on the appearance of an explicitly moral technology.[1]

In Britain and Australasia, however, the models of addiction and abuse underwent a transformation of an altogether different nature after the mid-1980s. 'Addicts' were to be re-imagined respectively as 'problem drug takers' and 'drug users'. With respect to Britain (and the same will be seen to apply to Australasia), a 'disease-based notion of addiction gave way to the notion of "problem drug taking" ... [involving] a broader perspective, moving away from a substance focus and recognising the personal, social and medical [including dependence] difficulties

---

1 Moore and Haggerty (2001) provide a useful analysis of the development of home drug-testing kits that regards them as appearing at the intersection of a morally-laden and disease-oriented framework provided by the War on Drugs, and a neo-liberal political rationality. The neo-liberal focus in turn integrates a focus on commodified technologies with a stress on the responsibility of families for governing their children in a setting that demonises drug use. This analysis shows very clearly how difficult it is to 'read-off' particular governmental techniques from political rationalities without paying attention to the specificities of the context. As will be argued in this chapter, in the Australian context, neo-liberalism is strongly associated with opposition to disease orientation, demonisation and intrusive measures.

which may be associated with the use of a range of drugs' (Glanz, 1994, p 157). This language of 'problems' and 'difficulties' heralded a shifting of attention away from power of the chemical substance. As well – unlike the situation in America where it is part of strategic thinking that 'drugs impair rational thinking' (ONDCP, 2000, p 6) – these new discourses began re-envisaging drug takers in ways that do not automatically assume their rationality and freedom to be diminished. A further contrast was to be drawn against the US strategic aim of creating a barrier to drug use that set apart addicts and 'abusers' of illegal drugs as a deviant and criminal populace. Indeed, 'drug abusers' were added to the pantheon of drug-related subjects in the War on Drugs, to counter the implication that addicted drug takers have an attenuated free will and thus are not fully subject to criminal law (Matza and Morgan, 1995). This further manifestation of the unstable medical/penal couple in such drug discourses overlapped extensively with the 'addict', particularly with respect to the determinist discourse of decline and pathology. Yet while contrasting on the issue of will, both addicts and abusers were subject to discourses of moral condemnation and otherness in the United States. This can be seen as running counter to the dialogue in other nations, especially the Australian and New Zealand versions, where harm-minimisation strategies were to constitute drug users and drug consumers as ordinary persons *at risk* from their drug use – whether or not that involved illegal or legal (specifically alcohol, tobacco and pharmaceutical) drugs. They appeared as normal subjects confronting unusual risks, harms, problems or difficulties rather than as actors making explicitly *moral* choices.[2]

Risk, choice and indeterminism

In 1992, the Australian federal government launched the National Drug Strategy (Task Force, 1992), cementing in place a 1980s harm-minimisation framework for the government of licit and illicit drugs. One of the striking things about this document, and its substantial accompanying programme, was that the terms 'addict', 'addiction' and 'abuse' scarcely appeared. A year later, in the *Victorian Drug Strategy 1993–98* (a state-based programme formally operating within this federal rubric of harm minimisation), 'addiction' and 'drug abuse' had entirely given way to discourses of 'drug use' (HCS, 1993). A few years later, much the same stance was adopted by the New Zealand *National Drug Policy* (NZ Government, 1998) and by

2 It is recognised that the term 'harm minimisation' refers to a great diversity of drug programmes, and many of these do not converge closely with those reviewed in this chapter. Fischer (1995), for example, shows that in German discourses, harm minimisation is integrated with prohibitionism. The national drug strategy 'clearly emphasizes the use of law enforcement, repression and criminal justice instruments as the main tools against the threat of drugs ... [the German federal government] has never left any doubt about its prohibitionist position and mainly promotes the vision of a drug-free society' (1995, p 391). Even so, as Fischer indicates, local harm minimisation policies in Germany often closely reflect the assumptions mapped out in this chapter. Thus in Frankfurt's model, it was stressed that the 'maximum amount of social and health assistance must be made available when dealing with drug addiction and drug users, and repressive interventions must be reduced to a minimum' (quoted by Fischer, 1995, p 396). It is worth stressing, however, that the focus on particular harm minimisation strategies in this chapter is not intended to suggest that they are representative or typical of a broader set. In keeping with the general analytical focus of the book, the concern, rather, is with the governmental implications of specific configurations of risk and uncertainty, particularly with respect to such matters as the subjectivities created or imagined, the forms of 'freedom' to be created, and so on.

the Major and Blair regimes in Britain with *Tackling Drugs Together* and *Tackling Drugs to Build a Better Britain* (HM Government, 1995; 1998). Here too, discourses on abuse and addiction were marginalised in favour of discourses of the 'drug user' (New Zealand) or 'drug misuser' (Britain). This shift was associated with a re-thinking, even of persistent drug use, in terms of choice. It restored free will to new categories of 'dependent' or 'problem' drug mis/users, and understood the process of becoming a drug consumer as involving rational decision-making. Rather than progressing from this foundation to a heavily moralised, prohibitive response, as in the US, it sought to *enlist* the rationality of these subjects. It sought to 'enable' or even 'empower' its subjects by imparting 'skills', providing 'information' and creating treatment resources through which these neo-liberal subjects could 'make informed choices' and achieve 'healthy and crime free lives' (HM Government, 1998).

In these regimes, instead of blanket imageries of addictions and abuses, there emerged a spectrum of qualified conditions and forms of 'use' or 'misuse', ranging in the Australian context from 'excessive use' and 'dependent use' ('problem misuse' in Britain) to 'informed use' and even 'responsible drug use' (see HM Government, 1998; Commonwealth Department of Human Services and Health, 1995). Even in some of its strongest warnings, Blair's *Tackling Drugs* displaces traditional narratives of pathological addiction and inexorable decline with the much more conditional observation that 'drug-taking can be harmful' (HM Government 1998, p 7), while the New Zealand (1998) policy refers to a 'continuum of harm associated with drug use'. The varieties of drug 'use' and 'misuse' in this discourse, it appears, are linked to variable degrees of risk and magnitudes of harm – they have no inevitable medical trajectory or blanket moral status attached to them. While these 'harm-minimisation' approaches all seek to deflect or reduce the acceptability of drug use on grounds of risk and harm, only infrequently is drug consumption (as opposed to trafficking) defined explicitly as morally or criminally culpable. In this there is a strong contrast with strategies formerly in place. In Britain in the 1980s, for example, campaigns such as 'Heroin screws you up' and 'Smack isn't worth it' depicted users as morally corrupt, unhealthy and helpless, and suggested a typical career of use, addiction and despair (Davies and Coggans, 1994, p 311). The key factor underlying the quite dramatic shift away from such imageries of abuse and addiction, it seems clear, is to be found in the development of forms of harm minimisation – that is, explicitly risk-based approaches that are inflected with neo-liberal technologies of freedom and self-government.

The National Drug Strategy, endorsed by all federal, state and territory governments in Australia, defines harm minimisation as aiming to 'reduce the adverse health, social and economic consequences of alcohol and other drugs by minimising or limiting the harms and hazards of drug use' (Commonwealth Department of Human Services and Health, 1995). More explicitly, the *Victorian Drug Strategy 1993–98* (HCS, 1993) states that '[t]he specific objectives of the Drug Strategy focus on changing behaviours and reducing other risk factors which have been shown to increase the potential for drug related harm … All objectives are defined in terms of risk factors linked to specific harms, with emphasis on prevention wherever possible and on minimising the negative impact of drug use problems where they occur'. Likewise, the British *Tackling Drugs* strategy is saturated with risk talk, stressing that 'action will be concentrated in areas of greatest need and risk'; that it seeks 'big reductions in crime and health risks'; that 'significant health risks are associated with drugs'; and so on. Such risk management strategies place an analytical and governmental grid across the social terrain they seek to govern that does not necessarily correspond to the grid laid down by prohibitive laws or medical regimes of addiction. For example, some harm-minimisation programmes stress that 'it is important to recognise that illicit drugs are, in functional terms, the same as legal drugs' (PDAC, 1996). While they recognise 'the devastating effects that illicit drug use can have', they do so in the context of observations that align them, in terms of harm, with licit drug use (HCS, 1993). Similarly, as part of its 'Vision', *Tackling Drugs* states baldly that '[a]ll drugs are harmful', while the New Zealand policy stresses that 'of all drugs tobacco and alcohol result in the most harm in New Zealand'.

Harm minimisation and normalisation

One of the major concerns of harm-minimisation policies is the capacity of prohibition's exclusionary categories and procedures to 'demonise' illicit drug users. For harm minimisation, legal exclusion and demonisation of drug use creates problems of 'deviance amplification' and resistance to effective intervention. Compulsion and coercion are regarded as creating resistance among the very drug using subjects upon whom the programme is intended to have its effects (for example, PDAC, 1996). The strategy of harm minimisation, therefore, is to 'emphasise voluntary treatment rather than punishment of users and to minimise the stigma of criminalisation of drug users' on pragmatic grounds (Task Force, 1992). Thus, in contrast to the Foucaultian sense of normalisation as bringing deviant subjects into conformity with a constructed norm (licit drug use or no drug use), 'normalisation' in the lexicon of harm minimisation takes on the meaning of rendering illicit drug-taking subjects normal subjects of government (Glanz, 1994, p 158). The point is made well by Strang (1984, p 1,203), suggesting that '[a]s notorious drugs (such as the use of heroin) become more widespread in a population, the people using them are likely to be more normal (statistically and in other senses) than the abnormal population who presented originally'. In consequence, 'if some of the drugtakers are becoming more normal then perhaps some of the drug services should do likewise' (Strang, 1989, p 143). This was to be achieved through 'the gradual shift from disease and criminal models', precisely because of an awareness 'that "drug addicts" and "alcoholics" can bear the brunt of problems in our community and can be the scapegoats of more severe social ills' (Task Force, 1992). Instead of coercive, long-term residential models, voluntary and short-term 'out patient' models became preferred options, and 'the view that drug misusers need to be dealt with by specialists was undermined' (Glanz, 1994).[3]

---

3   A governmental analysis would be rather less sanguine, or at least more agnostic, about the prospects for normalisation being translated into practice. That is, while normalisation is the stated objective, there is no guarantee that this, or any other governmental objective, will be reached. Thus in relation to attempts to normalise the mentally ill by releasing them into the community, Kemshall (2002, pp 96–99) notes that the reverse effect may result. Communities confronted by the mentally ill in their midst may respond with alarm and generate their own exclusionary responses.

As part of this normalisation strategy, even in such a comparatively anti-drug document as *Tackling Drugs for a Better Britain*, a distance is created between criminality and drug 'misusers' by stressing that 'all drug users do not commit crime' and that the aims of the programme include '[concentrating] our ... law enforcement effort on those who produce, process and sell [drugs]' (HM Government, 1998, p 8). With respect to misusers the strategy is one that 'enables' and 'helps' and with respect to potential users is not so much to prohibit but to provide guidance. The stress in *Tackling Drugs* (1998) is not on subordination to expertise, which is held to re-enforce dependency, but on assistance and enablement: '[h]elping drug-misusing offenders to tackle their problems and become better integrated into society' and intervention to 'enable people with drug problems to overcome them'. Such normalisation, we will see, is undertaken precisely in order to govern drug users more effectively, to align the wills of such subjects with the project of harm minimisation, and to align the distribution of risks and harms with the objectives of government programmes. These 'users' and 'misusers' – unlike 'addicts' and 'abusers' – are to be governed through the exercise of their freedom.

We have seen that the discourses of addiction and abuse focus on the presence (abuse) or absence/attenuation (addiction) of 'free will'. In these essentially binary models the subject is or is not a wilful law breaker, is or is not diseased, and thus is or is not a subject of governmental intervention. However, by regarding drugs as part of the generalised issue of risk management, harm minimisation operates within a *probabilistic* model that erodes the binary of free will and determinism or, more precisely, creates a form of freedom that is 'shaped' by probabilities (Hacking, 1991). Whether, with reference to alcohol, tobacco, pharmaceuticals or 'illicit drugs', harm reduction involves 'a recognition that drug use involves varying degrees of risk for the user' (DSEV, 1995). Thus *Tackling Drugs* (1998) stresses that 'almost half of young people are likely to take drugs at some time in their lives, but only one-fifth will become regular misusers (ie at least once a month), with a tiny minority of that group taking drugs on a daily basis'. In place of the addiction 'narrative of inexorable decline and fall' (Sedgwick, 1992), the drug user is understood to be free, but in an environment of varying risk. In this way of thinking, a subject is created who must make choices from among a range of risk-bearing alternatives. The drug user as informed choice-maker becomes the key form of subject through which government of drugs proceeds.[4]

---

4 There is little room for doubt that part of the genealogy of harm minimisation involves the intellectual formulations of social theorists in drug research. For example, the NDC development of processes of 'deviancy amplification' and the 'demonisation' of drug users (Young, 1971) are equally echoed in harm minimisation discussions (eg, PDAC, 1996). But perhaps more central, it is worth recalling that Howard Becker's classic essay, 'Becoming a marijuana user' (1965, p 85), deliberately eschews the language of addictions, instead referring to drug 'users', and regards users as making rational decisions in a process that is 'easy' and voluntary: 'anyone can become a marijuana user but nobody has to.' The convergence of this rational choice subjectivity of the 'user' with that of harm minimisation is significant, and indicative that however much rational choice models are regarded as conservative, this is not necessarily their effect. Much depends on how they are deployed. However, it should be recognised that whereas Becker stresses the element of pleasure, this usually is absent from harm minimisation discourses, which are largely silent on this 'positive' side of the felicity calculus (see more generally O'Malley and Valverde, 2004).

Drug use, empowerment and informed choices

Regimes of drug addiction and abuse both assume that drug taking begins with a rational decision to consume. However, the consequences – moral and medical – are so constituted that this decision is not represented as one that is simply a matter of free choice. In both cases the assumption is that the decision to take drugs should be constrained by moral condemnation and/or the threats of punishment and addiction. 'Just Say No!', as the most salient manifestation of such approaches, is an instruction: it does not suggest that the potential user should consult the spectrum of choices and select that which suits them, weighing up the probabilities and making a lifestyle choice. Thus, in the shadow of the War On Drugs, a marked contrast was created by documents such as *Tackling Drugs for a Better Britain* (HM Government, 1998) which urged that 'we need to ensure that young people have all the information they need to make informed decisions about drugs'. Consider also the following view from an Australian state's drug education programme:

> A harm minimisation approach acknowledges that many young people will use drugs at some stage in their life, making it critical that students acquire knowledge and skills that will assist them in making informed decisions about their drug use and so minimise any harmful effects associated with that use. (DSEV, 1995, p 1)

Here, potential users have been rendered choice-makers whose consumption choices cannot be governed by coercive regimes of legal or medical prohibition. The Victorian Drug Education Program makes no bones about 'accepting [that] drug use by young people is a personal choice that is not within the control of teachers or schools', while the New Zealand policy specifically notes that 'people are often highly resistant to "Just Say No" messages about drug use, even when they are aware of the health, legal and other risks associated with such use. Innovative strategies are needed to communicate to them the value of staying drug free' (NZ Government, 1998, p 10). In these instances, the shift toward government through choice is clearly founded on pragmatism. They are based on the belief that governing through a risk-informed freedom may be a more effective mode of aligning the wills of the governed than is the threat or practice of constraint; but both Australasian programmes – at least ostensibly – go beyond this to suggest that the discourse of rights genuinely applies to the decision to use drugs. In the New Zealand case (NZ Government, 1998, p 37) 'choices – which may be harmful to the individual – are legal and acceptable if the user does not unreasonably impinge on others. That is, individual choices are respected where the costs of the choices are not borne by others'. The Australian programme for secondary schools not only 'respects other's rights to make their own decisions' but, more importantly, deploys such freedom of choice as the key element in the self-government of 'responsible' users and potential users. For this reason, they 'should have access to accurate information and education programmes relating to drugs and drug use, on the basis that informed, skilled individuals are able to make better choices which help prevent drug problems' (HCS, 1993, p 5).

Buried in these models is a series of key assumptions. The first is that the freedom of the individual as a choice-maker is to be established and facilitated. The second is that these choice-makers can be assumed to make rational decisions that will accord with the aims of government providing they are given 'accurate' information and the skills required to make choices. The third is that the role of government is to provide access to the necessary skills and information. In this sense, there is an 'enhanced autonomy' of the self when compared with models of all previous liberalisms (Rose, 1996a); but as might be anticipated, the skills and the information to be presented are understood as aimed at minimising risks. Thus, *Tackling Drugs to Build a Better Britain* (HM Government, 1998) aims to 'increase levels of knowledge of 5–16 year olds about the risks and consequences of drug misuse', and urges that '[i]nformation, skills and support need to be provided in ways which are sensitive to age and circumstances, and particular efforts need to be made to reach and help those groups at high risk of developing very serious problems'. The Australian *Get Real* drug education package describes itself as providing:

> … accurate and meaningful information. It provides a framework for understanding the forces that shape choice. It develops an awareness of risk situations. It develops skills to avoid situations of risk and to manage them when they arise. It encourages open discussion about drug use. It is open to young people's views and experiences. It does not encourage, condone or condemn the use of drugs by young people. It develops skills that enable young people to influence and change their environments. It helps students understand that drugs perform many useful functions in our society. (DSEV, 1995, p 4)

Built into this array is a series of carefully developed tactics for governing at a distance, through shaping the choice-making freedom of potential and current users. The emphasis on providing accurate and meaningful information follows from the assumption that government is intended to work through the actions of choice-makers. Examination of the texts of harm minimisation policy indicates another layer to this strategy of self-government. It is noted frequently in the literature that provision of biased or incomplete information aimed at deflecting people from drug use has been found to be counterproductive (for example, PDAC, 1996). Information that distinguishes between illicit and licit drugs on the basis of the harmfulness of the former, for example, is found to limit the credibility of drug education, particularly among young people. Information that provides distorted and alarmist accounts of illicit drug use, such as tales of the inevitable slide from marijuana use into opiate addiction, is likewise found to discredit the programme because it can be refuted by experiences of users. Hence, *Tackling Drugs* (HM Government, 1998, p 8) goes to some pains to dismiss 'misconceptions' by asserting that 'all drug takers are *not* addicts; all drug takers do *not* commit crime' (emphasis in original). The provision of 'accurate information' is preferred partly because it is understood to govern more effectively. However, it is also clear that provision of accurate information alone is not regarded as sufficient, for evidence is produced to show that by itself it does not reliably reduce risk-taking behaviour (for example, PDAC, 1996; NZ Government, 1998).

It is at this point that 'responsible', choice-making drug users are to be *created* by government, for, as noted, such programmes are to provide 'skills' as an essential adjunct to information. The *Get Real* education package, for example, provides potential users with a 'framework for understanding the forces that shape choice. It develops an awareness of risk situations. It develops skills to avoid situations of risk and to manage them when they arise' (DSEV, 1995, p 4). Likewise, *Tackling Drugs* (HM Government, 1998, p 17) seeks to 'teach young people from the age of five and upwards – both in and out of formal educational settings – the skills needed to resist pressure to misuse drugs'. In particular these risk-managerial skills include building self-esteem, recognition of the importance of peer group influence on choice making, and skills for managing such pressures. These skills are specified and given shape on the basis of evidence indicating their role in reducing risky behaviour. Put another way, the choice-makers are being given skills to render them more autonomous, but this autonomy renders the subjects more able to isolate themselves from pressures other than those provided by harm minimisation. Thus the tolerance associated with freedom of choice is associated with a subtle process of aligning subjects' wills with those of the policy-makers. This is reinforced by the fact that the information about drug risks, appearing as objective and accurate, will present itself as no more than mapping out a quasi-natural order of risks. It does not take the form of an imposed order formed and policed by moral and political governance, for the risks appear as probabilistic events triggered by the failure of the user to take necessary avoiding steps. The governmental presentation of information appears as a technical service provided to enable individuals to chart their own course through the risk-laden domain of drug use.

'Dependent drug use' and the responsible addict

Most of what we have examined thus far enlists potential users/misusers and seeks to govern risks through their freedom of choice. Yet what of those who are – in the words of *Tackling Drugs* – 'problem misusers' or, in the Australian discourses, 'dependent drug users'? At first blush, drug dependency appears to be merely a synonym for addiction. Like many programmes governing addicts and abusers, the government of dependent users often operates primarily through methadone or other drug maintenance programmes. Surprisingly, however, harm minimisation discourses do not necessarily make dependence itself the target for governance. While methadone, for example, is regarded as ultimately delivering a way out of dependency, this is regarded neither as a necessary outcome, nor as the primary benefit, delivered by the programme. Indeed, it is emphasised in the information provided to potential participants that methadone maintenance involves not only continued dependence on opiates, with the associated biochemical risks, but a dependency that often proves significantly more difficult to break (HCS, 1995). Methadone programmes under harm minimisation regimes have as their primary target the governance of risks and harms generated by drug dependency. These risks, and the ways in which methadone programmes manage them, are identified quite clearly in literature made available to dependent users. These include the following: methadone is administered orally (usually in solution with a fruit juice) thereby reducing the health risks associated with injection; standard quality control by the administering agency prevents harms associated with drug adulteration; because methadone does not give the user a 'high', it may be used to stabilise the dosage required by users, thus breaking the spiral of demand for larger dosages at greater cost; because its effects are longer lasting than are those of other opiates (between 24 and 36 hours) methadone allows increased calculability of lifestyle, and normal patterns of work and life become possible – which in turn produces economic harm-reduction and associated risk reduction with respect to the need to commit crimes to finance drug use; because it is legally available at low cost, participation in a methadone programme reduces risks associated with the violation of criminal law (HCS, 1995).

Such 'benefits of the methadone scheme' are presented to the user alongside a series of other issues to be considered by a potential participant. These include not only the fact that the user remains opiate dependent, but also that there are requirements of the programme demanding a regularising of the user's lifestyle. For example, '[y]ou are committed to attending daily for your dose [and] travel or holidays can be difficult and must be organised well in advance' (HCS, 1995, p 4). There is not, as is sometimes implied by critics, a *secret* agenda of surveillance. As with the transmission of 'accurate' information to responsible users, the effects of the programme, and their associations with the governance of risk, are presented openly to the dependent user as matters for choice-making, rather than as matters to be concealed: 'Your treatment team can support, advise and listen to you but basically you have to decide whether methadone is right for you' (HCS, 1995, p 5).

Again, this voluntarisation and responsibilisation emerges out of the recognition that compulsory programmes fail to deliver results because of the fear, stigmatisation and hostility that compulsory treatment creates among users. Voluntary programmes, working through the rational choice users' preferences, and based therefore on their recognition of the risk reductions associated with enlistment in such programmes, are held to deliver better results. Governing through freedom of choice thus displaces government through coercion not simply on the basis of 'humanity' (although such ideas are certainly present) but primarily on the basis of optimising effective rule. Through their participation in the programme, methadone consumers are normalised, and as rational 'choice, calculating risk-takers, they enter the sphere of responsible drug use.

Uncertainty and the precautionary principle

In harm minimisation discourses, concerns with substantive 'conventional' legality and morality appear to be substituted by an amoral, pragmatist technology in which the distribution of efforts and resources is geared to the measured potential for harms. Thus in one governmental briefing paper, the question of how harms and risks may be 'assessed and weighted in comparison with each other' suggests that:

> If we had the ability to measure the harm with precision in terms of the severity, prevalence and the nature of the affected populations, we would be more able to appropriately tailor harm minimisation strategies. When comparing ... types of harm a common framework is required: estimates of the economic costs of different harms to the community can be made to compare and prioritise different types of harm, or measures such as 'person years of life lost' can be derived. (Commonwealth Department of Human Services and Health, 1995, p 8)

In this framework, problems for government thus appear to be identified and prioritised scientifically and objectively rather than in terms of the value commitments and arbitrary moralities of some political regime. Such discourses of harm and risk imply that the locus of harm creation lies neither in the properties of drugs nor in the characteristics of the user, but in the variable yet calculable relationships between them. It is for this reason, among others I will now discuss, that the governance of drug use is almost always expressed in terms such as 'drug related behaviours', 'drug related problems', 'drug related harms' and even '[d]rug-related critical incidents' (DSEV, 1995). The governmental categorisation of types of drug use and drug user is structured in terms of the probabilistic, risk-based understanding of how drugs and users are brought together. There is an attenuation of concern with the properties of drugs and the problematic free will of users, and an increased stress on the user's relationship to an array of risk factors. The minimisation of harm may involve a range of outcomes including abstention from drug use, reduced or controlled use, safer behaviours associated with drug use, or reduction of harmful consequences of drug use for the community. Inherent in this approach is the recognition of a continuum of risk for each drug, from high risk to low risk, along which the user can move.

The starting point here is close to, but distinct from, the traditional approaches to drug governance. In harm minimisation discourses, the governmentally relevant biochemical and psychodynamic effects of certain drugs – to produce hallucinations, to slow the pulse rate or to suppress respiration and so on – are clearly acknowledged, but are invariably linked to the volume and frequency of use. Management of the risks associated with 'the properties' of drugs, in other words, lies in the (self) government of their use – so that 'excessive use' or 'problematic use', rather than 'use' *per se*, emerge as sites of possible intervention (PDAC, 1996). How is 'excessive use' to be defined? For most of the modern era this has been defined in behavioural terms – for example, with respect to the inability of individuals to perform certain tasks (walking the white line) – or with respect to a certain state of the will (Valverde, 1998). In harm minimisation discourses, the answer is almost invariably given in terms of actuarial rates (for example, rates of brain damage, of foetal damage or motor co-ordination impairment related to levels of drug intake), on the basis of which a level is drawn up beyond which use is 'excessive'. In other words, government in terms of harm minimisation, even where concerned with the effects of drugs on the body, moves us away from an emphasis on the fixed biochemical properties of drugs, toward their actuarial rates of risk production, and thence to the government of risk-informed patterns of use.

What is particularly significant is that the level at which use is defined as 'excessive use' varies according to the risk in terms of which it appears as a 'factor'. In some cases this may be straightforward, as for example with respect to 'safe' levels for long-term health or for reaction times in driving a motor vehicle. In other cases, however, the risk factoring may become more complex. In Victoria, while the general level of use defining safe levels for driving is a blood alcohol content of 0.05%, for drivers in their first three years of licensed driving this figure is zero. This is based on the relationship between the risk factor associated with drug consumption and a second risk factor associated with accident rates for new or young drivers. In other words, the definition of problematic drug use in this context is produced socially by the articulation of two discrete risk factors, one of which has no intrinsic connection with drug use.

Such examples, discussed in more detail shortly, are linked with punitive and incapacitating interventions, such as licence confiscation, reflecting harm minimisation's limiting principle of harm to others. By and large, however, the category of excessive use *per se* remains – like other drug use – in the domain of self-government. The role of state governmental programmes is primarily advisory: to establish and broadcast the so-called 'recommended safe levels of usage', founded on expert evaluations of actuarial data, so that responsible users may moderate their risk-bearing behaviours in line with an officially endorsed risk calculus. However, this issue of the calculability of risk becomes particularly acute where 'polydrug use' is considered. Unlike 'excessive use', polydrug use emerges as a category for governance precisely because of its *unpredictable* nature. The combination of varying numbers of drugs, in varying volumes, ratios and sequences of usage, creates incalculable risks. Here the displacement of drug effects by drug-related risk in the centre stage of government is brought into sharp focus, for polydrug use – like excessive use – is regarded as 'high risk'. So much so that there is no recommended safe level of polydrug use (PDAC, 1996, pp 73–76). However, if the categorisation of 'excessive' use as 'high risk' is a tautology – for the actuarial risk level is used to define what is excessive – it is *the unpredictability and thus the ungovernability* of polydrug use that gives rise to 'the taming of chance' technique that is deployed to determine its governmental status.

This mobilisation of the precautionary principle differs somewhat from the instances discussed in Chapter 1, for there the critical issue was the matter of second-order risks – in a loose sense, the risk that risks exist. But the precautionary principle is deployed here, as elsewhere, where there is an unwillingness to accept uncertainty because the stakes are so high. Even so, in instances where the uncertainty relates to life itself, these harm minimisation policies do not intervene coercively: the drug consumer appears as a sovereign consumer of risks, entitled to take risks if willing to bear the consequences as long as these are visited only on the self. However, this stance undergoes a significant change when these situations concern the creation of risks to the well-being of others.

Harms to others: strategic moralisation

The minimisation of overtly moralising interventions has been seen to be central to the normalisation strategy of harm minimisation. Certainly, in the light of the material discussed thus far, it would be easy to regard the process involved as a strategic demoralisation. It already appears that a morally neutral stance is more or less consciously adopted to maximise the effectiveness of technocratic rule. However, while receiving far less attention, overtly moral and coercive strategies do have a definite place in harm minimisation literatures. Eschewed in relation to drug users, they are deployed with respect to two other categories of subject in the governance of drug problems – irresponsible users and drug traffickers – who expose others to risks as a result of their activities.

Responsible drug users, by implication, are assumed to be those who govern in an 'informed' way the risks of drug use. Such risks include the implications of their drug consumption for the welfare of others, and in this respect users are expected to deploy a form of reasonable foresight. Accordingly, the primary governing strategy deployed is to provide drug users with the information they need to avoid inflicting harms on third parties. For example, in the case of driving, this information includes data concerning the impact of alcohol and other drugs on drivers' reactions, and advice on suitable techniques for 'avoiding risk situations' – including the promulgation of the 'designated driver' model, the use of public transport when alcohol consumption is likely, and so on. At this point, the mobilisation of morality becomes salient, for the responsibility called for – for example in drink-drive advertisements – is clearly an overtly moralised responsibility. Advertisements aimed at responsibilising users depict the injuries suffered by innocent third parties in drink-drive accidents, the anguish and misery inflicted on their families, and almost invariably include the driver suffering extreme guilt and remorse. Drivers are, thus, morally manoeuvred to avoid drink-/drug-driving. Equally, friends and family are made morally responsible for ensuring that guests, loved ones and fellow drinkers do not drive if they are drink or drug impaired. While a key strategy to promote responsible self-use is a stance of moral neutrality (where risks are linked to the user), this shifts to a morally-valorised responsibility when the topic becomes governing the risks to others.

Linked with this moral shift comes the deployment of increasingly coercive interventions. The intrusive probabilistic technologies of random breath testing are now a routine part of everyday life for drivers, the vast majority of whom, in a legal sense, have not offended (Walsh and Trumble, 1991). Such interventions are justified primarily on the basis of their preventative or deterrent effect, and primarily with respect to the risks created for third parties. These technologies and justifications are clearly becoming more generalised. Thus, in the *Victorian Strategic Plan* (HCS, 1993) and reforms suggested more recently (PDAC, 1996), priority is given to developing effective random drug testing devices to 'shrink' the risk assessment 'gap' between the current capabilities for alcohol testing and those available for policing other drugs – which at present are effectively limited to more subjective means. The Victorian plan proposed to:

> amend legislation to allow law enforcement to test impaired drivers for drugs other than alcohol for the purpose of legal action, deterrent [*sic*] and investigation into drug driving impairment ... [including] changes to the Road Safety Act to allow Victoria Police powers to take blood and/or urine samples from drivers whose BAC does not correlate with the degree of impairment displayed by the driver. (HCS, 1993, p 24)

In addition, pre-emptive random drug testing is encouraged for a wider array of settings that are linked with driving. Major parties such as Vicroads (the state road transport authority), 'employer groups, transport unions, and the Road Transport Forum will develop new policies on drug use, guidelines for pre-employment medical examination and primary prevention and early intervention programs in the workplace' (HCS, 1993, p 24).

The effect of such interventions is to reintroduce prohibition, justified not on the basis of particularistic prohibitive moralities of the 'private self' and its pleasures, but out of a moral concern with exposing others to significant risk.[5] Zones of

---

5 Prohibition is by no means at odds with some readings of harm minimisation. Patricia Erickson (1990), for example, has argued that prohibition may be a major contributor to harm reduction by decreasing the general accessibility of the drugs to a population. Needless to say, were it demonstrable that prohibition significantly reduced aggregate risks across a population, harm reduction advocates would 'logically' opt for this (although in practice their allegiances may be governed by other factors). The likelihood is the such proof will never appear – if only because prohibition is articulated with so many considerations in drug harm minimisation, such as its side effects of demonising users, reducing users' preference for contacting official channels of assistance, and so on.

prohibition are thereby created, such as motor vehicles, certain occupations, workplaces or public spaces, entry to which is regarded as a matter of *choice* (cf Simon, 1987; O'Malley and Mugford, 1991b). People are free to consume drugs, and their freedom of choice in this specific respect is not problematic, but their entry to certain zones – defined by the association between those zones and risks to others – is prohibited. Even here, however, the primary response within harm minimisation discourses is not primarily or solely punitive. Much emphasis is placed on the effectiveness of exclusion, whether by entry-level detection or by responses to transgression which remove the risk – for example, licence cancellation coupled with driver education for drink drivers.

It is crucial to recognise that while elsewhere in the discourse of harm minimisation, new governmental categories have been created for drug use, organised around the problematic of risk, this is not the case with respect to 'drug traffickers', a term imported without change from law and order discourses. By and large, it is also the case that the modes for governing traffickers are also fully imported. New and more punitive sanctions have been put in place with respect to confiscation of the assets of persons convicted of trafficking, usually with reverse onus conditions attached (PDAC, 1996; Task Force, 1992). Indeed, the unusual harshness of such sanctions has been noted by many commentators (for example, Freiberg, 1992; Fox and Matthews, 1992). Equally, it is clear that all relevant policy documents adopt a morally condemnatory tone toward drug trafficking. Retention of the language of 'trafficking' – in the face of the explicit abandonment of associated discourses of addiction and abuse – suggests that the demonisation and moralisation being deliberately abandoned for the user is being retained and mobilised against the traffickers.

'Strategic moralisation' is thus a better description of harm minimisation responses to drug governance than the 'demoralisation' that sometimes is regarded as the identifying feature of risk management technologies (Simon, 1987). Such programmes selectively focus moral outrage and punitive responses on the basis of the criteria 'creating risks for others'. In the case of 'inappropriate use', the primary techniques are self-control through moral responsibility, linked with zonal prohibition and incapacitation. For traffickers, however, the response is severe punishment. Yet this distribution of morality and punitiveness is not at all unproblematic. The demonisation of suppliers occurs despite the fact that the view in harm minimisation literature is clearly that blanket prohibition is not necessarily an effective strategy, and may – where adulteration is a result of cutting the supply – be counterproductive (Blewitt, 1987; PDAC, 1996). This suggests that the deployment of moral responsibility is not so much pragmatic as symbolic (cf Garland, 1996). It is the traffickers who are held ultimately *responsible* for the creation of most drug-related risks, especially conditions leading to drug adulteration, black market price escalation, 'dirty' needle use, and violence and corruption. Moral responsibility has been directed away from drug users – who are governed most effectively by choice – and refocused on those defined as the creators of harm, the risk producers.

Governing the future

The probabilism of harm minimisation has been linked here to the general avoidance in such discourses of both 'drug addiction' and 'drug abuse'. Harm minimisation could escape these two discourses precisely because it partially avoided the determinism/free will polarity that Eve Sedgwick (1992, p 141) regards as their intellectual foundations:

> So long as an entity known as free will has been hypostatised and charged with ethical value, for just so long has an equally hypostatised 'compulsion' had to be available as a counter structure always internal to it, always being required to be ejected from it. The scouring descriptive work of addiction attribution is propelled by the same imperative: its exacerbated perceptual acuteness in detecting the compulsion behind everyday voluntarity is driven, ever more blindly, by its own compulsion to isolate some new, receding but absolutised space of pure voluntarity.

In some respects, 'free will' and 'compulsion' are displaced in harm minimisation by two parallel but distinct terms: 'choice' and 'risk'. If free will and compulsion exist at opposite ends of a spectrum, this is not the case for choice and risk, which are compatible and complementary terms. Indeed, as Luhmann (1993) has argued, risk implies or even requires choice on the part of subjects. In turn, choice emerges as a very particular formulation of 'freedom' for it always implies a partial closing down of liberty, and its restriction to a number of given possibilities rather than open selection from an unmarked terrain of possibilities. 'Freedom of choice' allows us to think in terms of variable degrees of freedom without necessarily raising the spectre of a constraint on action produced by an impaired or coerced will. In harm minimisation discourses, the dependent user, for example, is not imagined as having the same array of choices that is available to the non-dependent user, for their array has been narrowed by the reliance on gaining access to a drug supply; but they are still imagined as a choice-maker. New choices become necessary or open for the dependent user – such as choosing between enlisting in a methadone programme or not – which do not confront other users. Enlistment in such programmes is understood to increase the array of certain choices open to dependent users, for example with respect to types of lifestyle that are opened up, but is seen to close down others, for example those which depend upon a 'freedom' of movement unfettered by the need to arrange methadone supplies.

The imagery of the choice-making drug user is thus of a 'normal' subject who seeks pleasure through the consumption of drugs, but whose choices are conditioned by an *environment* of risk rather than a restrictive polity. The drug user is neither totally free nor compelled, but must make choices among risk-bearing options. The prudent individual takes on the role of governing drugs and, on the balance of probabilities, enjoys their pleasures in safety. The feckless individual bears costs to health and lifestyle that, on the balance of probabilities, are delivered by their own lack of responsibility. Prudence based on the advice of experts is the virtue that emerges from responsible drug use. In the process, however, as Ian Hacking observes:

> The erosion of determinism and the taming of chance by statistics does not introduce a new liberty. The argument that indeterminism creates a place for free will is a hollow mockery. The bureaucracy of statistics imposes order not just by creating administrative rulings but by determining classifications within which people must think of themselves and the actions that are open to them. The hallmark of indeterminism is that cliché, information and control. The less the determinism, the more the possibilities for constraint. (Hacking, 1991, p 194)

There is, then, a dark side to the expansion of choice that harm minimisation seems to deliver to a drug-using society. Now, it is not simply the addict who will be treated, nor the minority of users who are punished. *All* users are exposed to a regime of self-governance, constantly responsible for monitoring their behaviour, governing themselves without pause. Moreover, the probabilism of harm minimisation weakens the power to contest this regime. While tales of the inevitable slide into addiction could be refuted by counter examples from friendship networks, the evil vision of the free will drug abuser could be challenged by reference to harmless recreational users, what can challenge the depiction of a risk based on probability tables drawn from whole populations? The power to define risks and thus to shape self-governing drug use is moved to a more autonomous plane, more difficult to challenge from the resources of personal experience.

For all that harm minimisation establishes a regime of expanded choice for users, the new relations of expertise that are established have the potential to deliver the shaping of governance into the hands of technocrats. It is technocrats, in the form of health statisticians, who identify and map the terrain of risks through which the choice-making drug taker charts their course. It is educational programmers, psychologists and evaluators who develop the techniques of choice making that are held to maximise autonomy: the skills for resisting peer pressure, the development of self-esteem and so on. It is medical programmers and their evaluators who develop the techniques of health risk avoidance and reduction that are available to the choice-maker in formulating a personal programme of pleasure.[6] The 'taming of chance' thus appears in this domain as the *shaping of choice* and the *identification of risk*. More generally, I have argued, these two interlinked processes are key features of government in advanced liberalism, for as the domain of our security is increasingly passed over to the responsibility of the 'prudent' individual, then more and more of our lives and resources need to be given over to the government of our futures. Only the irresponsible or feckless will leave the future to chance when new probabilistic and risk managerial technologies allow for its taming. At the beginning of the 21st century almost every area of the person has become subject to risk managing technologies that 'allow' us to spread or reduce risk. Confronted by so many advanced technologies for governing the future, the individual's range of choices apparently expands. But the ambiguity of this choice should now be clear, for while each choice represents the creation of an option, each option represents a further shaping of 'freedom'. Harms that exist only in the *possible* future must increasingly be governed as if they are actually occurring problems or 'objective risks' in the here and now. Increasing commitment of time and effort must be given over to governing the future security of our physical health and fitness, employment, property, retirement, and mental faculties. More than this, they must be given over to governing the futures of all those others, the members of our

---

6 Such concerns not infrequently lead to considerable suspicion of harm minimisation and similar public health models. Jon Zibbell (2003), for example, has argued that despite the emphasis on drug users becoming 'experts of themselves', their knowledge and concerns are invariably subordinated to that of professional expertise. 'Empowerment' of drug users in such discourses is thus regarded as spurious, for no matter how important and relevant users' knowledge, their social or relational power is insufficient to give them more than a contributory or advisory role in their own government.

'families' and 'communities', whose futures are increasingly rendered the responsibility of self-governing individuals under advanced liberalism. Awareness of risks may extend our future and render it more secure. Yet the more that risks are identified and linked to current life practices, lifestyle choices and the acquisition of new commodities of security, so the present is consumed and governed by the future.

In the genealogy of liberalism the association between risk, uncertainty and freedom has been a central theme, in large measure because all of these ways of framing governance assume and valorise an *indeterminate* future. Only if the future is in some degree calculable can a 'free' individual chart a course. To be subjected to a future governed by random forces is not part of liberalism's vision of freedom. Under such conditions subjects become hostages to fortune. On the other hand, only if the future is in some degree incalculable can individuals have the 'freedom' to make rational decisions and take responsibility. To the degree that they are subjected to determining forces, whether of nature or politics, likewise subjects are rendered unfree. Uncertainty and risk appear as the two primary ways in which, historically, this partially determinate future has been imagined and governed by liberalism.

This may be taken to imply that risk and uncertainty were simply brought into being to resolve problems identified with liberal governance. Of course this is part of the truth. Actuarial insurance, for example, was encouraged and shaped by 19th century liberal governments seeking to foster thrift and independence among the mass of the populace. The invention of social insurance reflected a later attempt to govern harms that were identified by liberal collectivists as lying outside the effective control of individuals. As this example also indicates, however, it is possible to argue that such efforts to govern through risk and uncertainty have been formative as well as reflective of changes in historical liberalism. It was not simply 'liberals' but social theorists, statisticians and charitable agencies that identified the 'social' nature of problems, and actuaries who rendered social insurance a feasible solution. One of the major reasons for emphasising this point is to undermine any tendency to regard liberalism itself as a new engine of history (cf Frankel 1997). There is a fine line to tread between giving due force to the impact of major rationalities such as social liberalism and regarding them as the determinants of the nature and form of all governance that coexists with them. An emphasis on the genealogy of risk and uncertainty provides a counter to such determinist thinking. If rationalities themselves are regarded as assembled and invented, their own contingent formation will be seen to reflect the impact of technologies which they adopt, adapt and valorise. Retrospectively it might appear that rationalities simply bring technologies into being. But only relatively late in the development of rationalities does the flow of influence run decisively in this direction. This occurs primarily after intellectuals have rendered the jumble of ideas, critiques, practices, techniques and so on into something coherent, a recognisable 'rationality'.

Even so, government does not stay in one place for too long. While some commentators regard the influence of the professions and technologies of the welfare state as profoundly diminished by neo-liberalism (Garland 2001), it is not at all clear that this is so. Rather, as argued in Chapter 7, the 'social sciences' are now being translated into a new governmental context, often under the banner of risk-reduction. As in the field of crime prevention, the 'social' re-emerges in a new guise. Social democratic governance is revitalised in some contexts dominated by neo-liberalism, and neo-liberalism begins to change. Alongside this, new writings on managerialism, and new techniques that they advocate, have played a vital role in shaping an emergent Third Way. Innovation and risk-taking are now promoted in new ways. A revised image of the subject as a 'social entrepreneur' begins to overlay or elaborate the 1980s economic imagery of the entrepreneur as the agent of a market-led form of government. We can recognise a certain 'inventiveness in politics' that is reshaping neo-liberalism and its technologies, arguably, into something else (Rose, 1999a; 1999b).

As this book has also been at pains to argue, the relationship between risk and uncertainty cannot be regarded as one of mutual exclusion, nor can it be argued that risk is displacing uncertainty. Of course risk has become very prominent in ways that would have been surprising 50 years ago. In the 1950s far less emphasis was placed on the individual's responsibility for government of everyday risks. Quite possibly it is this change that has made risk so salient to many social scientists in recent years (O'Malley, 1992). However, in some respects, in the 1950s risk governed the lives of many people to an even greater extent than is the case now, through the apparatuses of social insurance and related technologies of social security. The subsequent transformation and reshaping of their domain has been a major theme in recent governmental analysis. This *redistribution and reshaping* of technologies of risk, it seems to me, is of greater significance than whether 'more' of our lives, or whether the lives of 'more' people, are governed through risk than was formerly the case. The converse of this is that it cannot be said that government through technologies of uncertainty has been diminishing in significance in the past 50 years. In the heyday of the welfare state, the uncertain technologies of the market and reliance on individual foresight often were regarded as problematic. They were to be assigned an important but comparatively restricted role. Science, planning and risk would magnify the creative powers and diminish the harms delivered by the free market, and they would improve on the protections provided by individual prudence. Subsequently, however, the ascendancy of neo-liberalism has re-centred uncertainty – and more precisely the uncertainties associated with the free market and the importance of individual self-reliance – in ways that also would have been thought surprising 50 years ago.

For such reasons, it is not at all clear that risk is becoming the dominant *telos* or organising principle of contemporary government, as many suggest (Dean, 1995a; Rose, 1999b). Doubtless it is a very salient principle; but the promotion of neo-liberalism and entrepreneurial governance has also pressed a new *telos* of creative uncertainty to the foreground. Rather than concerning ourselves about a possibly futile exercise in measuring whether risk is 'spreading', we should recognise that risk and uncertainty are *both* being valorised in new ways and forms. And they are being deployed in relation to different domains or functions of government than was the case in the post-war years. Not the least important of these changes is that both are mobilised to emphasise the choice and responsibility of individuals for the governance of their own futures and the futures of their families and 'communities'. The apparatuses of social security that once provided actuarial governance of harm are increasingly inflected by uncertainty. Unemployment insurance is translated into a contractual arrangement in which the unemployed cease to receive a guaranteed insurance benefit as of right. Now they are transformed into jobseekers, who must enterprise themselves in exchange for an allowance. Life insurance, once promoted as an actuarial technology promoting prudence, often is rendered a speculative 'financial product'. As part of this, the distinctions between insurance and financial speculation are broken down by governments and corporations eager to render 'policyholders' into 'stakeholders' or even 'shareholders'. 'Communities' are invented in order to take over 'their' responsibilities for governing crime risks, or for administering risk-based advice and care in relation to HIV, or for providing support and skills to young people and minorities. They are pressured to form quasi-contractual partnerships with police and other 'service providers'. They are given information and training in managing crime risks, health risks, and so on, and invited to contribute their own 'local' expertise. Drug addicts are made free and rational in order that they can learn about the risks of drug consumption and freely take a personal responsibility for harm minimisation. In their various ways, these responsibilising processes seemingly *democratise* government through the mobilising of risk and uncertainty. Individuals and communities are made free to choose how they will govern themselves in relation to a host of insecurities. Expertise in risk and uncertainty – dealing with everything from crime risks to financial investment – appears in an advisory capacity, often available in a commodified form. We are all to be 'empowered' by the provision of information and skills about how to secure ourselves.

Significantly, the trigger of this 'democratisation' of security is not simply hostility to, or distrust of, expertise, as the risk society thesis suggests. Experts in risk are among us in numbers greater than ever before, and their services are eagerly sought after – even though increasingly we pay in cash. However, they have been joined by other experts in security, whose knowledges come from diverse sources. If these experts often disagree with each other, this is not only (or necessarily) because the truth now evades scientific expertise in a world of modernisation risks. It is more to do with the fact that markets in expertise have been created in many fields to promote the provision of choice and to maximise competition. Western medicine and its battery of risk-diagnostic techniques are more active and extensive in their reach than ever. But in the marketplace of health they are joined by New Age therapies and ancient remedies. Private security forces now compete with public police, with whom they are also sometimes allied, and offer 'expert' services in crime prevention – once part of the police monopoly. 'Entrepreneurs' and 'stakeholders' are invited to question virtually all expertise and innovate their own solutions. Even economists are challenged by managerial experts in 'voodoo economics'. Few of these arriviste expertises are related to the undermining of traditional experts by modernisation risks; few of the mainstream expertises appear to be 'working' any less well than they used to work. Indeed, what characterises many of these challenges to mainstream scientific expertise is that they are promoted (or at the very least tolerated) rather than opposed by state governments. The picture of experts and governments in collusion in order to conceal the failure of forecasting in the risk society simply does not gel. Experts of differing kinds are pitted against each other in the domain that perhaps more than any other epitomises uncertainty – the 'free' market. They are pitted against each other in the name of democratisation and empowerment. Hence New Age proponents of 'inventive government' call for such reforms because:

> [w]e rely on professionals to solve problems, not families and communities. We let the police, the doctors, the teachers, and the social workers have all the control, while the people they are serving have none ... We create programs designed to collect clients rather than to empower communities of citizens. When we do this, we undermine the confidence and competence of our citizens and communities. (Osborne and Gaebler, 1993, p 51)

In this process there seems little of the idea that science, insurance or any other expertise is being undermined by modernisation risks, or that the idea of progress has been abandoned. The source of change appears to be political or governmental rather than to do with the contradictory logic of modernism. For this reason too, the challenge to experts is not specific to expertise in risk, technology or science. Nor is it the case that the challenge is occurring only where science is proving an ineffective predictor. Medicine is a good counter example to such claims, for it seems better than ever at identifying and diminishing risks. Yet this is a time in which 'alternative medicine' has flourished as never before. Rather, the challenge has arisen, I suggest, because in some measure the 'old' truths have come to be regarded by neo-liberal governments as *monopolies*. Faith in competition, and the preference for 'freedom of choice', allow new or formerly marginalised knowledges to surface in the marketplace. Looked at this way, the inevitable trajectory of government, impelled into the risk society by modernity's contradictions, dissolves. We simply do not know whether all of this will continue, accelerate or be reversed by some new shift in liberal (or other) government.

Yet this discussion raises another kind of governmental question. It is concerned with the kind of 'freedom' and 'democracy' that the current regime of risk and uncertainty is supposed to deliver. For classical liberals, the foundations of freedom were to be found in uncertainty, particularly in the institutions associated with the free market. The market would make subjects free by requiring them to become independent. In this they would be 'aided' by the practices of diverse disciplinary institutions that would train them to take on the 'yoke of foresight'. Laws of contract and tort would elaborate and enforce all manner of intellectual devices – 'reasonable foreseeability', 'expectations', 'voluntary assumption of risk', 'negligence', 'contributory negligence' and so on – through which entrepreneurs, traders and labourers would be instructed in the exercise of foresight. While a handful of 'entrepreneurs' would practise a creative uncertainty, most people were to practise a defensive regime of prudence; and so the lives of the masses were to be shaped by a governmental vision of the uncertain nature of the future. It is not so much that the future itself was to be governed or 'colonised', as some have expressed it. Quite the reverse was the case. The present was to be colonised by the future. The practice of freedom in the 19th century, paradoxically, was defined as subjection to the uncertain impact of things to come. As far as governments were concerned the *nature* of these uncertainties was known: the unemployment, sickness, injury or death of the breadwinner – such things that would 'foreseeably' interrupt earnings and thus threaten independence. In the name of this future, self-discipline and self-denial – techniques of defensive uncertainty – were imposed upon the present.

How differently things now appear. True, as in the 19th century, 'uncertainty makes us free'; but the uncertainty envisioned by neo-liberals relates to a situation in which we are all imagined to be entrepreneurs. We are exhorted to experiment and innovate, to become risk-takers, to 'reinvent' ourselves. This is meant both literally, in the sense that we should invest our capital in the speculative market, and figuratively, in that we should become entrepreneurs of civil society and of ourselves. It is seemingly positive and self-described as 'empowering'. It is, however, a kind of empowerment that is also colonised by a future mapped out by another rationality of liberal government. If our 19th century forebears were required to practise defensive uncertainty because government had determined that the future was uncertain, for the same reason we are now instructed to practice a creative uncertainty. Ushered in under the announced reality of 'globalisation' and the 'failure' of the welfare state, we are once again to be governed by a future represented as uncertain. This situation apparently has made it necessary that we abandon many existing traditions, solidarities and identities – for globalisation and uncertainty are about the only things said to be certain about the future. (A vision, curiously, shared by Tony Blair and Ulrich Beck.) Thus, when we are invited to reinvent ourselves, and to embrace uncertainty, there is a certain paradox invoked. The future is certain to be uncertain in *specific* ways. Of course there are enormous differences between the 19th century and 21st century uncertainties, and between the respective techniques that we are provided with to chart our course through them. Yet now, as then, the shape of the future is given to us by government. Our inventiveness can only be judged in a positive light to the extent that we adapt to it; and so the limits of this new freedom are revealed.

In contemporary government risk differs surprisingly little from uncertainty in these respects. In risk-based technologies, as Bernstein bemoans, the future also is mapped for us by authorities – if with a good deal more precision. 'Objective' harmful realities are shown to exist probabilistically 'out there' in the future, and we must chart our course between them. In broad contrast to risk under social liberalism, risk now charts out many probable harms that we must *personally* avoid. Perhaps as a consequence, risk technologies now have an even greater power to govern the interstices of life than was formerly the case. For much of the 20th century the governance of risk was centred in great institutions of the state and the insurance corporations. While under these regimens new risks were discovered and new risk technologies were invented to govern them, the pace of change was comparatively slow. The shape and domain of risk in the 1960s differed surprisingly little from that of the 1930s. In the years since, however, the revitalisation of uncertainty has been paralleled by a reinvention of risk. We are increasingly 'free' to govern ourselves through risk and choice, and thus we increasingly create demands for new risk-diagnostic tests, routines, equipment, and so on. These are 'needs' which *industry* now eagerly provides for, makes us aware of, and of course stimulates. The valorisation of markets and individual freedom has not only created new competitors to traditional experts in risk. It has also promoted a proliferation of risk expertise and risk paraphernalia, so that the rate of change in this field of individualised risk governance is doubtless unprecedented. If neo-liberals were opposed to technocratic domination by welfare state expertise, they have fostered a similarly pervasive domination through commodified expertise. Perhaps, too, they have stimulated a challenge to the authority of scientific definitions of risk and its governance.

Through risk the future colonises the present. Despite Bernstein's mantra, much the same is true for uncertainty, even as we are encouraged to become inventive. Nowadays, however, it is not that the yoke of foresight is being *imposed*. Rather, all of this enterprising and risk-reducing work is to be carried out as part of our self-fulfilment and lifestyle. Even our inventiveness and creativeness has been captured by a new regime of liberalism. The 'inner self', formulated and promoted by the Romantics in their resistance to utilitarianism, has been set to work on a rather different project of freedom.

A new age of uncertainty?

In the past year or so, a surprising convergence has occurred between a governmental analytics and the risk society theorists. Francois Ewald (2002, p 276) has argued that a new paradigm of insecurity has emerged that is linked to a science 'that is consulted less for the knowledge it offers than for the doubt it insinuates'. Like Ulrich Beck, Ewald sees major areas of life being affected by a new principle that focuses on the 'unpredictability' of substantial hazards:

> The precautionary hypothesis puts us in the presence of a risk that is neither measurable nor assessable – that is, essentially a nonrisk. While the logic of insurance and solidarity had reduced uncertainty to risk, in order to make the former systematically assessable, the logic of precaution leads us once again to distinguish between risk and uncertainty. Precautionary logic does not cover risk (which is covered by prevention); it applies to what is uncertain – that is, to what one can apprehend without being able to assess. (2002, p 286)

The precautionary principle has as its focus prevention by taking no chances. Even before a risk has been identified as such, the worst is assumed. All steps are to be taken to preclude a possible event, the precise nature of which is 'unforeseeable'. The most extreme form is argued to be 'development risk', in which, to borrow Keynes' phrase, 'we simply do not know' what will happen. Of course there is a calculation here. Genetic modification of foods, for example, is selected as a target for the precautionary principle because the kinds of harms that are *imaginable* would be unacceptable under any circumstances. This is distinct from, say, reasonable foreseeability in law, because there the unwonted event must appear 'reasonably' likely to occur. Here, on the other hand, any degree of likelihood would be too great to tolerate. Zero risk of an unacceptable harm is possible only where there is zero action. Thus while risk has been enormously productive of institutions, technologies of the self and new commodities, precaution is said to offer nothing.

While this sort of view has much in common with that of Beck, several significant differences emerge. The first is that Ewald does not assume that 'risk consciousness' has taken over the world and is displacing all other modes of governance. Ewald is clear that this is a new 'attitude' that joins 'prudence' and 'prevention' in our battery of ways for governing indeterminacy. Secondly, like Beck, Ewald regards precaution as concerned with risks of the sort that have been generated by the advance of science, industry and technology. In consequence, he restricts precaution to a specific domain, the 'context of scientific uncertainty on the one hand and the possibility of serious and irreversible damage on the other' (2002, p 284).[1] The specificity of Ewald's account is refreshing, as is the refusal to regard uncertainty and distrust of expertise as saturating the present. The restrained nature of the argument contrasts with Beck's view that turns not only science, but all of government and everyday life, on its head:

> A characteristic of the global risk society is a metamorphosis of danger which is difficult to delineate or monitor: markets collapse and there is shortage in the midst of surplus. Medical treatments fail. Constructs of economic rationality wobble. Governments are forced to resign. The taken-for-granted rules of everyday life are turned upside down. Almost everyone is defenceless against the threats of natures as re-created by industry. Dangers are integral to normal consumption habits. (Beck, 1999, p 143)

This is unconvincing to say the least. Medical treatments have failed for several hundred years. Shortages for some have always existed alongside surplus for others. Governments routinely have been forced to resign throughout the last couple of centuries. Constructs of economic rationality have wobbled and markets have crashed throughout the history of liberalism. Dangers were far more integral to normal consumption habits in the 19th century than is now the case. Of course, sociologists have a particular penchant for what Colin Gordon (1986, p 78) once called 'semiologies of catastrophe' – narratives of transformation and rupture, usually pessimistic, that imagine us to be on the brink of a global social and political watershed. Unfortunately, Ewald eventually proves unable to resist the temptation to join in. The precautionary principle becomes 'one of the primary instruments of "reflexive modernization" which, as Beck demonstrates, characterises postmodernism'. It comes to be the case that through this principle 'modern society thinks about its problems and questions its basic assumptions'. Indeed, 'along with the principle of precaution, the notion of reflexive modernization has become a central preoccupation of the international community' (Ewald, 2002, p 295).

Whether any of these statements is accurate is hard to judge. As with Ulrich Beck's work, no evidence is presented about whether 'modern society' (let alone a large number of people) has undergone such a change of consciousness. It is simply assumed to have happened. In practice, Ewald points to a small handful of examples in which this principle has become part of state or supra-state governance. This is not to deny that the precautionary principle has become a high profile regulatory resource, especially in the EC (Fisher, 2002). However, in most instances, as he suggests, the principle is put in place as a temporary measure until the risk can be determined (presumably by scientists). For the most part, the appearance of major and potentially catastrophic risks has not given rise to new reflections about the limits of science. At least as often, it has given rise to the

---

1   This qualification is important, for precaution takes a rather different form with respect to the security interventions developed post-9/11 (regarded by Beck (2002) as an instance of modernisation risks at work). Thus the Bush doctrine of 'pre-emption' claims that there is now a need 'to confront the worst threats before they appear'. However, it also argues that 'in the world we have entered, the only path to safety is the path to action' (*New York Times*, 16 December 2003). Action, a code word for military intervention, in turn, implies that the threats and their source are both imaginable, merely incapable of precise specification. Here we are in the familiar territory of uncertainty.

intensification of a search for security based on risk and foreseeability. In Chapter 1, for example, this was discussed with reference to the development of catastrophe insurance. In ways not even considered by Beck, this inventive institution has rendered disasters governable, despite his assertions about the uninsurability of modern catastrophes. Will they work? Will they fail? None of us knows, including sociologists of the risk society. Elsewhere, as in the threat of international terrorism, holes in the ozone layer, even global warming, there have been large-scale governmental mobilisations of the same kind to govern these threats. Whether any of these will 'work' or not is a moot question. In any case it is a question whose answer is largely outside the competence of any sociological analytic. Whether or not global warming is occurring, and if so whether it is reversible, are not questions which sociologists, *qua* sociologists, are competent to investigate or pronounce upon. The same point applies to whether or not the ozone layer is being repaired by the effects of new precautions, or whether security against terrorism will be 'effective'.

This is not to say that sociologists should be unconcerned about these issues. Of course they are vital *political* issues we cannot help but be involved in; but at what cost does social theory advance on the assumption that it too knows the future? What are *the dangers* of assuming that the logic of a contradictory modernism is propelling us into a risk society where precaution becomes the principal response to problems? What are the 'risks', for example, of sociologists assuming, with neo-liberals, that the future of globalisation and its consequences render the welfare state obsolete – that render welfare state governance of the (mal)distribution of goods into a *passé* charade that has been overtaken by the problem of the distribution of 'bads' (cf Beck, 1999, pp 73–80)?

In the meantime government, in all shapes and forms, acts. The problematisations, plans, techniques, apparatuses and routines that are deployed in the name of our security are for the most part recognisable by social analysts and already bear consequences for us. We need not guess about these, as we must about the future of 'reflexive modernisation'. In opposition to the kind of theory and politics practiced by risk society theorists, it is possible to provide an alternative, if less grandiose, project. In a limited way, this alternative is what has been attempted in this volume. It is neatly summed up by Wendy Brown, as follows:

> If history is without a forward-moving logic, then it bears no logical entailments for the future; no inference can be drawn from it about what is to be done or what is to be valued. As history is emancipated from metaphysics and thereby becomes radically desacralised, so too politics becomes a matter of opportunity, limits and judgment rather than unfolding historical schemes and transcendent ideals. A revitalized left politics would then grapple with constraints and openings rather than logics of power and history; it would develop strategies to counter specific regimes of rationality rather than countering specific policies within those regimes, on the one hand, or countering rationality, as such, on the other. (Brown, 2001, pp 117–18)

In trying to foreground the assembled nature of government and, in particular, the ways in which we are governed through configurations of risk and uncertainty, the non-necessity of any of the existing rationalities and technologies of government becomes more evident, as does their specificity. *Uncertainty* ceases to be a vague domain of the possible, a factual depiction of a murky future, an exercise in 'incalculability'. Instead it emerges as an array of specific demands upon subjects to live their lives in certain ways, instructions about how they should exercise foresight and thus practise their freedom. It appears as a range of invented techniques deployed by government in order to make us into the likeness of a specific image of a rational and free person. *Risk* ceases to be a literal depiction of the world that provides objective indicators of future harms. Instead it emerges as a diverse family of ways in which certain choices are presented to us, and through which practitioners of particular kinds of expertise define the future. Risk assigns us to categories, creates divisions among us and incorporates us in diverse solidarities of fate.

The meandering nature of the genealogies of risk and uncertainty reveal the arbitrary distinctions and moral politics that were inscribed into their formation. Their common focus on an assumed indeterminate future makes them key sites in which liberal freedom has been wrought into specific and limited formations. Risk and uncertainty occupy a principal place among the technologies of freedom, and their genealogies thus reveal how our freedoms are represented to us by those who paradoxically claim to know the future. The point, thus, is not to observe with Peter Bernstein that 'uncertainty makes us free', nor with Ulrich Beck that 'risk dims the horizon'. Even the patchy excursions this book has made into the genealogy of risk and uncertainty suggests the possibility that we can govern ourselves in other ways. Freedom is no more given by uncertainty than it is taken away by risk.

Bibliography

Abel, R, 'The political economy of informal justice', in Abel, R (ed), *The Politics of Informal Justice*, Vol 1, 1982, New York: Academic Press, pp 1–52

Abel-Smith, B and Townsend, P, *Poor and Poorest*, 1965, Harmondsworth: Penguin

Abrams, P, *The Origins of British Sociology 1834–1914*, 1968, Chicago: Chicago University Press

Aharoni, Y, *The No-Risk Society*, 1981, New York: Basic Books

Alcock, P, 'A better partnership between the state and the individual provision: social security into the 1990s' (1989) Journal of Law and Society 16, pp 97–111

Alexander, W, *A Brief History of the Equitable Life Assurance Society of the United States: Seventy Years of Progress and Public Service 1859–1929*, 1932, New York: James F Newcomb

Atiyah, P, *The Rise and Fall of Freedom of Contract*, 1979, Oxford: Clarendon

Atiyah, P, *The Damages Lottery*, 1998, Oxford: Hart

Avery, J, *Police: Force or Service?*, 1981, Sydney: Butterworths

Baker, T and Simon, J, *Embracing Risk: The Changing Culture of Insurance and Responsibility*, 2002, Chicago: Chicago University Press

Barry, A, Osborne, T *et al*, 'Liberalism, neo-liberalism and governmentality: an introduction' (1993) Economy and Society 22, pp 265–66

Baumann, Z, 'Social issues of law and order' (2000) British Journal of Criminology 40, pp 205–21

Beck, U, *Risk Society: Toward a New Modernity*, 1992, New York: Sage

Beck, U, 'The reinvention of politics: towards a theory of reflexive modernization', in Beck, U, Giddens, A and Lash, S (eds), *Reflexive Modernization*, 1994, Cambridge: Polity, pp 1–55

Beck, U, 'The politics of the risk society', in Franklin, J (ed), *The Politics of the Risk Society*, 1998, London: Polity, pp 2–35

Beck, U, *World Risk Society*, 1999, London: Polity

Beck, U, 'The terrorist threat: world risk society revisited' (2002) Theory, Culture and Society 19, pp 39–55

Becker, H, 'Becoming a marijuana user', in Becker, H (ed), *Outsiders. Studies in the Sociology of Deviance*, 1965, New York: Free Press, pp 41–58

Bentham, J, *The Works of Jeremy Bentham*, Vol 1, Bowring, J (ed), 1962, New York: Russell and Russell

Berlin, I, 'Two concepts of liberty', in Berlin, I (ed), *Four Essays on Liberty*, 1969, Oxford: Oxford University Press, pp 118–72

Bernstein, P, *Against the Gods: The Remarkable Story of Risk*, 1998, New York: Wiley

Beveridge, W, *Social Insurance and Allied Services*, Cmd 6404, 1942, London: HMSO

Blackstone, W (1767), *Commentaries on the Laws of England*, 1922, Philadelphia: Bisel

Blaug, M, *Economic Theory in Retrospect*, 1988, Cambridge: Cambridge University Press

Blewitt, N, *National Campaign Against Drug Abuse: Assumptions, Arguments and Aspirations*, 1987, Canberra: Australian Government Publishing Service

Blomberg, T and Cohen, S (eds), *Punishment and Social Control: Essays in Honor of Sheldon L Messenger*, 1995, New York: Aldine de Gruyter

Bottoms, A, 'Crime prevention facing the 1990s' (1990) Policing and Society 1, pp 3–22

Bougen, P, 'Catastrophe risk' (2003) Economy and Society 32, pp 253–74

Brabrook, E (Sir), *Provident Societies and Industrial Welfare*, 1898, London: Robinson

Brenner, R and Brenner, G, *Gambling and Speculation: A Theory, a History, and a Future of Some Human Decisions*, 1990, Cambridge: Cambridge University Press

Brett, J, 'The party on the road to nowhere', *The Age*, 17 July 1993, Melbourne

Brown, W, *Politics Out of History*, 2001, Princeton, NJ: Princeton University Press

Burchell, G, Gordon, C et al, *The Foucault Effect. Studies in Governmentality*, 1991, London: Harvester/Wheatsheaf

Cane, P, *Atiyah's Accidents, Compensation and the Law*, 5th edn, 1993, London: Butterworths

Carney, T and Hanks, P, *Social Security in Australia*, 1994, Melbourne: Oxford University Press

Castel, B, 'From dangerousness to risk', in Burchell, G, Gordon, C and Miller, P (eds), *The Foucault Effect. Studies in Governmentality*, 1991, London: Harvester/Wheatsheaf, pp 281–98

Ciro, T, 'Gaming laws and derivatives' (1999) Company and Securities Law Journal 17, pp 1–86

Ciro, T, 'Functional regulation and financial products. Regulatory interplay between financial derivatives and contracts of insurance' (2002a) Journal of Banking and Finance 13, pp 5–14

Ciro, T, 'Anti-speculation laws and financial markets regulation in Australia and the United States' (2002b) Journal of Banking and Finance 13, pp 15–28

Clark, G, *Betting on Lives. The Culture of Life Insurance in England 1695–1775*, 1999, Manchester: Manchester University Press

Clark, J and Newman, J, *The Managerial State*, 1997, London: Sage

Clarke, J, Gerwitz, S et al, *New Managerialism, New Welfare?*, 2000, London: Sage

Clarke, R, *Situational Crime Prevention. Successful Case Studies*, 1992, New York: Harrow and Heston

Clayton, G, *British Insurance*, 1985, London: Elek Books

Cohen, L and Felson, M, 'Social change and crime rate trends: a routine activity approach' (1979) American Sociological Review 44, pp 588–608

Cohen, S, *Visions of Social Control*, 1985, London: Polity

Collins, A, 'The pathological gambler and the government of gambling' (1996) History of the Human Sciences 9, pp 69–100

Collins, H, *The Law of Contract*, 3rd edn, 1997, London: Butterworths

Commonwealth Department of Human Services and Health, *Briefing Notes on Harm Minimisation and Drug Use*, unpublished material, 1995, prepared for the Department of Human Services and Health, Australia

Conley, M 'The "undeserving poor": welfare and labour policy', in Kennedy, R (ed), *Australian Welfare History*, 1986, Sydney: Macmillan, pp 281–303

Considine, M, *Enterprising States. The Public Management of Welfare-to-Work*, 2001, Cambridge: Cambridge University Press

Cornish, D and Clarke, R, 'Situational prevention, displacement of crime and rational choice theory', in Heal, K and Laycock, G (eds), *Situational Prevention. From Theory into Practice*, 1986, London: HMSO, pp 1–16

Cowing, C, *Populists, Plungers, and Progressives: A Social History of Stock and Commodity Speculation*, 1965, Princeton: Princeton University Press

Crawford, A, *Local Governance of Crime*, 1997, Oxford: Clarendon

Crawford, A, 'The growth of crime prevention in France as contrasted with the English experience: some thoughts on the politics of insecurity', in Hughes, G, McLaughlin, E and Muncie, J (eds), *Crime Prevention and Community Safety*, 2002, London: Sage, pp 214–39

Crossman, B and Fudge, J (eds), *Privatization Law and the Challenge of Feminism*, 2002, Toronto: University of Toronto Press

Cruickshank, B, 'Revolutions within: self government and self esteem' (1993) Economy and Society 22, pp 326–44

Cutler, T, Williams, K *et al*, *Keynes, Beveridge and Beyond*, 1986, London: Routledge and Kegan Paul

DSEV (Directorate of School Education Victoria), *Get Real. A Harm Minimisation Approach to Drug Education*, 1995, Melbourne: Directorate of School Education

Daston, L, *Classical Probability in the Enlightenment*, 1988, Princeton: Princeton University Press

Davies, J and Coggans, N, 'Media and school based approaches to drug education', in Strang, J and Gossop, M (eds), *Heroin Addiction and Drug Policy. The British System*, 1994, Oxford: Oxford University Press, pp 301–25

Dean, M, *The Constitution of Poverty*, 1991, London: Routledge

Dean, M, 'Governing the unemployed self in an active society' (1995a) Economy and Society 24, pp 559–83

Dean, M, *Critical and Effective Histories*, 1995b, London: Routledge

Dean, M, 'Putting the technological into government' (1996) History of the Human Sciences 9, pp 47–68

Dean, M, *Governmentality. Power and Rule in Modern Society*, 1999, New York: Sage

Defert, D, 'Popular life and insurance technology', in Burchell, G, Gordon, C and Miller, P (eds), *Foucault Effect. Studies in Governmentality*, 1991, London: Harvester/Wheatsheaf, pp 211–34

Deleuze, G, 'Postscript on control societies', in Deleuze, G (ed), *Negotiations 1972–1990*, 1995, New York: Columbia University Press, pp 177–82

Departmental Committee, *Report of the Departmental Committee on the Business of Industrial Assurance Companies* (Parmoor Report), 1920, London: HMSO

Dixon, D, *From Prohibition to Regulation. Bookmaking, Antigambling and the Law*, 1991, Oxford: Clarendon

Donzelot, J, 'The poverty of political culture' (1979) Ideology and Consciousness 5, pp 71–86

Doran, N, 'Risky business: codifying embodied experience in the Manchester Unity of Oddfellows' (1994) Journal of Historical Sociology 7, pp 131–54

Douglas, M, *Risk Acceptability According to the Social Sciences*, 1986, London: Routledge and Kegan Paul

Douglas, M, *Risk and Blame. Essays in Cultural Theory*, 1992, London: Routledge

Downes, D, Davies, B *et al*, *Gambling, Work and Leisure: A Study Across Three Areas*, 1976, London: Routledge and Kegan Paul

Drucker, P, *Post-capitalist Society*, 1993, New York: Harper Business

Dryden, J, *Addresses and Papers on Life Insurance and Other Subjects*, 1909, Newark, NJ: The Prudential Life Insurance Company of America

du Gay, P, 'Making up managers: bureaucracy, enterprise and the liberal art of separation' (1994) British Journal of Sociology 45, pp 655–74

du Gay, P, 'Entrepreneurial governance and public management: the anti-bureaucrats', in Clarke, J, Gewirtz, S and McLaughlin, E (eds), *New Managerialism, New Welfare*, 2000, London: Sage, pp 62–81

Dunning, J, *Insurance in the Economy*, 1971, London: Institute of Economic Affairs

Eghigian, G, *Making Security Social. Disability, Insurance and the Birth of the Social Entitlement State in Germany*, 2000, Ann Arbor: University of Michigan Press

Emery, H, *Speculation on the Stock and Produce Exchanges of the United States*, 1896, New York: Scribner's Sons

Erickson, P, 'A public health approach to demand reduction' (1990) Journal of Drug Issues 20, pp 563–75

Ericson, R, 'The division of expert knowledge in policing and security' (1994) British Journal of Sociology 45, pp 149–75

Ericson, R and Haggerty, K, *Policing the Risk Society*, 1997, Toronto: University of Toronto Press

Ericson, R, Doyle, A and Barry, D, *Insurance as Governance*, 2003, Toronto: University of Toronto Press

Etter, B, 'Mastering innovation and change in police agencies', in Etter, B and Palmer, M (eds), *Police Leadership in Australia*, 1995, Sydney: Federation Press, pp 278–309

Everingham, S, 'Benefits and costs of early childhood interventions', in Parliament of NSW (ed), *Crime Prevention Through Social Support*, 1998, Sydney: Parliament of NSW Legislative Council, pp 131–47

Ewald, F, *L'Etat Providence*, 1986, Paris: Grasset et Fasquelle

Ewald, F, 'Norms, discipline and the law' (1990) Representations 30, pp 138–61

Ewald, F, 'Insurance and risk', in Burchell, G, Gordon, C and Miller, P (eds), *The Foucault Effect. Studies in Governmentality*, 1991, London: Harvester/Wheatsheaf, pp 197–210

Ewald, F, 'Two infinities of risk', in Massumi, B (ed), *The Politics of Everyday Fear*, 1994, Minneapolis: University of Minnesota Press, pp 221–29

Ewald, F, 'The Return of Descartes's malicious demon: an outline of a philosophy of precaution', in Baker, T and Simon, J (eds), *Embracing Risk: The Changing Culture of Insurance and Responsibility*, 2002, Chicago: University of Chicago Press, pp 273–301

Ewick, P, 'Corporate cures: the commodification of social control' (1993) Studies in Law, Politics and Society 13, pp 137–59

Fabian, A, *Card Sharps, Dream Books, & Bucket Shops: Gambling in 19th-Century America*, 1990, Ithaca: Cornell University Press

Farrington, D, 'Early development prevention of juvenile delinquency' (1994) Criminal Behaviour and Mental Health 4, pp 209–27

Feeley, M and Simon, J, 'The new penology: notes on the emerging strategy of corrections and its implications' (1992) Criminology 30, pp 449–74

Feeley, M and Simon, J, 'Actuarial justice: the emerging new criminal law', in Nelken, D (ed), *The Futures of Criminology*, 1994, New York: Sage, pp 173–201

Felson, M and Clarke, R, 'The ethics of situational crime prevention', in Newman, G, Clarke, R and Shoham, G (eds), *Rational Choice and Situational Crime Prevention: Theoretical Foundations*, 1997, Aldershot: Ashgate, pp 197–218

Ferguson, R, 'The Horwitz thesis and common law discourse in England' (1983) Oxford Journal of Legal Studies 3, pp 34–45

Ferguson, R, 'Commercial expectations and the guarantee of the law: sales transactions in mid-nineteenth century England', in Silverman, D and Rubin, G (eds), *Law, Economy and Society 1750–1914*, 1984, pp 192–208

Fine, B, *Social Capital Versus Social Theory*, 2001, London: Routledge

Fischer, B, 'Drugs, communities, and harm reduction in Germany. The new relevance of "public health" principles in local responses' (1995) Journal of Public Health Policy 16, pp 389–411

Fisher, E, 'Precaution, precaution everywhere: developing a "common understanding" of the precautionary principle in the European Community' (2002) Maastricht Journal of European and Comparative Law 9, pp 7–28

Floud, J and Young, W, 'Dangerousness and criminal justice' (1982) British Journal of Criminology 22, pp 213–28

Foucault, M, *Discipline and Punish*, 1977, London: Peregrine

Foucault, M, *The History of Sexuality*, 1984, London: Peregrine

Foucault, M, 'Governmentality', in Burchell, G, Gordon, C and Miller, P (eds), *The Foucault Effect. Studies in Governmentality*, 1991, London: Harvester/Wheatsheaf, pp 87–104

Fox, N and Matthews, I, *Drug Policy. Facts, Fiction and the Future*, 1992, Sydney: Federation Press

Frankel, B, 'Confronting neoliberal regimes' (1997) New Left Review 226, pp 57–92

Fraser, N and Gordon, L, 'A genealogy of dependency: tracing a keyword of the US welfare state' (1994) Journal of Women in Culture and Society 19, pp 311–36

Freiberg, A, 'Criminal confiscation, profit and liberty' (1992) Australian and New Zealand Journal of Criminology 25, pp 44–81

Freiberg, A, 'Guerillas in our midst? Judicial responses to governing the dangerous', in Brown, M and Pratt, J (eds), *Dangerous Offenders. Punishment and Social Order*, 2000, London: Routledge, pp 51–70

Gabel, P and Feinman, J, 'Contract law as ideology', in Kairys, D (ed), *The Politics of Law*, 1982, New York: Pantheon, pp 172–84

Garland, D, *Punishment and Welfare: A History of Penal Strategies*, 1985, Aldershot: Ashgate

Garland, D, 'Penal modernism and postmodernism', in Cohen, S and Blomberg, D (eds), *Punishment and Social Control*, 1995, New York: Aldine, pp 181–209

Garland, D, 'The limits of the sovereign state: strategies of crime control in contemporary society' (1996) British Journal of Criminology 36, pp 445–71

Garland, D, *The Culture of Control*, 2001, Oxford: Oxford University Press

Garland, D and Sparks, R, 'Criminology, social theory and the challenge of our times' (2000) British Journal of Criminology 4, pp 189–204

Geason, S and Wilson, P, *Crime Prevention: Theory and Practice*, 1988, Canberra: Australian Institute of Criminology

Geason, S and Wilson, P, *Designing Out Crime: Crime Prevention through Environmental Design*, 1989, Canberra: Australian Institute of Criminology

George, V, *Social Security: Beveridge and After*, 1968, London: Routledge and Kegan Paul

Giddens, A, *The Third Way and its Critics*, 2000, Cambridge: Polity

Gilbert, B, 'The decay of the nineteenth century provident institutions and the coming of old age pensions in Great Britain' (1965) Economic History Review (Series 2) 17, pp 550–63

Glanz, A, 'The fall and rise of the general practitioner', in Strang, J and Gossop, M (eds), *Heroin Addiction and Drug Policy. The British System*, 1994, Oxford: Oxford University Press, pp 148–63

Gordley, J, *The Philosophical Origins of Modern Contract Doctrine*, 1991, Oxford: Clarendon

Gordon, C, 'Question, ethos, event' (1986) Economy and Society 15, pp 73–78

Gordon, C, 'Governmental rationality: an introduction', in Burchell, G, Gordon, C and Miller, P (eds), *The Foucault Effect. Studies in Governmentality*, 1991, London: Harvester/ Wheatsheaf, pp 1–53

Gosden, P, *Self Help: Voluntary Associations in the 19th Century*, 1973, London: BT Batsford

Gough, I, *The Political Economy of the Welfare State*, 1979, London: Macmillan

Greco, M, 'Psychosomatic subjects and the duty to be well' (1993) Economy and Society 22, pp 357–72

Green, J, *Risk and Misfortune. A Social Construction of Accidents*, 1997, London: UCL Press

Green, S, 'Negotiating with the future: the culture of modern risk in global financial markets' (2000) Environment and Planning D: Society and Space 18, pp 77–89

Greenberg, D, 'The cost benefit analysis of imprisonment' (1990) Social Justice 17, pp 49–75

Greig, D and Davies, J, *The Law of Contract*, 1987, Sydney: Law Book Company

HCS (Victorian Government Department of Health and Community Services), *Victorian Drug Strategy: 1993–98*, 1993, Melbourne: Health and Community Service, Promotions and Media Unit

HCS (Victorian Government Department of Health and Community Services), *Methadone Treatment in Victoria. User Information Booklet*, 1995, Melbourne: Health and Community Services, Public Health Branch

HM Government, *Tackling Drugs Together*, 1995, London: HMSO

HM Government, *Tackling Drugs to Build a Better Britain*, 1998, London: The Stationery Office

Hacking, I, *The Taming of Chance*, 1990, Cambridge: Cambridge University Press

Hacking, I, 'How should we do the history of statistics?', in Burchell, G, Gordon, C and Miller, P (eds), *Foucault Effect. Studies in Governmentality*, 1991, London: Harvester/Wheatsheaf, pp 181–96

Haggerty, K, 'From risk to precaution: the rationalities of personal crime prevention', in Ericson, R and Doyle, A (eds), *Risk and Morality*, 2003, Toronto: University of Toronto Press, pp 193–214

Hall, J, 'Burglary 1985: the insurance industry viewpoint', in Mukherjee, S (ed), *Burglary. A Social Reality*, 1986, Canberra: Australian Institute of Criminology, pp 241–54

Hamburger, P, 'The development of the nineteenth-century consensus theory of contract' (1989) Law and History Review 7, pp 241–329

Handy, C, *The Age of Unreason*, 1989, London: Arrow

Hannah-Moffat, K, 'Moral agent or actuarial subject. Risk and Canadian women's imprisonment' (1999) Theoretical Criminology 3, pp 71–95

Harries, J, *William Beveridge. A Biography*, 1977, Oxford: Clarendon

Hart, H and Honoré, T, *Causation in the Law*, 2nd edn, 1987, Oxford: Clarendon

Heal, K and Laycock, G, *Situational Crime Prevention: From Theory Into Practice*, 1986, London: HMSO

Heelas, P, 'Reforming the self', in Keat, R and Abercrombie, N (eds), *Enterprise Culture*, 1991, London: Routledge, pp 72–92

Heimer, C, 'The racial and organizational origins of insurance redlining' (1982) Journal of Inter Group Relations 10, pp 42–60

Heimer, C and Staffen, L, *For the Sake of the Children. The Social Organization of Responsibility in the Hospital and the Home*, 1988, Chicago: University of Chicago Press

Higgins, V, 'Calculating climate: "advanced liberalism" and the governing of risk in Australian drought policy' (2001) Journal of Sociology 37, pp 299–316

Home Office, *Tackling Crime*, 1989, London: HMSO

Home Office, *Protecting the Public: The Government's Strategy on Crime in England and Wales*, 1996, London: HMSO

Homel, R, 'Pathways to prevention', in Parliament of NSW (ed), *Crime Prevention Through Social Support*, 1998, Sydney: Parliament of NSW Legislative Council, pp 91–100

Horwitz, M, *The Transformation of American Law*, 1977, Harvard: Harvard University Press

Hudson, B, 'Punishment, rights and difference', in Stenson, K and Sullivan, R (eds), *Crime, Risk and Justice*, 2000, Exeter: Willan, pp 144–72

Hunt, D, 'Strategic management in policing', in Etter, B and Palmer, M (eds), *Police Leadership in Australia*, 1995, Sydney: Federation Press, pp 40–74

Institute of Life Insurance, Life Insurance Association of America *et al*, *The Economic and Social Contributions of Life Insurance to the Nation*, 1959

Jerry, R, *Understanding Insurance Law*, 2nd edn, 1996, New York: Matthew Bender

Johnson, P, 'Credit and thrift and the British working class', in Winter, J (ed), *The Working Class in Modern British History. Essays in Honour of Henry Pelling*, 1983, Cambridge: Cambridge University Press, pp 30–45

Johnson, P, *Saving and Spending. The Working Class Economy in Britain 1870–1939*, 1985, Oxford: Clarendon

Kanter, R, *When Giants Learn to Dance*, 1990, London: Unwin Hyman

Keat, R, 'Introduction. Starship Britain or Universal Enterprise', in Keat, R and Abercrombie, N (eds), *Enterprise Culture*, 1991, London: Routledge, pp 1–20

Keeler, J, 'Social insurance, disability, and personal injury: a retrospective view' (1994) University of Toronto Law Journal 44, pp 275–352

Kempf-Leonard, K and Peterson, E, 'Expanding realms of the new penology. The advent of actuarial justice for juveniles' (2000) Punishment and Society 2, pp 66–96

Kemshall, H, *Risk in Probation Practice*, 1998, Aldershot: Dartmouth

Kemshall, H, *Risk, Social Policy and Welfare*, 2002, Buckingham: Open University Press

Kemshall, H and Maguire, M, 'Public protection, "partnership" and risk penality' (2001) Punishment and Society 3, pp 237–54

Kercher, B, *Debt, Seduction and Other Disasters. The Birth of Civil Law in Convict New South Wales*, 1996, Sydney: Federation Press

Kercher, B and Noone, M, *Remedies*, 1990, Sydney: Law Book Company

Kewley, T, *Social Security in Australia 1900–72*, 1973, Sydney: Sydney University Press

King, D, *In the Name of Liberalism: Illiberal Social Policy in the USA and Britain*, 1999, Oxford: Oxford University Press

King, M, 'The political construction of crime prevention: a contrast between the French and British experience', in Stenson, K and Cowell, D (eds), *The Politics of Crime Control*, 1991, Newbury Park, CA: Sage, pp 87–108

Kinsey, R, Young, J et al, *Losing the Fight Against Crime*, 1986, New York: Basil Blackwell

Knight, F, *Risk, Uncertainty and Profit*, 1921, New York: AM Kelley

Knights, D and Verdubakis, T, 'Calculations of risk: towards an understanding of insurance as a moral and political technology' (1993) Accounting, Organizations and Society 18, pp 729–64

Kreitner, R, 'Speculations of contract, or how contract law stopped worrying and learned to love risk' (2000) Columbia Law Review 100, pp 1096–127

LSEC (London Stock Exchange Commission), *Report from the Commissioners on the Stock Exchange*, Cmd 2157, 1878, London: HMSO

Labour Party, *Labour Believes in Britain*, 1949, London: British Labour Party

Labour Party, *The Future of Industrial Insurance*, 1950, London: British Labour Party

Lake M, *Transcripts of Public Human Rights Debates*, 1990, Melbourne: National Centre for Socio-Legal Studies

Letwin, S and Letwin, W, *Every Adult a Shareowner*, 1986, London: Centre for Policy Studies

Levi, R, 'The mutuality of risk and community: the adjudication of community notification statutes' (2000) Economy and Society 29, pp 578–601

Levine, H, 'The discovery of addiction. Changing conceptions of habitual drunkenness in America' (1978) Journal of Studies on Alcohol 39, pp 43–74

Luhmann, N, *Risk. A Sociological Theory*, 1993, New York: Aldine de Gruyter

Lurie, J, *The Chicago Board of Trade, 1859–1905*, 1979, Chicago: University of Illinois Press

McLaughlin, E, 'The democratic deficit. European Union and the accountability of the British police' (1992) British Journal of Criminology 32, pp 473–87

McLaughlin, E and Murji, K, 'The end of public policing?', in Noaks, L, Maguire, L and Levi, M (eds), *Contemporary Issues in Criminology*, 1995, Cardiff: University of Wales Press, pp 82–105

Maclean, B, 'In partial defence of socialist realism. Some theoretical and methodological concerns of the local crime survey' (1991) Crime, Law and Social Change 15, pp 213–35

Matthews, R and Pitts, J, 'Introduction. Beyond criminology?', in Matthews, R and Pitts, J (eds), *Crime, Disorder and Community Safety: A New Agenda?*, 2001, London: Routledge, pp 1–25

Matza, D and Morgan, P, 'Controlling drug use: the great prohibition', in Blomberg, T and Cohen, S (eds), *Punishment and Social Control*, 1995, Chicago: Aldine de Gruyter, pp 229–44

Maurer, B, 'Repressed futures: financial derivatives' theoretical unconscious' (2002) Economy and Society 31, pp 15–36

May, C and Cooper, A, 'Personal identity and social change' (1995) Acta Sociologica 38, pp 75–85

Mayhew, P, Clarke, R et al, *Crime in Public View*, 1979, London: HMSO

Meredyth, D, 'Corporatising education', in Dean, M and Hindess, B (eds), *Governing Australia*, 1998, Melbourne: Cambridge University Press, pp 20–46

Merkin, R, 'Gambling by insurance. A study of the Life Assurance Act 1774' (1980) Anglo-American Law Review 9, pp 331–63

Miller, L, 'Looking for postmodernism in all the wrong places. Implementing a new penology' (2001) British Journal of Criminology 41, pp 168–84

Miller, P and Rose, N, 'Governing economic life' (1990) Economy and Society 19, pp 1–31

Moore, D and Haggerty, K, 'Bringing it on home. Home drug testing and the relocation of the war on drugs' (2001) Social and Legal Studies 10, pp 377–95

Morrah, D, *A History of Industrial Life Assurance*, 1955, London: George Allen and Unwin

National Crime Prevention, *Pathways to Prevention. Developmental and Early Intervention Approaches to Crime in Australia*, 1999a, Canberra: Commonwealth Attorney General's Department

National Crime Prevention, *Hanging Out. Negotiating Young People's Use of Public Space*, 1999b, Canberra: Commonwealth Attorney General's Department

National Crime Prevention of Canada, *Preventing Crime by Investing in Families*, 1997, Ottawa: National Crime Prevention of Canada

National Crime Prevention Institute, *Crime Prevention*, 1986, Louisville: National Crime Prevention Institute

New Zealand Government, *National Drug Strategy*, 1998, Wellington: Government Printer

Normandeau, A and Leighton, B, *A Vision of the Future of Policing in Canada*, 1990, Ottawa: Solicitor General Canada

Novas, C and Rose, N, 'Genetic risk and the birth of the somatic individual' (2000) Economy and Society 29, pp 485–513

ONDCP (Office of National Drug Control Policy), *National Drug Control Strategy 2000*, 2000, Washington, DC: Office of National Drug Control Policy

O'Connor, J, *The Fiscal Crisis of the State*, 1973, London: St Martin's Press

O'Malley, P, 'Social justice in the client state' (1989) Social Justice 16, pp 4–14

O'Malley, P, 'Legal networks and domestic security' (1991) Studies in Law, Politics and Society 11, pp 165–84

O'Malley, P, 'Risk, power and crime prevention' (1992) Economy and Society 21, pp 252–75

O'Malley, P, 'Risk and responsibility', in Barry, A, Osborne, T and Rose, N (eds), *Foucault and Political Reason*, 1996, Chicago: Chicago University Press, pp 189–208

O'Malley, P, 'Consuming risks. Harm minimisation and the government of "drug users"', in Smandych, R (ed), *Governable Places. Readings on Governmentality and Crime Control*, 1999a, Aldershot: Dartmouth, pp 191–214

O'Malley, P, 'Volatile and contradictory punishment' (1999b) Theoretical Criminology 3, pp 175–96

O'Malley, P, 'Genealogy, rationalisation and resistance in "advanced liberalism"', in Pavlich, G and Wickham, G (eds), *Rethinking Law, Society and Governance: Foucault's Bequest*, 2000, Oxford: Hart, pp 38–62

O'Malley, P, 'Risk, crime and prudentialism revisited', in Stenson, K and Sullivan, R (eds), *Crime, Risk and Justice*, 2001, Exeter: Willan, pp 89–103

O'Malley, P, 'Imagining insurance: risk, thrift, and life insurance in Britain', in Baker, T and Simon, J (eds), *Embracing Risk: The Changing Culture of Insurance and Responsibility*, 2002, Chicago: University of Chicago Press, pp 97–115

O'Malley, P, 'Moral uncertainties: contract law and distinctions between speculation, gambling and insurance', in Ericson, R and Doyle, A (eds), *Risk and Morality*, 2003, Toronto: University of Toronto Press, pp 231–57

O'Malley, P and Mugford, S, 'The demand for intoxicating commodities: implications for the War on Drugs' (1991a) Social Justice 18, pp 49–75

O'Malley, P and Mugford, S, 'Moral technologies. The political agenda of random drug testing' (1991b) Social Justice 18, pp 122–45

O'Malley, P and Palmer, D, 'Post-Keynesian policing' (1996) Economy and Society 25, pp 137–55

O'Malley, P and Valverde, M, 'Pleasure, freedom and drugs. The uses of "pleasure" in liberal governance of drug and alcohol consumption' (2004) Sociology 38, pp 25–42

O'Malley, P, Weir, L et al, 'Governmentality, criticism, politics' (1997) Economy and Society 26, pp 501–17

Ogus, A, 'Great Britain', in Kohler, P and Zacher, H (eds), *The Evolution of Social Insurance 1881–1981*, 1982, New York: St Martin's Press, pp 150–264

Osborne, T, 'Security and vitality: drains, liberalism and power in the nineteenth century', in Barry, A, Osborne, T and Rose, N (eds), *Foucault and Political Reason*, 1996, Chicago: University of Chicago Press, pp 99–122

Osborne, T and Gaebler, T, *Reinventing Government. How the Entrepreneurial Spirit is Transforming the Public Sector*, 1993, New York: Plume Books

PDAC (Premier's Drug Advisory Council), *Drugs and Our Community. Report of the Premier's Drug Advisory Council*, 1996, Melbourne: Victorian Government

Palmer, A, *Principles of Evidence*, 1998, London: Cavendish Publishing

Palmer, G, 'New Zealand's accident compensation scheme. Twenty years on' (1994) University of Toronto Law Journal 44, pp 223–73

Palmer, M, 'The likely environment in the year 2000 and beyond', in Etter, B and Palmer, M (eds), *Police Leadership in Australia*, 1995, Sydney: Federation Press

Passfield, L, 'Special supplement on industrial insurance', *New Statesman*, 13 March 1915

Paulus, I, *The Search for Pure Food*, 1975, London: Martin Robertson

Peters, T, *Thriving on Chaos: Handbook for a Management Revolution*, 1987, New York: Knopf

Peters, T, *Liberation Management*, 1992, New York: Knopf

Peters, T and Waterman, R, *In Search of Excellence*, 1982, New York: Harper and Rowe

Poovey, M, *Making a Social Body. British Cultural Formation 1830–1864*, 1995, Chicago: University of Chicago Press

Porter, T, *Trust in Numbers: The Pursuit of Objectivity in Science and Public Life*, 1995, Princeton, NJ: Princeton University Press

Potas, I, Vining, A *et al*, *Young People and Crime*, 1989, Canberra: Australian Institute of Criminology

Power, M, *The Audit Explosion*, 1994, London: Demos

Pratt, J, 'Dangerousness, risk and technologies of power' (1995) Australian and New Zealand Journal of Criminology 28, pp 3–32

Pratt, J, *Governing the Dangerous*, 1998, Sydney: Federation Press

Pratt, J, 'Emotive and ostentatious punishment. Its decline and resurgence in modern society' (2000a) Punishment and Society 2, pp 417–41

Pratt, J, 'The return of the Wheelbarrow Man. Or the arrival of postmodern penality' (2000b) British Journal of Criminology 40, pp 127–45

Price Waterhouse, *A Guide to the UK Insurance Industry*, 1990, London: Graham & Trotman

Priest, T, 'The new legal structure of risk control' (1990) Daedalus 119, pp 207–20

Productivity Commission, *Australia's Gambling Industries*, 1999, Summary

Pryke, M and Allen, J, 'Monetized time-space: derivatives – money's new imaginary' (2000) Economy and Society 29, pp 264–84

Quick, J, *The Annotated Workers Compensation Act 1914*, 1915, Melbourne: Maxwell

Rand Corporation, *Diverting Children from a Life of Crime*, 1998, Washington, DC: Rand Corporation

Rapp, R, 'Risky business: genetic counselling in a shifting world', in Rapp, R and Schneider, S (eds), *Articulating Human Histories*, 1995, Berkeley: University of California Press

Reddy, S, 'Claims to expert knowledge and the subversion of democracy. The triumph of risk over uncertainty' (1996) Economy and Society 25, pp 222–54

Reichman, N, 'Managing crime risks: toward an insurance based model of social control' (1986) Research in Law and Social Control 8, pp 151–72

Rose, N, *Governing the Soul*, 1989, London: Routledge

Rose, N, 'Government, authority and expertise in advanced liberalism' (1993) Economy and Society 22, pp 283–99

Rose, N, 'Governing "advanced liberal democracies"', in Barry, A, Osborne, T and Rose, N (eds), *Foucault and Political Reason*, 1996a, London: UCL Press, pp 37–64

Rose, N, 'The death of the "social"? Refiguring the territory of government' (1996b) Economy and Society 25, pp 327–56

Rose, N, 'Governing risky individuals: the role of psychiatry in new regimes of control' (1998a) Psychiatry, Psychology and Law 5, pp 177–95

Rose, N, 'Living dangerously. Risk management in mental health care' (1998b) Mental Health Care 199, pp 263–66

Rose, N, *Powers of Freedom: Reframing Political Thought*, 1999a, Cambridge: Cambridge University Press

Rose, N, 'Inventiveness in politics' (1999b) Economy and Society 28, pp 467–93

Rose, N, 'Government and control' (2000) British Journal of Criminology 40, pp 321–39

Rose, N, 'The politics of life itself' (2001) Theory, Culture and Society 18, pp 1–30

Royal Commission, *Royal Commission to Inquire into Friendly and Benefit Building Societies*, Fourth Report (Northcote), Cmd 961, 1874, London: HMSO

Ruhl, L, 'Liberal governance and prenatal care. Risk and regulation in pregnancy' (1999) Economy and Society 28, pp 91–117

Ryden, I, 'Recent changes in social security in Sweden', in Reynolds, E (ed), *Income Security in Canada: Changing Needs, Changing Means*, 1993, Montreal: Institute for Research on Public Policy, pp 189–202

Saint-Jours, Y, 'France', in Kohler, P and Zacher, H (eds), *The Evolution of Social Insurance 1881–1981*, 1982, New York: St Martin's Press, pp 93–149

Sandon, M, *Ministerial Statement: Safety, Security and Women*, 1991a, Melbourne: Parliament of Victoria

Sandon, M, *Safety and Security*, 1991b, Melbourne: Ministry of Police and Emergency Services

Secretaries of State, *Caring for People. Community Care in the Next Decade and Beyond*, 1989, London: HMSO

Sedgwick, E, 'Epidemics of the will', in Crary, J and Kwinter, S (eds), *Incorporations*, Vol 4, 1992, Cambridge: MIT Press, pp 130–42

Select Committee, *Report from the Select Committee on the Friendly Societies Act 1875*, 1889, London: British Parliamentary Papers

Select Committee, *Committee on Industrial Assurance and Assurance on the Lives of Children under Ten Years of Age* (Cohen Report), Cmd 4376, 1933, London: HMSO

Simon, J, 'The emergence of a risk society: insurance, law, and the state' (1987) Socialist Review 95, pp 61–89

Simon, J, 'The ideological effects of actuarial practices' (1988) Law and Society Review 22, pp 771–800

Simon, J, 'Governing through crime', in Friedman, L and Fisher, G (eds), *The Crime Conundrum. Essays in Criminal Justice*, 1997, Boulder, CO: Westview, pp 171–89

Simon, J, 'Managing the monstrous. Sex offenders and the new penology' (1998) Psychology, Public Policy and Law 4, pp 452–67

Simon, J, 'Fear and loathing in late modernity: reflections on the cultural sources of mass imprisonment in the United States', in Garland, D (ed), *Mass Imprisonment. Social Causes and Consequences*, 2001, New York: Sage, pp 15–27

Simon, J and Feeley, M, 'True crime. The new penology and public discourse on crime', in Blomberg, T and Cohen, S (eds), *Law, Punishment and Social Control: Essays in Honor of Sheldon Messinger*, 1995, New York: Aldine de Gruyter, pp 147–80

Simpson, A, 'Innovation in nineteenth century contracts' (1975) Law Quarterly Review 91, pp 247–78

Simpson, A, 'The Horwitz thesis and the history of contracts' (1979) University of Chicago Law Review 46, pp 533–601

Sparks, R, Girling, E *et al*, 'Fear and everyday urban lives' (2001) Urban Studies 38, pp 885–98

Stanko E, 'When precaution is normal: a feminist critique of crime prevention', in Gelsthorpe, L and Morris, A (eds), *Feminist Perspectives in Criminology*, 1990, Milton Keynes: Open University Press, pp 123–48

Steffensmeier, D and Harer, M, 'Is the crime rate really falling?' (1987) Journal of Research in Crime and Delinquency 24, pp 23–48

Stenson, K and Watt, P, 'Governmentality and "the death of the social"? A discourse analysis of local government texts in south-east England' (1999) Urban Studies 36, pp 189–201

Stimson, G and Oppenheimer, E, *Heroin Addiction: Treatment and Control in Britain*, 1982, London: Tavistock

Strang, J, 'Changing the image of the drug taker' (1984) Health and Social Service Journal 11, pp 1202–204

Strang, J, 'A model service. Turning the generalist onto drugs', in MacGregor, S (ed), *Drugs and British Society*, 1989, London: Routledge, pp 134–48

Sugarman, S, *Doing Away With Personal Injury Law*, 1989, New York: Quorum Books

Task Force on Evaluation, *No Quick Fix. An Evaluation of the National Campaign Against Drug Abuse*, 1992, Commissioned by the Ministerial Council on Drug Strategy

Thatcher, M, 'The Airey Neave Memorial Lecture' (1980) Commentary 2, pp 7–14

Thatcher, M, *The Downing Street Years*, 1993, London: Harper Collins

Thompson, E, *Whigs and Hunters. The Origins of the Black Act*, 1977, London: Allen Lane

Thurgood, P, 'Safety, security and women', paper presented at the Crime Prevention Seminar, Ministry of Police and Emergency Services, Melbourne, 30 August 1991

Tilbury, M, Noone, M *et al*, *Remedies. Commentaries and Materials*, 1993, Sydney: Law Book Company

Tilley, N, 'Crime prevention in Britain, 1975–2001: breaking out, breaking in and breaking down', in Hughes, G, McLaughlin, E and Muncie, J (eds), *Crime Prevention and Community Safety: New Directions* 2002, London: Sage, pp 12–36

Tolley, S and Tregeagle, S, 'Children's family centres. Integrated support services to prevent abuse and neglect of children', in Standing Committee of Law and Justice (ed), *Crime Prevention Through Social Support*, 1998, Sydney: Parliament of New South Wales Legislative Council, pp 83–90

United States Congress, *Fictitious Dealing in Agricultural Products. Washington: Committee on Agriculture*, 1892a, Washington, DC: House of Representatives, 52nd Congress, 3rd Session

United States Congress, *Options and Futures Washington: Committee on Judiciary*, 1892b, Washington, DC: United States Senate, 52nd Congress, 2nd Session

Valverde, M, 'The dialectic of the familiar and the unfamiliar: the "jungle" in early slum travel writing' (1996) Sociology 30, pp 493–506

Valverde, M, *Diseases of the Will. Alcohol and the Dilemmas of Freedom*, 1998, Cambridge: Cambridge University Press van Antwerp, W, *The Stock Exchange from Within*, 1913, New York: Doubleday Page

Viscusi, W, *Risk by Choice. Regulating Health and Safety in the Workplace*, 1983, Cambridge, MA: Harvard University Press

Waine, B, *The Rhetoric of Independence. The Ideology and Practice of Social Policy in Thatcher's Britain*, 1991, Oxford: Berg

Waine, B, 'Workers as owners. The ideology and practice of personal pensions' (1992) Economy and Society 21, pp 27–33

Walklate, S, 'Gendering crime prevention: exploring the tensions between policy and process', in Hughes, G, McLaughlin, E and Muncie, J (eds), *Crime Prevention and Community Safety: New Directions*, 2002, London: Sage, pp 58–76

Walsh, J and Trumble, J, 'The politics of drug testing', in Coombs, R and West, L (eds), *Drug Testing. Issues and Options*, 1991, New York: Oxford University Press, pp 27–47

Walters, W, *Unemployment and Government. Genealogies of the Social*, 2000, Cambridge: Cambridge University Press

Weber, M, 'The Stock Exchange', in Runciman, W (ed), *Max Weber: Selections in Translation*, 1978, Cambridge: Cambridge University Press, pp 374–77

Weir, L, 'Recent developments in the government of pregnancy' (1996) Economy and Society 25, pp 372–92

Welsh, B and Farrington, D, 'Value for money? A review of the costs and benefits of situational crime prevention' (1999) British Journal of Criminology 39, pp 345–69

Wightman, J, *Contract: A Critical Commentary*, 1996, London: Pluto

Wilson, A and Levy, H, *Industrial Life Assurance. An Historical and Critical Study*, 1937, Oxford: Oxford University Press

Wilson, G, 'Business, state and community: "responsible risk takers", New Labour, and the governance of corporate business' (2000) Journal of Law and Society 27, pp 151–77

Windeyer, W, *The Law of Wagers, Gaming and Lotteries in the Commonwealth of Australia*, 1929, Sydney: Law Book Company

Wynne, B, 'May the sheep safely graze? A reflexive view of the expert-lay knowledge divide', in Lash, S and Wynne, B (eds), *Risk, Environment and Modernity*, 1996, New York: Sage, pp 44–83

Yeatman, A, 'Interpreting contemporary contractualism', in Dean, M and Hindess, B (eds), *Governing Australia*, 1998, Sydney: Cambridge University Press, pp 227–41

Young, J, *The Drugtakers*, 1971, St Albans: Paladian

Zelizer, V, *Morals and Markets: The Development of Life Insurance in the United States*, 1979, New York: Columbia University Press

Zelizer, V, *The Social Meaning of Money*, 1994, New York: Basic Books

Zibbell, J, 'Can the lunatics actually take over the asylum? Reconfiguring subjectivity and neo-liberal governance in contemporary British drug treatment policy', unpublished manuscript, 2003, Department of Anthropology, University of Massachusetts

Zollner, D, 'Social insurance in Germany', in Kohler, P and Zacher, H (eds), *The Evolution of Social Insurance 1881–1981*, 1982, New York: St Martin's Press, pp 1–92

Index